AITCHISON MEMORIAL TRUST

THE GOODMAN LECTURES

1973–1982

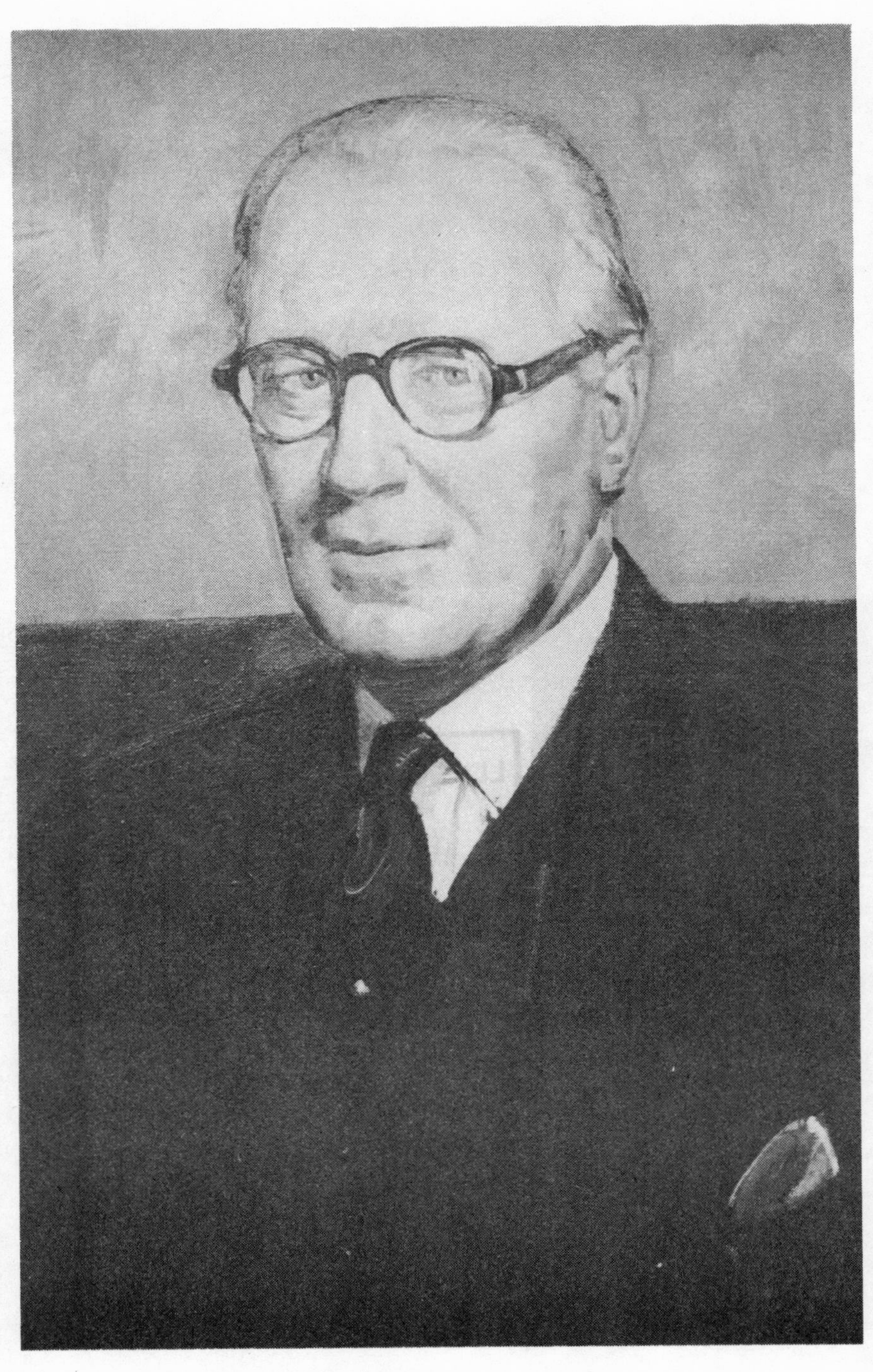

Irvine George Aitchison, M.A. LL.B. F.S.M.C. F.B.O.A.
(from the portrait by Ruskin Spear, R.A.)

Aitchison Memorial Trust

The Goodman Lectures

1973–1982

AT THE ROYAL SOCIETY
6 CARLTON HOUSE TERRACE
LONDON S.W.1

THE AITCHISON FUND

Phototypeset by
Falcon Graphic Art Ltd, Wallington, Surrey
Printed in Great Britain by
Billings, Worcester

ISBN–0–951 0376–0–9

Contents

THE GOODMAN LECTURES

PREFACE

This small book contains the first ten 'Goodman Lectures' delivered since they were established as a happy method of commemorating the memory of Irvine Aitchison. Modesty demands that I exclude any reference to the merits or demerits of the first lecturer, but it will be observed that the remaining lectures were delivered by people about whose qualifications there can be no argument. They covered a wide variety of topics and it is hoped to maintain this variety in ensuing years.

The lectures have been an outstanding success and have annually become a modest feature of the London scene. They have always been exceptionally well–attended and I can remember no occasion when they were not enthusiastically received. It would be invidious to grade their order of popularity but the trustees will be well satisfied if they can maintain that level of interest in future years.

Irvine Aitchison was a remarkable man and a distinguished member of an important profession, whose principal preoccupation was not the making of profit but the supplying of a good and adequate service to the public at large. He was keenly and scientifically interested in ophthalmic matters and established a business known and respected throughout the nation which has, under the auspices of his successors, grown from strength to strength. It can now probably claim to be the largest group of opticians in the country, and possibly even in the world.

The notion of establishing this lecture was a singularly happy one. I knew him well and he was a man who took pleasure in academic discussion and would, I think, have been peculiarly pleased by the method that has been devised to pay tribute to his memory. He was supported in his interests by a charming and talented wife who, alas, survived him all too briefly.

I am very happy indeed to have been associated with these lectures and regard it as a signal honour – thoroughly undeserved – that they should bear my name. I hope the association may continue for many years.

Goodman

FOREWORD
BY THE TRUSTEES OF
THE SOCIETY OF OPTICIANS AITCHISON MEMORIAL FUND

The Society of Opticians was founded in 1937 and is actively involved in the development of the vital services offered by opticians to the public. In 1966 the members of the Society formed the Aitchison Memorial Trust (a registered educational charity) to commemorate one of its co-founders and its first Chairman.

Irvine George Aitchison, M.A., LL.B., (Cantab)., F.S.M.C., F.B.O.A. Barrister-at-Law, led a distinguished life of wide ranging interests. In 1911 he assumed responsibility for the firm of Aitchison and Co., on which he built the foundation of an international optical group retiring as Chairman in 1964. He was an active member of the Society's Executive Committee until his death in 1965. He also played a prominent part in promoting the Opticians Act 1958 and was a founder member of the General Optical Council.

Outside his business interests, his great loves were ski-ing and mountaineering and he was particularly proud of his ski ascent of the North Eigerjoch in 1938, a feat not previously accomplished. He was very active in the affairs of the Ski Club of Great Britain and of the Alpine Ski Club and was largely instrumental in keeping these institutions alive during the difficult war years and indeed for rebuilding them after the war. He was elected President of the Ski Club of Great Britain in 1944, a post which he held until 1946, and was made an honorary member in 1948. He also served as President of the Alpine Ski Club from 1946 to 1949. It is difficult to convey to those who never met him what he meant to his friends; to his widow, Lord Goodman wrote, 'He was a man of great integrity, of humour, and with a sense of values as rare as it was valid'. Integrity was perhaps his most striking characteristic.

In 1973, because of his personal regard for Irvine Aitchison, the Rt. Hon. Lord Goodman, CH., kindly consented to the

Trust sponsoring a series of lectures to be known as the Goodman Lectures. He gave the first of these himself with Lord Snow as Chairman and has taken the chair at subsequent lectures, with the exception of 1977.

These lectures would not have been possible without the personal involvement of Lord Goodman. A solicitor by profession and a Cross-Bencher, Lord Goodman has been consulted on many issues by Ministers of both main political parties. He has been a member of a Royal Commission, a Parliamentary Commission and a great number of Committees of Enquiry – of which he has chaired several. As a mediator, his skills have been called upon in diverse and numerous fields. He was Chairman of the Arts Council of Great Britain from 1965–1972; of the Newspaper Publishers Association from 1970–1976; of the Housing Corporation from 1973–1977; and of the National Building Agency from 1973–1978. His current appointments include the Chairmanship of the English National Opera Limited, The Association for Business Sponsorship of the Arts, The Theatres' Trust, The Theatre Investment Fund, and Motability, and the Deputy Chairmanship of the British Council. He has been Master of University College, Oxford since October 1976.

The lectures, all of which have been given by kind permission at the Royal Society, have attracted audiences of widely varied interests and responsibilities, they have been regularly reported in the national press and copies of them are to be found in many reference libraries. In short they have developed a place of their own in learned circles. This has only been achieved by the very high standard of the speakers, each of whom has been an acknowledged leader in his own field. The Trustees believe that these lectures should reach an even wider audience and have therefore decided to publish the first ten in book form.

Each lecture stands on its own and each contributes to the understanding of the world in which we live and its future. We

are grateful to all who have given freely of their wisdom and time. We hope and believe that you, the reader, will be equally grateful.

M.D. Ballantine, F.B.C.O.
R.T. Harris
R.B.Thorpe, F.B.C.O.
N.H. Wingate, F.B.C.O., F.A.D.O.

Trustees

The Rt. Hon. The Lord Goodman, C.H.
(from the portrait by Graham Sutherland, O.M.)

THE FIRST GOODMAN LECTURE

'Coming to Terms with Science'

delivered by

The Rt. Hon. The Lord Goodman, CH.

Tuesday, 22nd May, 1973

CHAIRMAN The Rt. Hon. The Lord Snow, CBE.

LORD SNOW:

Ladies and gentlemen, first of all if you can't hear, for God's sake demonstrate, and we shall try and adjust these microphones.

There is a curious convention that in fact you say, if you are introducing a well known person, that he needs no introduction. I have suffered from this. I remember some years ago on a very hot afternoon in New York State by the Hudson River precisely that happening to me. I should say that the Chairman was a very old man, but he began with this well known phrase: "Our guest this afternoon needs no introduction". I was about to give a Commencement Address to a very well known College which had been written about by a notorious female writer, I won't reveal the name, but you would know it if I told you. This distinguished old gentleman went on, saying I needed no introduction, and I was about to give the Commencement Address and receive an Honorary Degree. He gave a sort of sketch of someone's biography which bore a faint resemblance, though not a very accurate one, to my own, and then with a flourish said: "I now give you our guest, Sir Charles Russell". I claim to be one of the every few men alive who has actually

received an Honorary Degree in a false name.

I am not going to do that about Lord Goodman, and in fact I am going to indulge myself by saying just a bit about him. It is a commonplace that he is one of the best influences in English public life. We all hear it, and it is true. We all know he is a man of almost infinite goodwill. His energies, his kindness, his intelligence, are at anyone's disposal. And this is fine, there is not enough goodwill in our harsh and gritty world. But that would be insipid if it were not illuminated by something quite different – the sharpest, most brilliant, the most incisive intelligence which any of us know. Goodwill is splendid, but it wants something to redeem it from the kind of ordinary charitableness which ordinary decent men can achieve, and Lord Goodman has far more than that. I know of literally no-one who can produce more ideas, more sparkle, more intellectual stimulus in the whole of our society. That is one of the things which we treasure him for. We treasure him for many others, but that is one. Some idiot in a profile, I think it was, said he was intelligent but not intellectual. If that is true, the word "intellectual" has been absurdly debased. It means that stupidity is a kind of concomitant of the intellectual life, which is not a thing the friends I grew up with would very willingly accept. In fact, intellectualism has come to mean that you have to have contemporary foolish tastes, swim with the tide, be one with fashion. Lord Goodman has never done that. He has got exceptionally independent tastes; he in fact can sympathise I think rather more than I can with contemporary folly, but nevertheless his own intellect is fine, and if, as I say, the word "intellectual" means anything, of course he is one, and dominant among them.

Very shortly we are going to hear him speak. In the House of Lords he is the only speaker I have known who, when he is up, as we say, people flock into the Chamber. Normally the House of Lords is completely deserted; you get a few desolate figures on these red benches, in various bars, restaurants and whatev-

er. They are not often there; they come to vote, but otherwise there are two or three desolate figures on the benches who are just about to make speeches. When Lord Goodman gets up, the House is packed. He speaks normally completely without notes, and that is regarded as a conjuring trick in the House of Lords. I happen to do the same thing myself, nothing like as well, nothing like as fast, nothing like as interestingly, but I think even my humble efforts are regarded as a conjuring trick. The normal process in the House of Lords is to read your speech very dully and then sit down. I believe, and I am sure you believe, that the worst spoken speech is better than the best read speech. To my astonishment I find Lord Goodman has some notes tonight. I have never known that before, and I am quite certain he will not use them.

He is going to speak to us on "Coming to Terms with Science". I am fascinated, and I am sure you will be, by what he is going to say. I have talked to him on many things, but I have never talked to him on this topic. He may say something absolutely shattering, so dismaying that I shall be angry with him for a long time, but anyway I am delighted to be here, I am delighted to be with the Society of Opticians, and it is a privilege to introduce an old and admired friend, Lord Goodman.

LORD GOODMAN:

Mr. Chairman, Ladies and Gentlemen, after those introductory remarks let me say you have probably got a severer migraine than me. It is impossible in any lecture I give you this evening to realise any expectations that might have been aroused by that delightful and charming but wholly extravagant assessment of my qualities. May I say, in a determined effort to embarrass Lord Snow and to some extent by way of reciprocity that I am enormously honoured by his taking the Chair here this evening.

This afternoon I reached a very firm assessment about

myself which differed very sharply from the words you have heard from Lord Snow, and it was that in coming to give this lecture here I was undoubtedly certifiably insane, and if there were to be any scientists on the premises I would like to have avoided giving it by another rapid route. I realised all at once that I had been defeated and caused to put myself in a position of very great danger by sheer typical vanity. The opportunity of talking on a scientific topic in this building was irresistible, and it was only when I had selected the topic and was preening myself on how I was going to talk on it that I realised that I knew absolutely nothing about science, and I was thinking about changing the topic when it suddenly dawned on me that what I wanted to say came better from a total scientific ignoramus than someone who was trained as a Fellow of this Society.

I am a total scientific ignoramus. My scientific education, if that word could be used to ennoble a few desultory pieces of instruction I received, which consisted of some instruction in Chemistry, a topic in which I did contrive to obtain a London matriculation pass which I shall never be able to explain, and some even more desultory instruction in Physics, and something called Biology which consisted of bringing a live frog, destroying the poor creature, and by some process which I suppose is called Anatomy seeking to determine how the creature proceeded by way of motion and the other attributes as a poor live frog. I have never understood anything about science. I have never been able to relate one scientific topic to another, I never knew how mathematics realted to physics, and how physics related to anything else. I never understood the theory of the fact that the earth is alleged to go round the sun. As far as I am concerned, the sun can go round the earth, or both can be totally stationary. These propositions are equally acceptable to me, and I certainly would not worry about them at any time of day or night. I understand nothing about the great scientific developments in my life-time. I heard, I think

when I was an undergraduate, that Rutherford had split the atom. The atom to me was a unit of nothing, and he had contrived most beautifully to make two units out of what to me was nothingness. I admired his achievement enormously.

I never disparage a scientist. That would be terrible, something in the nature of a positive sacrilege. I have the greatest respect for scientists, but no knowledge of them and no knowledge of their activities. Hence I am ideally suited to deliver this address.

What I want to talk about is really a myth, that at this moment we live in a society which on the whole contains a negative imperfection. I don't believe that society is on the point of collapse, or indeed that the world we are living in is necessarily much worse than the world which existed twenty, thirty, fifty years ago. In fact there are signs of improvement. I think poverty has been reduced, I think starvation has been reduced, I think that education is on the whole somewhat improved. But the fact remains that there are large areas about which we should have more reservations, and those areas are areas where the concentrated attention of people who know what the thing is about would be of enormous value.

What I am going to say to you is to put forward the view of a man who, having no scientific knowledge, can only fumble his way towards the belief that a better understanding between the humanist and the scientist is something that ought to be achieved. It is very appropriate that Lord Snow should be in this Chair this evening, as it was he, I think, who raised the question and challenged the existence of the two worlds, the scientific world and the humanistic world. I think he took the view, very rightly, that the estrangement between them was a very dangerous and unnecessary thing for the body politic in which we live, and he was assailed by one particular humanist in violent terms, and a most edifying and learned exchange took place between them. It was at the time of the Watergate scandal and the Lonrho case, and all these delightful things

were going on, but I think in a way it is an argument which needs to be reviewed. I think it is dangerous to record a cleavage between the two worlds as a bad thing, that it necessarily does not exist, and that more does not need to be done to foster a partnership.

This is really the theme of what I am going to say, and to a very large extent it depends on the belief that the scientists' participation in our affairs today is a remote one, and is one where on the whole he carries on in his own way without any special commitment to the needs of the society, because what he is doing is purely scientific activity about which he really has a volition which is beyond his control in many matters. Now, this is not in any sense an attack on scientists, it couldn't be, no sensible man would attack a scientist. It is an expression of a view that scientists are not understood by the rest of us, we are so ignorant of what they are doing and so incapable of proferring to them the proper terms of a special relationship in which they can play their proper part. This is really what I am anxious to develop this evening.

Now, why is it that science has taken a distinct flow, in terms of knowledge, from the humanities? I think one has to look at the way that science develops. I know as little about the history of science as I know about the substantive quality of science. But I know enough to know that the important century for demonstrating the present shape of our educational system, of our intellectual system, of the things we understand and know about, was the nineteenth century. In the nineteenth century there were, of course, important scientists at work. People like Pasteur, Lord knows how many others, were all working very hard indeed to produce prodigies of achievement of which, on the whole, the rest of society were reasonably indifferent and reasonably uninformed.

The nineteenth century was a society where education reposed, in this country at least and I think throughout the world, mainly in the middle and upper classes. It didn't repose

in the working classes, it didn't repose in the proletariat. As a result, these middle classes and the upper classes regaled themselves with the humanities to an extent which has been unequalled since then, and is unlikely to be. They read an immense amount of excellent literature which was then emerging. They read Dickens' works, each section of it as it emerged, and I don't think in the whole of the human history there has been a situation where tough, vigorous, strong men wept their hearts out over the death of someone like Little Nell. In New York, I believe, they were waiting by the quayside for the arrival of the boats, and the people were standing on the quayside demanding to know whether Little Nell had been killed or not, and scrambling to get the issue which revealed this terrible news. This, I think, was a good thing. It showed that they had heart, it showed that they had literary appreciation, it showed that they had very marked concern indeed for the things on which we set value. But they did not really have an interest or an understanding of science.

I except the medical sciences. That is in a sense, and I think few would disagree, not a pure science. It is half a science and half an art, and obviously there are always hypochondriacs expressly concerned with the question of what medical advances might be made. But leaving that aside, I do not believe that in the nineteenth century any great understanding of science existed except that there were a number of people at work who were doing good and benevolent work, and I will turn to the question of the good and benevolent work in a moment. There were people who were doing good and benevolent work which was useful to society and to the harm of society.

We have for many years until very recently held the belief that scientific advances and scientific achievements were something that a section of society which was on the whole of service to us, in servitude to us in the best possible sense, was producing for our benefit. They were producing anaesthetics so

that we knew we would not suffer as people had suffered in the past from the heaviest pains of operations. They were producing all sorts of advances in locomotion, advances in printing, advances in development. The application of science to the engineering processes and the designs of the engineers were, in our view, wholly beneficial. Even when you have got a troubled society, when you have got a man like Darwin, most people would have accepted what he did as something that was beneficial to mankind. He caused doubt in areas where, on the whole, doubt did not give rise to too much pain and too much distress.

Some time in the 1920s there was an interesting action – interesting in the field of litigation – somewhere in Tennessee, I think, when there was a prosecution of a school teacher who had taught Darwinism and was prosecuted as it was regarded as illegal and improper. At that time, informed and professional opinion was outraged at the situation, as it ought to be. I am not sure that today we might not find an argument in favour of the prosecutors. We might well take the view that the Darwinian theories had taken something away and not put anything back. This is, of course, a highly reactionary proposition, and I would only air it to select audiences of this kind who won't spread it abroad.

The fact thus remains that our attitude towards science which, as I say, was an attitude of believing that somewhere, somehow, we could harness to our service a collection of benevolent gnomes like the little creatures who came to repair the shoemaker's uncompleted output in the fairy tale, and they were doing good and virtuous work on our behalf. This I believe to be the picture of science that existed, certainly throughout my youth. I saw scientists as quite remarkable people who did me a lot of good, who could produce splendid toothpastes, who could produce cough lozenges and all the things that I required and needed for my mental and physical welfare, and in no circumstances at all would give rise to any

serious risk to my health or welfare. This was the belief we retained, even after the first world war. I think, though, there was the beginning of questioning and the beginning of doubt then. I think when people saw that science had contrived to produce aviation, that science had contrived to produce submarines, and other things which were of benefit to us when they were destroying the enemy but which were of less benefit to us when the enemy was destroying us, then I think the first few qualms began to emerge and the first feelings of doubt began to arise within us.

It was then, I think, that we might have started to formulate the belief that on the whole we needed to investigate the morality of all human activity, and it was then, I think, that we made the fundamental mistake to which we still adhere, which was the belief that science had arrived at a morality of its own. We have today, I think, come to realise – and again, it is no reproach to the scientist – that the scientist has no code of morality, and that science is morally sexless. The scientist is not concerned with morality. The scientist is concerned with pursuing some quest where his interest has been aroused, where his knowledge has been aroused, and he has a belief that he is about to fulfil an intellectual purpose that is self-propelling.

I believe that we have put ourselves into a position of some difficulty. We humanists – not the scientists, who have never made the claim that there is a scientistic code of morality – rather naively assert that there is such a code, and it is something upon which we can rely. I think we have found ourselves in a position of great difficulty on that account. We are making assertions for the scientist that the scientist has not the remotest wish to make for himself. My own recollection of science is almost a matter of mental cameos. I think of Watt sitting in front of a kettle, I think of Newton having an apple descending on his head. I think of poor Galileo being interrogated and giving some historic answer to the effect that he did

not believe what in fact he did believe. All these things I recollect by way of cameos, but when you come to look at all these situations, no scientist has sought to inform his views or beliefs with an orderly moral code, with the express intention of telling them how society should be organised. I would not presume to speak for scientists, but most scientists would look on it as arrogant, they would not consider it as part of their duty to say in the production of an explosive that it was either instructive or beneficial or useful, but if it could be used in order to obtain ore from mountains, it could be used in order to destroy human beings. They would not presume to suggest that what they are discovering are things that have a relevance in relation to man's firm belief that the society in which we live needs direction. It must be remembered that until a few years ago we were on the way to believing that we were so advanced and so sophisticated in our approach to human organisation and government that direction was an unnecessary element.

Hence we came, I think on that account, to rely more and more on the notion that scientists have something to tell us about what route to take. I believe the scientist has a lot to tell us about what route to take if we work with him in incorporating and enmeshing into our social notions the value of his work in accordance with our own established and virtuous beliefs. I don't think the scientist has anything to tell us if all we do is sit back and watch and admire what it is he says he is producing, as an abstract activity which may or may not be put to some use but even so is being incorporated into a social scheme.

Well, I said when I started talking to you that I was giving you the unformed and rather elementary views of a man who knew nothing about science. What I am saying to you is that I instinctively feel. I am not saying to you anything I could prove or establish or which needs to be proved or established. But I think it does need to be said that our society having reached the point where we are confronted with very many grave dangers, when we are confronted with many grave situations where the

harnessing of the unique quality of scientific thought that is available to us could be of special advantage, that we ought to find the means of establishing a dialogue between the scientists and the non-scientists that will enable us to harness these talents to the general advantage of everyone. I don't believe we have found any such means.

There are perhaps three matters I would like to allude to in terms of scientific advancement that indicate the sort of thing I have in mind. The discovery of television was one of the great social discoveries of our time. It is ironic if you ask any of the people who sit in front of the television screen for hour after hour after hour absorbing the unbelievably inept material that is put out night after night after night, hardly one of them, if any of them, could tell you the name of a single engineer concerned with the manufacture and discovery of this remarkable achievement. They could tell you the names of the unhappy performers whose antics unhappily take away an immense amount of pleasure from our evenings if we are sufficiently ill-advised to watch them. There is no problem at all about identifying any of them. What they would not know is the name of the man who had produced the instrument which made all this possible. This is not of itself important. What is important is that this immensely powerful social machine, this method of communication infinitely more effective, infinitely more cogent than any method of communication previously invented, has been flung into society without any sense of direction, any attempt to determine its efficacy, any attempt to determine its effect. We do not know what television is doing to our society, and we are making not the slightest effort to find out. There are those who think television is doing great injury to our society. Others hold the happy belief that it is the best influence that has yet emerged. Anyone who holds that belief, in my view, must be a singular creature indeed. There are people who do hold that belief, and hold it even without the added advantage of incurring great material

benefits. It is true that most of the people who express that belief in a coherent and convincing form are people who have a financial interest in the institution, and none the worse for that. It is a really terrible thing that we should have something of this kind, something that suddenly emerges, develops with lightning speed, in a decade where we have established a pattern of living quite different from the pattern of living that existed a decade ago, for many millions of people in this country, and we do not know what it is doing. We do not even know what it is doing to their eyesight. One thing that can be determined by those who go blind is that they are giving external evidence and proof that something is going wrong, but we have not the least idea what it is doing to their minds. This we do not know, and have made no attempt to find out.

The Government has recently declared that, in relation to the institution of television and broadcasting, it was unnecessary in their view to have any form of enquiry. I do not know if the sort of enquiry that is normally established by Governments to establish this sort of thing is of the slightest value. Usually a group of gentlemen is selected, selected because no-one is able to identify any particular prejudice or preconception they have publicly uttered. The fact that they privately hold prejudices of the strongest character is of complete irrelevance in that direction, and of course the report that ultimately emerges is merely an expression of the views that they hold of which the Government was not conscious at the time when they reported.

There is not a shadow of doubt, shade of doubt, that we do need to enquire into this with meticulous care, and we need, if I may use the word, to hold a highly scientific enquiry. We need to know what the effect is of having this for hour after hour after hour in a particular sitting room where parents and children sit together ceasing to converse. I am not one of those people who utter the platitude that television kills conversation. I do not believe that before the invention of television in

most lower and middle class homes in England there was scintillating conversation between parents and children. I have a belief that this is a total misconception, but the fact remains that people are now being reduced to a condition where they are incapable of speech. Children attending schools are now found to be so defective in their capacity to speak and to organise the outward expression of their thoughts that this is a serious deterioration in the situation from a few years back, and we are allowing this to happen without any attempt to investigate it on a scientific basis.

This is one of the immensely powerful and influential inventions which many of you gentlemen – because I detect to my considerable surprise and consternation a considerable number of scientists in the audience – this is one of the inventions for which you are responsible for which you should have retained a continuing responsibility. You ought not to have let it loose, and there are many other things you ought not to have let loose.

Now let us touch on another matter – and here again I may be regarded as a reactionary creature – and that is the visit to the moon. Astronomy was for many years probably the most kindly of all the sciences, since it involved no special activity. You stood in front of your telescope and you observed what there was to observe. You did not have to travel anywhere, you did not have to instal yourself in a machine or a rocket, no-one had to light a paper at the end of it and send you spinning into the atmosphere. It was a civilised activity in which to engage. All of a sudden there was a sensational change. People suddenly decided that they had to go to the moon. The argument propounded in favour of going to the moon was the argument propounded by the gentleman who said he had to climb Mount Everest because it was there. That, if I may say so, was a damned silly answer. I am not sure that I would have taken any positive action to prevent anyone going to the moon. I would have said, indeed that if you go to the moon I am able

to tell you what in fact was ultimately found out, that there is nothing there. But that, if I may say so, is quite a different aspect of the matter.

They set off to the moon, they arrived on the moon. Television has shown them stumbling all over the moon. They have finished off a number of charming myths and legends. We no longer believe it is made of green cheese; all kinds of nice little notions we had were pulverised on the day they took their first step on it. I doubt whether the fact that they put their first step on it justified, in terms of value, the loss of all those nice little notions, but what I do feel is that this continuing activity should be watched with special care and special concern.

I do not believe that the travels to the moon will end up without tears. I believe that unless it is invigilated, it will end up with a great many tears. We shall find that it is not the best and serious interests of knowledge that are the motives that the scientists have, but the secondary motives of people who can see possibilities that are too horrifying to comment on and certainly are beyond my range of knowledge to comment on.

This is just one of a number of hundreds of scientific activities where scientists have plunged into an activity without serious thought of its consequences. Probably the most terrifying of all – and it would be impossible to embark on this discussion without mentioning it – was, of course, the use of the atomic bomb. How the atomic bomb came about I have no idea. It was an excellent illustration of the total ignorance of the rest of mankind of what the scientists were doing. The cobbler was asleep in his room, probably, as the fairy tale cobbler was, not too well. The gnomes were working away with a frenzy, not repairing his shoes but preparing for his total destruction, and they were doing it with a completely disinterested viewpoint. They were not interested in whether the cobbler was destroyed or not, that was no part of their responsibility. They were interested in the question that there was a possibility of producing a situation where an explosion

of such magnitude, the harnessing of immense artificial power of such strength was possible, that it could be used to produce electricity for great cities, and could be used to destroy to an ash every great city in the world. This happened without any of us knowing. We had no idea. It only burst upon us in a newspaper during the war. I remember in those days I was in the Army, and nobody was more innocently and peacefully engaged during the war than I was. I had the great satisfaction of being able to say that I had done no damage to the human race throughout six years of service. Whether I had done any good to the human race was arguable.

But other people were at work – were at work in circumstances where not a word of reproach can possibly be said to them. No-one can reproach them, no-one can say that they did anything wrong, no-one can say that they were not following their destinies. In the great mass of mankind, even today the number of scientists in this country is surprisingly few. When I was looking up some statistics, I found that in 1954 the number of registered scientists was something less than 100,000. It is a tiny proportion of the population, if that figure is right, and I believe it was right, but these gentlemen were doing what they had been engaged to do and what they had been trained to do, and what their natural talents and energies compelled them to do. They had no choice in the matter. But someone should have been watching them. The atom bomb should not have been allowed.

Some of you may have read, and may remember, President Truman's biography where he discussed whether or not he should have made use of the atom bomb, whether he should have decided in favour of using it. The arguments, of course, were relatively simple on each side. The main argument, to which I do not think he gave sufficient heed, was that once you have used it, there is no conceivable case for not using it again. That is really the argument, the argument which now bedevils the whole of mankind. But his argument was a different one. It

was that if he did not use the atom bomb and did not destroy the Japanese opposition at that moment then great numbers of innocent people would meet their deaths because he had refrained from using the instrument in support of his own people and his own troops. We can see the moral dilemma. I think it would have required a man of even greater moral capacity than President Truman, and I rate him as one of the best of the American Presidents and a man of high courage, to have decided not to use. it. Many people would have reproached him. Widows, and mothers of American soldiers who had died as a result of that decision, had they known of it would have said he made the wrong decision. The wives and mothers of American soldiers who might die would have urged him to use it. But the fact remains that that decision was made on the say-so of one man with no scientific knowledge reinforced by the views of a number of scientists who obviously wanted to see it used. There were many scientists in the United States of America who were conscious of the dangers involved and who wished to withdraw from the whole transaction. There were scientists in this country who wished to withdraw from the whole transaction.

When history comes to be written, dozens of people who have been regarded as people who have committed enormities against their own country will emerge as people having the major moral dilemmas of their time. I can see the difficulties that confronted them, and I believe that they have stated the best scientific case that has been stated in history, in defence of wishing to disseminate this knowledge for the benefit of the whole of mankind.

We can now look on these things much more coolly than we did in those days. We can now see that decisions of this kind touch the future and the happiness of everyone alive and everyone to be born hereafter. It is impossible today, I think, to assess the consequences of the decision to have used the atom bomb. Much of the social unrest, much of the social rebellion

against the establishment, much of the refusal to accept the standards of previous generations by younger people, stem directly from that decision. They do not rationalise it as I am trying to rationalise it this evening. Some of them do, but the great majority of them sense that a decision was made by their predecessors which is injurious to their welfare, and which should not have been made. That decision arose from a failure to have a sufficient understanding and sufficient liaison between the scientific and the non-scientific aspects of the nation.

If there had been discussions at all levels about the degree of investigation and research necessary to produce this hideous discovery, if people of all shades of opinion, of sound moral opinion, had been able to urge their views, the situation could have proceeded on very different lines. This is my firm belief and conviction, absolute conviction, that derives from having seen what happened, not having known anything about the discovery, not having had the slightest opportunity – or at least, I wouldn't have had in those days – of airing a view. I am absolutely positive of what my view would have been, and what I venture to think a large number of you in this audience would have agreed with and would have been equally vehement and vocal in trying to prevent the thing happening.

Now I have reached the end of a few brief remarks. I do not want you to believe that I have sought to give you any formulated picture of my ideas of what scientists ought or ought not to do. What I should like you to believe is this, that I have the unformed view that the relationship is wrong. I have the unformed view that while the relationship is wrong, great dangers will beset mankind. You who are scientists have great powers and capacities beyond human description. We who are not scientists can only walk willingly after you urging you to stop or slow down for a moment while we can see what it is that you are carrying in your heads. You do not stop because you see no reason to stop. We cannot pursue you because we do not possess the necessary speed. While this hopeless race is

progressing, then the human race is indeed in very great danger. This may sound too portentous an observation to be included in what was to have been a rather amiable and kindly lecture in memory of an amiable and kindly man. I do not think one could do a better service to the memory of an amiable and kindly man than by seeking to instil in you the notions and doubts and disquiet and anxiety that exist in my own mind on this topic.

Thank you very much.

LORD SNOW:

My Lords, ladies and gentlemen, what did I tell you? Do you wonder the House of Lords is electrified, and have you realised that Lord Goodman in that speech has said exactly twice as much as any normal man would have said in making any normal speech, simply because he has used twice as many words.

He has kindly said he is prepared to answer questions for a short time. There is at least one of the most distinguished scientists in the world in the audience, and several more who are competent to intervene. It would be nice if they did say something – if not, of course we can get along. If they do want to ask questions, could we have some sort of microphone, because this room probably is not good for hearing speeches from the floor. Not that we want speeches from the floor, but it is very difficult to hear what is being asked. Any takers?

SIR DESMOND HEAP:

My Lord Chairman, I am not a scientist. I happen for better or worse to be a lawyer, and I am one of those who so warmly agreed with Lord Goodman in that positive tour de force with which he regaled us tonight when he said it was something in the nature of an assault when man put his foot on the moon. There is so much in the words of the Mikado when the lady said: "Behold her frame, the placid dame, the moon's 'celestial highness', there's not a trace upon her face, of diffidence 'or

shyness'". I feel there was a terrific invasion of the moon when man put his foot right upon her. I have often though there may have been better things for a man to do than put his foot on the moon.

The question I would like to ask Lord Goodman is, I wonder if out of this great thing, this great action of going right up to the moon, is there not something in the nature of a fall out by what was learned by that most terrific, horrific, scientific achievement which in future will enable doctors and surgeons from this knowledge to be able to carry out better operations of most modest proportions than they would ever have been able to do if some man had not carried the flag forward right up to the moon? In other words, isn't there something in the slipstream in the job of getting there? Haven't we all learnt something that may be of benefit to mankind, universally and on a more modest scale?

SIR PETER MEDAWAR:

I should like to ask Lord Goodman a question which I think he is better qualified than anybody else in this country to answer. How in practical terms could these conversations have taken place before the detonation of the first atom bomb. He reckons that consultations should have taken place, and we must accept his rebuke that they did not, but how could they have happened as a matter of practical policy? I am sure no one could know better than he does how they could have happened, and I wish he could explain. Thank you.

LORD PLATT:

It seems to me that there is another division. It is not simply between the scientists and the humanists, but it is between people who really do things and make things and conduct experiments and get on with their daily work, and the people who manage them. This is a very dangerous split, I think, in our society at the present time. There are a large number of firms now in which the directors acknowledge that they are there not to make cloth, but to make money, and some of

them, I think, do not even know what goes on in their own factories.

In the same way, I think this question of the atomic bomb was a political decision, and what is wrong is that the politicians are out of touch with the scientists. The scientist knows that he can do this, and then he is threatened with all the political arguments that someone else is going to do it if we don't. As Professor Blackett, who was President of this Royal Society in whose premises we are privileged to meet, pointed out, one of the big arguments for using the atomic bomb was that America wanted to show the power to Russia because of what was going to happen after the war, and I don't believe that Truman's decision was entirely one of which was going to do more or less good at the time the bomb was used.

QUESTION:

Lord Goodman, I speak as a simple engineer and not as a scientist, but it seemed to me that your method was absolutely admirable addressed to the scientists of the world and the masses of the world, to get together and sort out their mutual impact. Where I lost track was how you imagine that message can be got forward to the scientists of individual sovereign states, and the masses of individual sovereign states, the various sovereign states having quite fundamental cultural differences in what they regard as true, pure and just. I think this goes right beyond the question of the bomb, and runs through the whole of your theme.

SIR ALISTAIR PILKINGTON:

Lord Goodman has been talking about the mistakes we have made in the past. It would be of tremendous interest to hear him talk about how we might meet a real situation in the future. As an example, it occurred to me that it is likely we can choose the sex of a child before the end of the century. It would interest me to hear how Lord Goodman feels this partnership between the humanist and the scientists should actually operate, coming up against real major problems like this.

LORD SNOW:

I think you have given Lord Goodman enough for any single man, even he. But I want to ask a question of my own, which really relates to the last question but one. I think I was probably the only person here who has even a tiny hand in the atomic bomb, that is, I was feeding scientists into this project so I knew vaguely but not in detail about this, and I knew in fact from the beginning of 1944 on that the thing would probably work. I think the question of one gentleman about the nation's state is very real. Nearly everybody I knew, Einstein, Niels Bohr and the rest, felt that if the Nazis possibly have it, then whatever the cost we had to have it. There was no moral choice there. The question of using it was quite different. I have always thought that was wrong, and shall think that until I die. I am sure that if Lord Goodman had been in the position that anyone was who was concerned with the actual technique of making it he would not have hesitated. Einstein did not hesitate, Niels Bohr did not hesitate, and so on. The question of use, which was the question Sir Peter Medawar asked, is an entirely different problem altogether, and one where I think the politicians went very wrong.

Now, Lord Goodman.

LORD GOODMAN:

There were a number of very interesting questions, and to some of them I can give a sort of composite reply.

I don't know how to organise the situation where this does not happen. I believe the first requirement before you can cure a situation is to diagnose it. I have been doing an elementary job of diagnosis, right or wrong. I believe that if we identify the nature of the problem, we go some way towards correcting it.

One thing I think is evident from a number of the questions. That is that our political organisation will have to take a different shape if we are to put this right. It is perfectly clear that our political organisations have got all their priorities wrong. They are concerned with spending hours and hours

about minor amendments to the Companies Act, and what should happen in relation to supplies of oil and petrol and so forth, when there should be a political organisation which is concerned with these matters which are crucial to the survival of mankind. I would say that I don't know how to put it right, but I believe diagnosis is the first requirement and a rapid change in our political organisation is necessary if we are to recognise that this matter takes a much higher priority than the ordninary affairs of Government.

I think I can then answer a good many of the questions pretty quickly. There was the gentlemen who is an engineer and made the point very valuably that scientists serve sovereign states. I made the point earlier on that I think there are obligations to mankind which transcend the obligations to sovereignty. It is an extremely difficult problem, a delicate problem, and I don't think one can say more than that. I think that if there is a community of people who between them can contrive to destroy the world, considerations of sovereignty become very puny and very meagre. This is my answer to that.

Sir Alistair Pilkington was concerned, again with the question of how the partnership was to operate, and here again I give my original reply – I don't know, but I think we have got to re-organise some of our considerations of government.

The same applies to Sir Peter Medawar. His was obviously a relevant question. Here you have indicated a number of stern and strong views, but what are you going to do about it? The answer is, I can't do more than tell an influential audience what I think about it, and hope someone amongst them will implement it and find the means necessary.

Lord Platt said it was a political decision, and here again it really is making the same point, that politicians who make these decisions are by themselves inadequate to make such decisions. A means must be found of buttressing them with knowledge and moral fibre and all the other commodities which need to be instilled into human conditions if we are to

survive as a human race.

There is also the question about scientists and religion. I have never known a scientist who challenges religion. It is no part of the scientific precept to challenge religion. The scientist provides you with a mine of information which you can, if you can understand it, apply to organised and accepted religious beliefs; religions can be affected in the light of science, but this has nothing to do with the scientists. The scientist is not concerned with diminishing religion or damaging religion, he is only concerned with the scientific facts.

I have tried to deal with the questions, except Lord Snow's question which is that he believes that if I had been concerned in the decision to use the atomic bomb I would, as he did, have acquiesced in its production. I am afraid I would. There is very little doubt that the terrible thing is that so many of these discoveries are made under the urgent coercion of war conditions. This changes human beings in a most marked fashion. If you are under a risk of extermination, and everyone you know and love is under a risk of extermination, you can't make a considered and objective decision. Obviously we must find a means of ensuring that decisions of this magnitude are not made at such moments of time.

Lord Briggs M.A B.Sc (Econ) F.B.A.

At the time of the lecture Professor Asa Briggs was Vice-Chancellor of the University of Sussex. He was created a life peer in 1976 in which year he was appointed to his present post as provost of Worcester College, Oxford. In 1978 he was appointed Chancellor of the Open University.

'Education and Health'

delivered by

Professor Asa Briggs

M.A (Oxon), B.Sc (Econ), Hon. LL.D., Hon. D.Litt., Hon. D.Sc,
Vice-Chancellor of the University of Sussex.

Tuesday, 18th June, 1974

CHAIRMAN The Rt. Hon. The Lord Goodman C.H.

LORD GOODMAN:

Ladies and gentlemen, it was the late Francis Bacon – not the present one, but Shakespeare's amanuensis, who said that a talkative judge was like an ill-tuned cymbal. A talkative chairman is far worse: he is like an ill-tuned orchestra. He prevents the audience from hearing what they have come to hear. I will be very brief. I have suffered from chairmen who said that they would only say a "few words", and then gave a personalised view of what "a few" means.

This is the second lecture in memory of the late Irving Aitchison.

Professor Asa Briggs belies his very mild and gentle appearance. He is one of the best brains in the country and one of – if not the most – distinguished academician in the country. He displays great versatility in public and university affairs. If you have got a television set you will not have failed to see him, to admire his dexterity, his great command of language.

Such descriptions can be a great disadvantage for a speaker

before he starts on the "centre court". Quite often it causes a "needle" in the early game, but you will not be disappointed in Professor Briggs. He is already in a high position, hanging securely to the wheel in somewhat turbulent seas, but never in fear of shipwreck. He is a model of what a Vice-Chancellor should be in these growing universities. He is a writer of great distinction. His history of the BBC shows how immensely readable history can be: it is as interesting as a piece of fiction. If you have not read it, a small appreciation of his presence this evening would be increased sales next week!

I look forward to a very interesting lecture. I will not tell you what he is to say, or to speculate on it, but will call on him to say it.

PROFESSOR ASA BRIGGS:

It is a very great privilege indeed to be invited to give the second of the Goodman Lectures under the benevolent and enlightened auspices of the Aitchison Memorial Trust.

At the same time, I am only too well aware of the difficulty both of following in Lord Goodman's footsteps – he gave the first of these lectures last year – and of doing full justice to having him as Chairman sitting at my side.

He chose last year with characteristic quiet and highly rational audacity to speak as a non-scientist about "Coming to terms with Science".

I have imitated his example tonight, at least to the extent of imitating his audacity. Education and Health are both big subjects about which everyone knows something. They are part of the style of daily discussion, though that discussion is often prejudiced and rarely profound. At least I can open up a few lines of thought tonight. Nothing that I can say tonight should be taken as definitive or exhaustive. The more I meditate on the subject I have chosen, the more disparate, even contradictory, the lines of thought appear.

When looking at the record of last year's lecture, I noted that

Lord Snow uttered some very wise words at the beginning, in introducing Lord Goodman, when he said that the "worst spoken speech is better than the best read speech". I am not going to read my speech, but I am going to use notes as I am reassured to know that Lord Goodman – who like me does not normally use them – did last year.

Without them – even with them – it is very easy to ramble in talking about "Education and Health". It is too possible to fall back on platitudes about ignorance and disease. There can be invincible ignorance and irremediable disease, but tonight I will concentrate on the aspects of social control which lead to good education and good health.

Why did I choose the subject? I was fascinated by Lord Goodman's incursion into the question of science and the non-scientist, but the reason for choosing this theme was personal. On Christmas Eve a few years ago I was drawn into the subject of the problems of nursing, about which I knew very little. From this I was drawn into a wider examination of some of the problems of health.

At first sight, the problems look like organisational problems. They are, to a very great extent, in the way they are being interpreted as the National Health Service is being reorganised. Part of the remit was to ensure, in the case of the Nursing Committee, "that the best use is made of available manpower to meet present needs and the needs of an integrated health service".

No one could tell me on that Christmas Eve, when the late Dick Crossman asked me to do the job, what the "integrated Health Service" might be. The upheaval has continued ever since, and an enormous organisational exercise is needed to cope with it. There are enormous administration problems which loom large: inequalities of provision for different groups and in different parts of the country; the somewhat terrifying inadequacies of provision with regard to the aged, the chronically sick, the mentally ill and the mentally handicapped. These

are all problems which bedevil real progress in the field. All of them are in no way separable from the general social problems which influence standards of life in the 20th century.

I started with this complex of organisational problems, and in my life I have become interested increasingly in these and in the way that organisations operate. But I was drawn at once into deeper problems about the role of care in contemporary society. Nursing is not only a caring profession – a term some people do not like – but it is increasingly the most important, the one that has helped to define this. The more complicated society becomes, the more it needs care for individuals.

So one moves from the problems of organisation, with clear outlines, to the rather difficult ones of suffering, deprivation and care. I turned back to Tolstoy's words on the death of Ivan Ilyich: "Something dreadful was happening to Ivan Ilyich, something novel, something of such great moment that nothing of greater moment had ever happened to him. And he alone was aware of this: the people about him either did not understand or did not care to understand, and went on thinking that everything in the world was just as it always had been. It was this that terrified him more than anything else." I have the feeling that such states of consciousness are neither specifically Russian or tied to any particular economic or social context: they are common to most people.

So you are drawn to the needs of individuals and groups, to the quality of care. Such a line of thought naturally leads to asking more basic questions about direct care, in relation not only to what forms of care but in relation to care for whom and when – into the continuity of care. As I have said, one is drawn not only into suffering, into deprivation, but into the relationship between management and care. There seems to me to have been too much thinking – although one understands the basis of it all – about the managerial models in relation to the Health Service and not enough attention paid to these prob-

lems of care for which the management is essentially instrumental.

I went on from this to the pivotal relationship in modern society about the standard of care and the access to it in relation to an integrated Health Service which encompasses hospital and community, and the changing methods of the service provided. I carried out this exercise, with my colleagues, on the basis that education mattered a lot. The education of nurses seemed to be the key to the quality of nursing in the future. So, also, the doctors and any other of the so-called para-medical professions.

You can see the various lines of enquiry opened up in my mind, and it seemed appropriate tonight to put this into relation with the development of education as a whole. I found myself getting to know more about the details of structure, the profile of a profession, and also the attitudes of a group. Being a historian by trade, I wanted to see this in historical perspective, not only in the recent historical perspective, through Florence Nightingale's eyes, but in more distant historical perspective, to set the 20th century against earlier experience, which is necessary to evaluate the particular qualities of the moment in time in which we are living. I found myself turning back to the relationship between medicine, health and society in different periods.

I also found out something about myself in the process of enquiry. I found that in terms of values I was attaching an immense importance to what is now called the "health sector", in jargon terms. It seemed to be just as challenging, if not more so, than the "education sector", just as much in need of investigation, speculation, reorganisation.

I found that my attitudes were not the same as those of the doctors. I began to feel more and more that health education should be considered as a whole, and that it should not just be the medical that was treated as a whole, with the education of the other professions treated as ancillary. There should be

some kind of common strategy even when the education was differentiated. There should be increasing – and not diminishing – concern for the social services within this health and welfare set-up. The segregation between the social worker and the clinician, the controversial consequences of the Seebohm Report, should not be allowed to lead to the complete segregation of these groups. The recruitment to all should be more open, and more attention should be given to the motivation of the recruits rather than their paper qualifications at the point of entry.

I began to feel increasingly that where the emphasis must be placed in the long run is not on the kind of contribution nurses made in the hospital or in the community service, but on the concept of positive health in society. Health education in the narrower sense of the word, as used by health educators through the ages, with a preventive element in it, seems to be a basic ingredient in all forms of health development.

Very little appears to have been written about some of the conditions for the development of positive health in a society. We have to study ways of life, to get at questions of this kind; to look at the ways of life in our society and the risks they carry with them; the complaints that are not conveniently labelled as diseases; the restrictions on human performance which prevent the realisation of potential; what may in current jargon be called the "ecological" as well as the "technological" approach to health. At this point I began to be very uneasy about the concept of "health sector" with which I had started.

As one of my colleagues at Sussex, John Fowler, has put it: "The well being of the individual human organism is affected by the whole social order of which it is a part, for example by the nature and quality of the food supply, by the presence of unnatural substances in working and residential environments and by socially determined habits such as tobacco and alcohol consumption. Health is appropriately regarded as a biological indicator of well being, to be coupled with monetary indicators

such as *per capita* income. Because health is affected by the whole social order, it is not realistic to attempt to isolate all the major determinants of health as a technical sector. We can discuss health in relation to the whole social order, and in relation to those activities specifically directed towards its improvement".

If one moves away from the concept of a sector of health, to an attempt to state the whole problem, it is in collectivist terms, but it can also be stated in individual terms, which are not so familiar to us. I wanted to get back to the individual terms, and I had to go back to the Classics to find some of the right statements, which gave some notion of balance, or strangely enough to Russian literature. I went back to the passage from Martial: "Cascellius extracts an aching tooth. Hyginus burns away the hairs that hurt the eyes. Hermes is a very Podalirius in curing hernia; but tell me Gallus, where is he that can help my harassed person?" So there was great difficulty in finding someone to deal with the whole.

Compare Ivan Karamazov's doppelganger in Dostoievsky: "I've consulted all sorts of doctors. They can diagnose excellently. They will tell you all your symptoms. They have your illness at their finger tips. But they've no idea how to cure you. I happened to come across a very enthusiastic medical student. 'You may die' he told me, 'but at least you'll have a very good idea of what you are dying of'."

This was before the Revolution. We no longer think in these kinds of terms about the relationship between disease and health, and know far more about cure than about care. But there are problems in relation to what the Greeks were thinking of when talking about "balance"; what the Russians were thinking of when expressing dissatisfaction with the "imbalance".

I had a brief word with Lord Cohen of Birkenhead, one of the great minds of our time. He said that the whole essence can be summed up in the phrase "mens sana in corpore sano".

That was the link between what I was thinking personally about health and about education. Do we get "mens sana" through education any more than we get a healthy body from the doctor? We do not. For all the vast public expenditure on education, we do not achieve by it as much as the most sanguine people hope. It is still the case that the healthiest man does not see the doctor and that the most wise – though not necessarily the most knowledgeable – is not a university graduate. This does not mean we should suspend, postpone or even limit our educational activities, but should be sceptical about the results they will achieve.

It is not difficult for a Vice-Chancellor to justify his making such comments, although these days a Vice-Chancellor is expected to talk more of vice than of education. I have always resisted the word "educationist". It sounds pompous and pretentious, and seems to me to confuse knowledge of systems and understanding of objectives. But looking at education in parallel to heatlth, although spending an enormous amount on education from the school right through to the university and beyond, we should realise it is an activity which involves something more than a sector of life, even if divided into primary, secondary and tertiary. There are so many things outside the education system which affect the people in it – family background, mass communication – which influence both children and adults inside and outside the home, sometimes reinforcing what the education system does or providing a counter influence. Many early aspirations have their roots in our families. There is very little that school or university can do to change them. As to the mass media, they are by no means clear about their influence in this direction, any more than the people who write about them are. There is a clear distinction made between "educational" influence and "educative" influence. It is a useful dichotomy. The former is premeditated and positive. The latter is diffuse and often unplanned.

Given therefore that it is misleading to think entirely of an

"education sector", we have to do a lot of re-thinking about it, as we have to do about the problem in relation to health which I earlier identified.

My own thinking about education has been just as strongly influenced by my own experience as has my recent experience in relation to the Health Service. I have become convinced of the importance of the continuity of education as a concept, just as much as the continuity of care. It is not an activity concentrated in a particular period of one's life or in any particular institution. It goes through stages. It has a different rhythm according to the learning activities of the individual which are very complex and about which we know nothing.

A somewhat similar process goes on at a more sophisticated level at university, so there is a great arc between what a child does at 3-7, and what an adolescent does at 17-20. We now realise how important it is to continue education at the adult stage. In 40-50 years universities may well become multi-age institutions concerned with people of all ages, rather than just with a particular age group between 17 and 20. What happens to people in the later stages of their life has always tended to be ignored, just as it is in the field of health.

I have mentioned the aged chronic sick and the mentally handicapped aged. We fall behind Germany and France in the rehabilitation services connected with health, which have become major services within their systems. This has emerged through my interest in adult education, re-interpreting it in the school and university systems. The Open University is of tremendous interest in showing what can be done.

The second line of enquiry is the relationship in education between the communication of specialised knowledge, on which our very complex modern society depends, and other knowledge, particularly at the university level. What is the knowledge we should have in common? How much should we have? When should we start? The more specialised we become, how are we to understand the limits of our specialisation and

the divergent and convergent specialisations which are part of the same cluster? Should we not find the things in common and review the learning process in relation to them?

This issue also arises in our thinking about health, particularly about the role of the general practitioner as compared with that of the specialist within the Health Service. In this country we attach an immense amount of importance to general practitioners as something more than a congeries of specialists. In this country we are in a position to be able to say more useful things about the relationship between the specialist and the generalist than is the case in most other countries.

The third line of enquiry is the question of how we in education can really distinguish between the problems concerned with the development of the individual – making him a more educated person – and those concerned with the transmission of bodies of knowledge. Without the latter, in a hard way, it is impossible to create effectively new knowledge. So there must be a very hard core to the educational process. But we must always be thinking how to relate it to the specific needs of the individual.

Here again there are interesting points with relation to the whole story of health, where the great bio-chemical revolution of the last 60 to 80 years was associated with the development of hard knowledge, so that we have been able to do extraordinary things with mortality. Other people have been responsible for the things we have been able to do in relation to birth. But this has been accomplished through the development of science and the laboratory.

Earlier on, why did people's mortality rate decline? Usually because of forms of improvement – improved standards of living, the impact of the sanitary idea as a moral idea, and the transformation of the environment. In our educational system today it is quite easy to have the moral concern comparable to that which animated the sanitary reformers of the nineteenth century. It is not missing from our own graduates. But there is

some willingness to go soft on some of these major issues. The more I have thought about them, the more I am convinced – and it is very appropriate to say this here – that we must never lose this concept of there being communicable developing knowledge which is to some extent independent of the person communicating it.

The quality of education is compared to the quality of care. It is essential to put the quality questions foremost in the way we think both about health and education. There is great difficulty in measuring this and defining this, particularly in education. Nevertheless everyone would agree that however much we might talk about access to education, flexibility of education, equality within the system, democratic control of the system – and all these four points are relevant to health – if quality is overlooked or under-priced then the system itself will lose its fire, its power. It is not simply a matter of resources but is essentially one of people.

My last personal thoughts about education inexorably have led me to the old question of what constitutes an educated man. It has to be reframed in every generation. There are more answers to it than to the question about what constitutes a healthy man, for which there are very few accounts – "strong as a horse", "as sound as a bell", "as fit as a fiddle" – these are very curious phrases. Nearly all those we apply to education come from agriculture – "culture", "seminal" – agricultural metaphors in their origin. Here we are getting to something profound about the relationship of the continuity of thought to these fundamental activities of human beings in every generation.

At present when we ask "what is an educated man?" we should add "in a pluralistic society such as our own, in the 20th century". The Renaissance man would feel ill at ease. What is a healthy man? What is a healthy man in an affluent society, but with strains and stresses unknown before? Our plurality may be less and our affluence may be very attenuated in the future

compared with what it is now. But the plurality and the affluence are dominating and controlling influences on the context within which the question should be put.

My line of enquiry has involved me in helping to create a new university, together with my colleagues, and this is a very rare privilege in any period. All the way through we realised we were dealing with the problem of objectives and not just of management, although the two interact in many ways. We had to have a secure framework if we were to get viable answers. I am not too happy myself about the results in general of this kind of fundamentally necessary endeavour. I am increasingly conscious of the pressures, internal and external, which may push us backwards rather than forwards in the next few years. At one time it was said that quantitative education, as in the Health Service, had peaks which pointed up to Heaven, that the dynamics of the system had changed. I am now much less sure. What stands out so much is not just the superiority of the old institutions which were already there. They can be very easily idealised or mythologised. What stands out is the extreme difficulty of graduates in new institutions at this period of time – in education as much as in anything else – when every old institution is being challenged: religious, economical, political. But if there is not a willingness to take risks and venture out, universities will be totally irrelevant. A good university is not necessarily a quiet one. But all depend on some basic conception of order, if they are to inject knowledge and to enhance new knowledge. That must be associated with freedom, which is the life blood of the whole exercise.

Let me move away from the personal experience, my own not very conventional and not very fashionable way of putting it, to the way it is being put conventionally at the present time. We have systems of education and health which are making immense calls on our national resources. In both cases there is talk of a crisis or of showdowns. Last week the *Daily Telegraph* ran the headline "Health Service on verge of

breaking down warn GP's", and "Students to get rid of, – Universities to close". The difference was that Dr. Rowse was wanting less money to be spent on education and the GP's wanted more money to be spent on health. In the same week university Vice-Chancellors were pointing to the threats to the financial future of universities and the *British Medical Journal* was supporting the doctors, and saying; " 'Crisis' may be an overworked word, but it is an accurate diagnosis of the political and financial condition of the Health Service at the present time." In both cases, attention was being focused directly on this year and next as the years of social emergency linked with the economic one. That is the way in which the issue is increasingly being posed.

As in the case of the economic crisis which is immediately responsible for restricting the supply of resources in education and health, this is not exceptional in this country, but the vast expenditures that we have in this country do raise fundamental immediate questions. Even before the latest feverish inflation, the gross expenditure for health and welfare and education had both passed beyond the £2500m – more than 5% of the gross national product. Recently they have roared further ahead, with resources failing to keep pace with inflation. These huge sums do not cover the whole of the direct spending on these two sectors. The sale of patent medicines over the counter amounts to another £100m. Private education also adds very substantially to the bill. These are huge sums of money.

One can play indefinitely with figures. They are the kind that astronomers used to employ to put man in his proper place in the universe. But thinking about these has been changed just as radically as the expenditures themselves. As the totals have risen sharply over the last 25 years, there has been a growing sense that both the health and education services, as they used to be called, constitute two joint systems. Hitherto in the 19th and early 20th century they were thought of as clusters of scattered activities – hospitals, schools, community services,

etc., sometimes unrelated, with many providers, many motives behind their provision, many sources. Now they are thought of as systems. A "system" is just as calculated to put an individual in his place as are the large figures involved in working out the total cost.

In thinking about the transformation which leads to this, I am reminded of the other dramatic transformation in the early 19th century when people began to talk for the first time of a "factory system". In present conditions it relies on co-ordination rather than competition, the opposite to the factory. There is bound to be a preoccupation with management and planning. Increasingly the global sums set aside by the community become a matter of politics and their distribution becomes a matter of norms identified on a sophisticated or unsophisticated basis, which take little account of local requirements. An immense amount of activity goes into the system management itself.

Education is a binary system divided up into stages. In health it is an integrated system, with local health and hospital brought into it together, but community care and continuous care is also brought in. How recent all this talk of a "system" in relation to health and education actually is. The Robbins Report in the early 1960's wrote vaguely of the system of higher education in this country "if it can be called a system". The hardening of the so-called "binary system" of education, with universities on the one side and polytechnics on the other, was still in the future except in the minds of a few elite in Whitehall.

Although the Porritt Committee of the BMA was proposing new area health boards in 1962 it was not until the late 1960's that the debate on integration within a comprehensive system opened out and quickened, and attempts were made to explain what "integration" really meant.

To understand systems and their workings we turn increasingly, not only in Whitehall, to systems analysts rather than to historians. But I am bound to note that very few people

in this country, including the system analysts, look at the same time at the development of a health system and an educational system in relation to each other. Each system, still in change, still involving large numbers of unknowns, still open ended, is taken on its own and examined on its own terms. It is not surprising therefore that there is so much concentration on operational management – necessary though this is – and so little understanding either of the human and social processes at work in a period of large-scale institutional change, or of the goals.

When the health system and the educational system are ever considered together, they tend to be thought of as competitors for scarce national resources: more hospitals or more schools, more community care or more further education. I have never heard anyone refer to the Robbins Report and the Porritt Report in the same context. Yet both systems have developed under common pressures, springing from within the heart of society, in the family, in the first instance, yet influenced also in the course of growth by professional considerations and large-scale governmental policies.

It is useful at times to put the two together rather than pull them apart. There would have been no Robbins Committee had there not been a much publicised "bulge", a demographic bulge with a substantial increase of numbers in the 18 to 21 year age group, and awareness of the bulge made policy-makers speculate also about what was called the "trend", a movement in attitudes and behaviour influencing the demand for higher places in higher education.

From that emerged the beginnings of a new concept of "system". Would the health care system have come if the numbers of people over 65 had not increased so much – to 9 million or 15% of the population – in the 1950's, when half the men in this country were living until just past 70 and half the women living until past 75? The very presence of the young in the demographic bulge and of the aged at the other end of the

spectrum have led to many pressures and options. So far the pressures have come from the parents and the teachers, not from the old, in working out these problems.

But these issues are at the very heart of our society. The same kind of questions are coming to the forefront: freedom and control, access and equity, quantity and quality, and the role of institutionalisation itself, the environment of the school or the hospital. There has often been a very loose and incomplete discussion about "regionalisation" with regard to education, a concept already achieved in the Health Service. It is interesting to see if there are to be similar developments in the educational system. In the next few years it will become increasingly necessary to note that both the health care and educational systems are perhaps best thought of as sub-systems, increasingly complex and expensive sub-systems, both related to the economic system on the efficiency of which they depend for their material resources.

In health care, the feeling of restraint applied to activity has always been strong, yet there is perhaps more talk than ever of rationing scarce resources and achieving cost effectiveness, and in higher education the mood is very different from what it was when the Robbins Report was published. This is the challenge lying ahead in the future.

In conclusion, to try to pull together a few thoughts of my own about that objective way of stating the problem rather than my own personal views expressed at the beginning. In thinking about education within the health professions, it is very useful to go back to some of the landmarks which are there in the documents of the past, some forgotten, some unimplemented, some extraordinarily well said. I look back to the Goodenough Report, produced in 1944, when this country was at war:

"Properly planned and carefully conducted medical education is *the* essential function of a comprehensive health service. If such a service is to have continuing vitality, it must be

founded on highly developed and vigorous systems of general and professional education for members of the medical and allied professions, and it must evoke the enthusiastic and intelligent co-operation of the general public. The spirit of education must permeate the whole of the health service . . . We think it is advisable to stress the dependence of a successful health service on medical education, partly because current discussions show signs of a tendency to concentrate prematurely on the detailed structure of such a service to the neglect of its essential foundation, and partly because problems of medical education and research are not the exclusive concern of the medical schools and the medical profession. They are of vital importance to the nation, and the general public should maintain a lively and understanding interest in them. Indeed, the nature and results of the arrangements made for training medical practitioners, and for increasing their knowledge and skill after qualification can rightly be judged only in relation to the individual and collective needs".

In the passage of time we might wish to widen the reference of this statement, but it still rings true. Professor Tawney, writing of education said that "educational problems cannot be considered in isolation from the aspirations of great bodies of men and women for whose sake alone it is that educational problems are worth considering at all."

One has only to look at some of the documents to get some of the clarion calls for effective action.

Secondly, the problems of health and education systems will not be met by the infusion of more and more men and women and more and more resources. They require more thinking, as related to the school, university, polytechnic, health centre. It must be well grounded and well informed, but there must be places of initiative where new ideas – the difficult ones – can be carried out. All the emphasis in stopping overlapping and making sure that everyone is fairly treated is very necessary, but there is a very strong argument for separate initiative and

for diversity of response, for experiment within the system. The whole pattern of health and education looks very different if you are within an innovating centre from what it does if you are in a place where the working of the system is regarded as the only going concern. Businessmen should be clearly aware of the concept of enterprise, just as important in relation to health and education as is the concept of system, which means very little to most businessmen in their daily operations.

Thinking on these lines, it is difficult to reconcile macro and micro planning, the planning of the small and large systems. It is also difficult to keep it flexible, even more so than in France, in being willing to try out different systems.

As the professions have responded to these professional, economic and social changes, there is a growing conflict between many of them to tighten their boundaries, to increase their nominal admission standards, to stiffen their licensing arrangements, to find themselves in argument with the people who might go into the professions. One of the points in the nursing report is that it is not formal paper qualifications at entry which really matter, although they may be a useful indicator, but the motivation, in the kind of way which allows a very genuine concern not only for standards but for objectives. So, all these points seem to arise when one is seeking to fit together a general picture with a personal picture, in relation to this subject.

LORD GOODMAN:

Professor Asa Briggs has said that he will be happy to answer any questions.

QUESTION:

Would the speaker feel that the conception of the Health Service, in the first place, would have been far better if greater emphasis had been placed on preventive medicine, a check-up every five years for people rather than spending money on surgical and other hospital services?

PROFESSOR ASA BRIGGS:

I think it is important and useful to start with that as a basic objective. If it had developed in a different way, through the community centre, earlier in the history, there might have been a different kind of development generally. I have been tremendously impressed by the experiment being worked out in the University of the Negev in Israel, where Dr. Prywes is trying to relate the whole thing from prevention to treatment, using teaching at every stage. But broadly speaking, I agree that ultimately the answer may be found that through preventive care of every kind it is possible to cut down much of the cost which at present occurs due to the inadequacy of such check-ups.

QUESTION:

You mentioned that many of the wise may not be graduates and also that there is a problem in relating the graduate who probably thinks that the wise have not sufficient knowledge or education. Have you any idea on bridging the gap, as it is quite a problem for employers?

PROFESSOR ASA BRIGGS:

Unfortunately, knowledge very easily goes with a kind of arrogance. Also, we have built up within 20th century society a very clearly delineated conception of the expert. I myself believe that it is only when one is concerned with a practical set of preoccupations that one can really develop the right kind of dialogue. It requires a very considerable amount of patience on the part of the person who is wise rather than knowledgeable. We can take some comfort from the fact that knowledge itself is changing rapidly whereas wisdom seems to be a quality found in equal quantities – or the lack of it – in each generation. There is in fact a field of thought where it does not matter very much in the short run whether one is wise or not. But increasingly, in relation to the big problem areas which are subjects of research, wisdom seems to be coming into the determination of those areas as much as in life generally. I

think this relationship is going through a pretty bad patch at the present time. Patience and a more shared educational experience of people of different ages would help in the long run to make this more effective.

QUESTION:

Have you any comments on the fact that we entrust a very large sector of our educational sector to elected representatives, whereas in the Health Service this is strongly resisted?

PROFESSOR ASA BRIGGS:

On the whole, this is a very interesting comment on the health service. There is current debate as to whether there should not be a stronger elected element in it. It takes up a tremendous amount of time, problably even more so than the education side which has always claimed people's time very much. In general, one would look in the long run towards a more important elected element in both, but it should not be just associated with a theory of representation. It is absolutely essential, if we are to get this in health or education, to have some educative element in relation to the people who are serving. In a field such as health you could not have it turned into a sort of battleground such as one can find even in some areas of education. In the long run, there will be an increase in the elected element in both, and I would hope that it would be associated with some kind of educational programme.

QUESTION:

Would you comment on the difference between education and health in the sphere of service given? In the educational field it is very much a personalised service, but in the health field there is very much a commercial approach. On the publishing side of the health field it is dead-end and materialistic as compared with the service.

PROFESSOR ASA BRIGGS:

One of the fundamental issues is not just the influence that the commercial motive plays but the whole question of research. If I had been speaking longer I would have wanted to

emphasise that teaching and health both involve enormous research expenditures, and in both there is a very real relationship between the teaching and the research. I think that the educational sector, for a whole number of reasons, has been open to a kind of argument and debate of a really broad type never applied to the health sector until very recently. It is only for 70-80 years that we have had a bio-medical revolution, and only for 150 years, with a few distinguished exceptions, that we have moved from almost a belief in magic to some form of social control. For education, on the other hand, a very real interest developed over a long period. The more you get these vast expenditures on health and education, the more you have to look at the question of service on one side and cost-effectiveness or value for money on the other. In such practical terms I would want to sort out the issue, but there is this contrast. You were right to raise the position of the publisher, but there has been a big change in recent years, where this has been brought within the market sector as the organisations have grown.

QUESTION:

How far do you think the increasing financial dependence of the health service and the educational system upon aid from the State is likely to constitute an unhealthy development in our health system and a constricting factor in our education system?

PROFESSOR ASA BRIGGS:

I think it would be constricting if it were to carry with it a threat to independent initiative and a variety of sources of intiative. Undoubtedly such a danger exists within the systems. But I also think that if one really looks at human needs in terms of different social groups, and looks at the way in which the health service deals with particular groups at the present time, it just nibbles away at some of the problems of deprivation which are so important regarding health. With education where huge sums are also spent, we have only just started to

move the mass of the population of the country into the position where they could have the chance to make the full use of their individual potential. I think that the idea of the community's involvement in both education and health is absolutely fundamental, but I believe that it is possible within both these systems to produce bureaucratic structures more easily than where there are more varieties of motivation and even of finance. We must make them both free from some of their inherent dangers if they are to be really effective long term instruments.

QUESTION:

Would you look at a problem facing us within the next two years? The lines of thought on health education and training and those on the health service will come together in the preparation of directives from the Common Market. We will be facing a situation where we must align the training and education of the professions in relation to the other eight – the former six countries. Have you any views on this problem?

PROFESSOR ASA BRIGGS:

These are very important discussions. I hope that the British view will be positively expressed in them, as it has been in relation to the medical ones which have taken place, that it is no good proceeding by some kind of mathematical way in saying that if you do X hours of this and Y hours of that you have the basis of the qualification. The emphasis which has been placed on this within the discussions on doctors' qualifications has been the right one, that the quality of the education is just as important as the quantity, and the more you apply formulae the more unsatisfactory the position becomes. In France there is a very peculiarly conservative medical profession and it is difficult to forge ahead with the kind of new ideas about education if there is to be a very bureaucratic Ministry-dominated approach. I regret that in some of the discussions which have taken place some continental countries have only been represented by people from

government departments. The most important thing we can do is to bring in the universities, the polytechnics, and the professions themselves where necessary. If we are to go ahead with some of this harmonisation, every profession will have to spend a lot of time working out its own strategy in relation to the talks. I do not think it should be left to civil servants.

LORD GOODMAN:

Obviously we could continue this fascinating exchange for the greater part of the night. Before calling for a formal vote of thanks, I would say that Professor Briggs has amply vindicated what I said about him at the beginning. He has the verve, the elan, the enthusiasm which denotes a dedicated man. Never before did we need a discussion of these fundamental matters so much as we do now. There is a hysteria calling for remedies beyond the nature of the ailment. Therefore wise and informed men should indulge in discussion. It is with special gratitude, therefore, that I call for the vote of thanks to him.

Lord Swann F.R.S.

At the time of his lecture Sir Michael Swann, (as he then was), was Chairman of the British Broadcasting Corporation, a post he held until 1980.

From 1965–73 he was Principal and Vice-Chancellor of the University of Edinburgh and since 1979 has been Chancellor of the University of York.

He was created a life peer in 1981.

THE THIRD GOODMAN LECTURE

'Coming to Terms with Mass Communication'

delivered by

Sir Michael Swann, F.R.S.,

Chairman of the B.B.C.

Tuesday, 1st July, 1975

CHAIRMAN The Rt. Hon. The Lord GoodmanC.H.

LORD GOODMAN:

Ladies and gentlemen, this is the third Aitchison Memorial lecture. Ordinarily, I would say that we have this evening a Speaker who follows in the splendid and distinguished tradition of his two predecessors, but it would be a little difficult for anyone as modest as myself to say that. I will only say we have an exceptionally distinguished and attractive speaker.

We have had three lectures. The first I gave myself, and called it "Coming to Terms with Science." It was a lecture in which I gave a faint inkling of my own massive ignorance of anything to do with science, but I felt I owed it to Irvine Aitchison to touch on some scientific form of subject, because primarily and basically he was a scientist. The second lecture was given by Professor Asa Briggs, who is, of course, a distinguished humanist. The third lecture is given by a very great scientist , a man of very great scientific achievement who is now, strangely enough, best known to the world for something quite different. He has entered into the world of the humanities.

Perhaps if he was asked to define those activities in those precise and slightly competing terms, he would say he is engaged in a "battle of the humanities", if I may express it in that fashion.

In 1973, something very remarkable happened to the BBC. What happened was that peace and repose settled upon it. Until that year there had been the most animated, interesting and exciting warfare going on between the Government and its Opposition, the Corporation, and everyone concerned in it. It was perhaps not specially edifying, but it was quite amusing. We have to reproach our speaker tonight that he has removed from us that element of entertainment that existed before 1973 in the constant warfare that went on. How he did that, I do not know. It is by sheer force of personality.

We have in our speaker tonight a most remarkable man who was a scientist and a member of this distinguished organisation – and it is appropriate we should have a Fellow to give the third lecture. He probably never thought at any time that his energies would be diverted from the real scientific activities in which he excelled and in which he obviously delighted, and all of a sudden he finds himself engaged in one of the most important creative and administrative tasks the country has. He was called upon, one might almost say, to rescure the BBC from the constant friction, the constant hostilities, the constant difficulties that arose within that organisation because it had failed to come to terms with Government.

I hope one day, perhaps in a lecture, when he feels able to tell us more than at the moment the 30-year rule permits and the outcome of the Crossman Diary controversy has been resolved, we will have a talk from Sir Michael about "Coming to Terms with Government". He has done this with superlative success. He has been able to turn his mind and the minds of people at Broadcasting House and Television House to their real task of producing broadcasting and television programmes, so that they are not distracted, and we are not distracted,

hour by hour by differences of opinion between men and their masters. I think this is a very great achievement.

But he has done something more. He has achieved, in the relatively short space of time he has been there, the total respect of the people who work for him and the people with whom he works. He has earned their affection and their respect, and he has earned their confidence that he will stand by them as long as they make sensible decisions. Throughout his life he has had a reputation for being sensible. This is a reputation which, if I may so so, nowadays is both rare and not always popular.

He deals with students, and managed somehow to avoid student problems and student conflagrations and student battles. He does this, not by the popular present-day formula of agreeing to everything the little dears ask for. By no means. He does this by exercising a sensible domestic control, and saying "When you ask for something sensible and necessary you can have it; when you ask for something preposterous you will get a clip on the ear." That is why this splendid blend of common sense, reason and knowledge, etcetera, has achieved the result at the BBC he achieved in his previous incarnation as Vice-Chancellor of a famous university.

I look forward immensely to hearing what he is going to say to us tonight. He has told me I suggested the theme for his lecture. If I do so I am very pleased, but it strikes me as a very provocative theme, and I have not the least idea what it means. I am certain he will give it a very real meaning, and a very sensible meaning, and we can look forward to it with great pleasure.

Before I conclude, I had better say that he has kindly said, as in the case of the previous lecturers, that he will answer a few questions. I hope the questions will be of the kind which do not involve departures from good taste and good sense. He is obviously not going to impart information of the character which can only be imparted by the *Sunday Times* in its most

belligerent mood. I can only say he has kindly agreed to answer appropriate questions.

I have very great pleasure in calling upon our Speaker. Thank you.

SIR MICHAEL SWANN:

Lord Goodman and Mr. Bateman, my Lords, ladies and gentlemen, it is a familiar situation, I suppose, to find myself having to move off to the rostrum on the left but being regarded as being on the right! It would be equally familiar if the situation was reversed.

Lord Goodman has made a whole lot of remarks which are totally unjustified, and I am not going to say anything more about them, save to thank him. But I do want to say that it is an honour to give this lecture, and it is a source of some concern to have to give it under the Chairmanship of Lord Goodman who, as you all know, is not only a master of the spoken word, but the man who gave the first of these lectures. Nevertheless, it is a source of some satisfaction that he gave the first lecture, as he said himself, audaciously, on a subject about which he knew nothing, namely, science. After all he started life as a lawyer – and don't we know it at the BBC, because occasionally people who do not like us go to seek his advice.

I also am going to talk audaciously about something I know very little about, having started as a scientist but having moved off into areas altogether far distant from this Society and its noted lecture hall. I should perhaps interject, because Lord Goodman said a word or two about it, that in one way or another television has caused me quite a lot of trouble in my life. For reasons I cannot remember, but way back in 1958, I used to do rather a lot of television. In those days I was just a junior academic, and I was drawn aside by my erstwhile professor at Cambridge, who said: "Swann, if you go on mucking about like this with the mass media, you will never get into the Royal Society." It is a source of some satisfaction to

me that I did indeed get into the Royal Society, and later on, into the BBC.

The title for this third Goodman Lecture, "Coming to Terms with Mass Communication", is not mine, though it is one I freely accepted. It comes, in fact, or so I believe, immediately, from the Aitchison Memorial Fund Trustees, and the more I have thought about it, the more I have come to realise how difficult and subtle a question it is. Does society ever really come to terms with any form of technology, or any form of social organisation? In the sense of absorbing them wholly harmoniously, the answer is quite certainly no.

We are apt to look back nostalgically to bygone days, the Edwardian era or the 18th century, or Elizabethan times, or Rome or Greece, and imagine otherwise. But that calm and golden stability, if it existed at all, was enjoyed by very few. And I don't doubt that even the enormous dynasties of Egypt or China were not as stable as they now look to people who know rather little about them.

But the important phrase in the Trustees' Lecture title is "coming to terms with", and it is inevitably the case that society has to come to some sort of terms with every human activity. The only question is, *what* sort of terms? They can be repressive, or easy. They can be changing, or relatively stable. They can be satisfactory or unsatisfactory, to either side, in varying degrees and in different respects. They amount at the end of the day to a deal or a contract between society as a whole and this or that activity or segment of society.

Consider first of all modern medicine, the most powerful offshoot of all from modern science. In the immediate sense, society has found no difficulty at all in coming to the most favourable and harmonious terms with it, not surprisingly. Techniques that have made death in childbirth an extreme rarity instead of a commonplace, that have made childbirth itself a less painful, or even a painless process, that have prevented half or more children dying in infancy, that have

prevented or greatly mitigated almost every human ailment, and doubled and nearly trebled our average life span all these are readily welcomed, and no questions asked.

But that is not quite the end of the story. The dramatic progress in medicine has only been achieved by a range of large and immensely costly services for research, development and treatment, and after a century or more of virtually unimpeded growth these have acquired great momentum, and become powerful vested interests. Since, moreover, knowledge inevitably outstrips practice, there is continuing pressure to extend the services yet further. But now, when the National Health Service, with all its ancillary and underlying support, absorbs something approaching one sixth of public expenditure, the end of the phase of growth is inevitably in sight. Society, in short, has got very soon to decide just how much more it is prepared to pay for its health. The decision will be a very difficult one, politically, socially, and ethically. But there is no doubt that quite soon we shall have to come to a fresh set of terms with medicine.

Nor are the problems restricted to questions of the cost of medical services. We take for granted all the benefits of medicine, and scarcely notice that as a result, we have a population of elderly and retired people which is far higher than it was even 50 years ago, and will soon be much higher yet. But we have by no means absorbed all the implications: first and foremost, I suppose, the need for a relatively smaller working population to work harder, and forgo some of their rewards for the benefit of the relatively much larger population of old people. We shall need, in short, to come to fresh terms with other sectors of society, because of the terms we struck in the past with medicine.

Difficult as it will be to deal with the problems of medicine, there are much more difficult ones already upon us – most intractable of all, the relations of Government and industry. Within the lifetimes of most of you here today, we have of

course seen a great change in the terms on which we accept capitalism. So great were the advantages it brought in the wake of the industrial revolution that its unacceptable face was largely ignored 100 years, even 50 years ago. Slowly this has changed, in part due to the growth of Trade Unionism, and its link with the Labour Party, in part due to changes in public opinion. The terms on which we accept private enterprise are now, by more or less universal consent, greatly stiffened. By contrast, the terms conceded fairly early on to Trade Unionism have changed rather little. In spite of this, Trade Unionism, as a mechanism for regulating the employer-employee relationship in a free society, continues to work quite well over much of private industry, even if it creaks in some areas. But it has ceased to work so well in one area for which of course it was never designed – within the state monopoly corporations. These are areas where financial and commercial constraints operate with difficulty, so that the normal limitations on wage claims are wanting. And of course, as one Union after another has discovered, it is an area where strikes can bring the whole country to disaster.

It was inevitable that the Labour Government in the late 60's should attempt to redraw the terms by new legislation, even though they were forced in the end to retreat. And it was equally inevitable that the last Conservative Government should try again, though they were unseated by a particularly powerful Union. In the circumstances I personally believe that the second attempt of the Labour Government to redraw the terms of the much maligned Social Contract was a wise one. But as we all know, it has not worked.

Clearly there must be fresh attempts to come to new terms, and if a centralist solution, such as most people fervently hope for, cannot soon be found, then the terms, whether far left or far right, are likely to be repressive and unchanging. At the very least the Trade Unions' right to free bargaining and strikes would be removed from them. One has only to look round the

Communist and Fascist countries of the world to see the terms these countries have struck with Labour.

I have not chosen these two facets of society, medicine and industry, at random. I want in due course to return to them in the context of the mass media. But they illustrate as well as any the changing nature of the terms on which society accepts any new advance, or any active social group. I want now to turn to the broad terms on which society has accepted the mass media, and later to look at some of the problems in detail.

The first mass medium was, of course, the printed word in book form, and the consternation it produced from time to time in Church and Government circles is well known. Restrictions of all sorts were imposed, and some, like the Vatican Index, even lingered on into the present century.

The restrictions on the printed word in newspaper form are less well known, but on and off throughout the late 16th century, the 17th and 18th centuries, and indeed well into the 19th century, they existed, with licences and censorship gradually giving way to heavy taxes that were not finally abandoned until 1855.

All this is not really very surprising. Books and newspapers expanded the extent to which information, ideas and comment could be spread round the country by a hundredfold or a thousandfold. A writer or an editor could speak to audiences far beyond the dreams of kings or emperors, and they did indeed pose a very major threat to older styles of Government. But gradually the style of government changed, and along with growing education and growing suffrage, newspapers won the terms from society that they enjoy today.

The terms are not particularly easy, nor, I am sure, are they immutable. Every Government, and most institutions, complain about the Press – its unfairness and the extent to which it makes Government at every level more difficult. But we tolerate it, for one reason above all, that it represents one of the most powerful protections we have against oppression from

any source – particularly from Government, and in lesser degrees from local government and all our other institutions.

No one, I am sure, imagines that the Press is universally wise and fair; nevertheless, it does manage, sooner or later, to expose a surprising lot of foolish or unjust happenings in society, whether they stem from malice, or much more usually, from thoughtlessness and inefficiency. And democratic society must welcome this for its own sake, and if it is a wise society, welcome it as a safety valve and an advance warning system of trouble ahead.

But, of course, there is an essential precondition: a free Press is only acceptable, if taken as a whole, it reflects somehow or other, *all* the interests and concerns of society. A Press which only reported in terms favourable to left or to right, to Trade Unions or to employers, would obviously be little or no better than a Press managed by Government, and reporting only in terms favourable to Government. And it would have lost any claim to be an essential part of the democratic process.

Charges that the Press's presentation of our national life is indeed lop-sided are not lacking. It is a regular complaint of the left wing that newspapers are biased towards industry and the right because of their private ownership. In the strict sense of views expressed in editorial columns, this may even be true. In the more important matter of news coverage I doubt very much if it is true. The faults and follies of industry are no less widely reported than those of Trade Unions, and Conservative Governments do not regard the Press any more kindly than Labour ones.

The recent Referendum campaign was instructive. Almost every editor came down, in the end, on the pro-Market side. But even the most pro-Market papers in fact reported anti-Market speeches and published anti-Market articles. The anti-Market case did not go by default in the Press, no matter what the anti-Marketeers may say.

Whatever the shortcomings of the British Press - and top of

my list would be inaccuracy and sensationalism - the fact is, I believe, that it does try rather hard to live up to the famous precept of C.P. Scott, that facts are sacred, however free comment may be. And even if matters were much worse than I think they are, it would not be a cause for reorganising things. In our present free enterprise system, any group that feels it is being done down, can start up its own newspaper, and if the public wants to read its reports and its comments, the new venture will flourish. The Press really does reflect the basic ethos of free enterprise, that the public can choose what it wants, and that it will pay people to produce it. Anyone, in short, who thinks that British newspapers are not reflecting what people want and believe, can readily prove himself right – or of course wrong. There is unfortunately only one such major experiment to watch at this moment – the new *Scottish Daily News*, which a workers' cooperative has set up in Glasgow, with Government help, in the ashes of the old *Scottish Daily Express*. But it is too soon to reach any conclusions about it.

Imperfect as the Press may be, society has co-existed with it on terms that have been regarded as broadly satisfactory for a century or more. But there are two factors that may bring about a change. The first of these stems from the shaky financial basis of the Press in Fleet Street. In part this is due to the uncertain element of advertising revenue, but in the greater part from chronic overmanning and resistance to new technologies.

The history behind this is long and complicated, but the outcome has been that on the print side Fleet Street has an alarming degree of overmanning. There is something of a conspiracy of silence over the whole affair: unions are reluctant to let the facts be published; editors freely admit that they tone down their comment to avoid confrontation. As a result, no one knows whether a quarter, a half or even more print workers are being maintained in partial idleness. But that it all contributes greatly to Fleet Street's financial problems is not in

dispute. And only now, with dire trouble round the corner, are one or two national newspapers starting to do anything about it. With some goodwill on both sides, the problem is soluble; but if it is not solved, and a few more national papers fold up, the basis of a free Press, namely the wide diversity of separate outlets, would be very seriously undermined, and pressure for some form of regulation by Government would be difficult to resist.

The second factor that could lead to Government's taking a hand in the Press, stems from the potential power of a handful of Unions to determine what is or is not printed. The National Union of Journalists, to their credit, have not sought to censor the news, though they have, in pursuit of a pay claim, applied a rather blanket 'blacking' on certain sources of news. Nevertheless, elements within the Union have openly spoken of their intention to step up such pressures; though whether such moves would command support is doubtful.

Certain of the print Unions however have, more often than is generally realised, refused to print items that they thought were not in their or the Trade Unions' interest. Sometimes editors have resisted such pressures, sometimes they have insisted on leaving blank spaces to indicate the hand of censorship. But in general, and almost by definition, there is once again a conspiracy of silence. One would like to know the full facts. It is, of course, the existence of these pressures that underlies the concern of editors at Mr. Foot's Bill dealing with the closed shop, and why, led by our Chairman today, Lord Goodman, they have been resisting the inclusion of editors themselves within the regulations.

In fairness, it should be said that in the past, though I suspect no longer, proprietors and editors have themselves been guilty of such censorship. But there are a lot of newspapers, and very few Unions, so that union power, if it ever grew to be a major censor of the news, would be a greater menace than editors. One can only hope that the journalistic ethos will prove strong

enough to resist these pressures; for if it doesn't there will, once again, be cause for Government intervention. One way and another, therefore, it is at least possible that a long period of relative stability in the relations of society with the Press is coming to an end.

Since broadcasting was born 50 years ago, in the middle of this period of stability, one might have expected its relationship with society to have been based on that established for the Press. But the constraints of the physical world would have determined otherwise. There are so few wavelengths available for broadcasting, other than on a strictly local basis, that the Press-type solution of multiple diverse private outlets is impossible. individuals or groups cannot set up a broadcasting station as they can set up a newspaper, so that Governments must license the use of wavelengths, and national broadcasting is inevitably a monopoly or near-monopoly affair.

The inherently monopolistic nature, coupled with the immediacy of broadcasting, and its vast audiences make broadcasting a formidable creature for Governments and society to absorb. It is not therefore surprising that the majority of countries in the world, even some that have a moderately free Press, control it tightly. But most of the western democracies have evolved structures that give it a fair measure of freedom.

The watchword, in these countries, is impartiality and balance – as between political parties, between both sides of industry, and all the other sections and interests in society. But this is more easily said than done. Indeed, after 2½ years as Chairman of the BBC, I am clear that it cannot be done to the satisfaction of everyone. What looks balanced and fair in the Labour Party looks unfair to Conservatives, and what looks fair to industrialists looks biased to Trade Unionists. Nor is life any easier outside politics. What seems a very reasonable coverage of sport to X is an intolerable BBC obsession to Y. And what strikes A as a good modern play, is a basinful of crude obscenity to B.

Turning to the political problem, within a fairly standard framework of governing bodies appointed by Governments, three solutions have been pursued in the democracies. One, the most unusual, and so far as I know unique, but in some ways the most logical, is to be found in the Netherlands. A very wide range of organisations – the 'societies' as they are called – provided they can muster enough paying members, can and do get access to the air under the umbrella of a central coordinating organisation which provides also a substantial fraction of the basic programme. Political groups, religious groups and all sorts of others thus have their own say. It looks a splendid idea, but the results, as even the Dutch admit, have been disappointing.

I hesitate to say why. Perhaps it has something to do with fragmentation of effort, and the troubles of coordinating these fragments in the network output; and with disputes over the boundaries of the responsibility of the central organisation for news, and the responsibility of the different societies for comment on public affairs. But although the structure exerts a lasting fascination for academics and critics, it has never been copied anywhere else in the world.

The second solution, and by far the commonest, is to maintain balance by building a balance of politicians into the governing bodies of the organisations. The system ought to work, but does it? Not, so far as I can judge, as well as one might hope.

The chief trouble, it seems, is that if one builds in party political balance at the top, it starts to spread downwards – as attitudes at the top of any organisation inevitably spread downwards. As a result, broadcasters can get appointed, not because they are the best ones, but because of their party affiliations. And in the long run, colleagues who ought to be collaborating to make the best programmes are in fact divided by Party loyalties, and Germany and Italy in particular are both wrestling with these problems at the present moment.

The third solution, evolved in Britain, and copied in a few Commonwealth countries, is a curious one at first sight. It rests not in meeting the problem head on, but, one might say, in abolishing it. The BBC has become an organisation that, in a party sense, is wholly non-political; and the political battle has been replaced with a common ethos of balance and impartiality. This does not mean that the BBC only recruits people with no political views. No doubt the staff are as politically committed or uncommitted as others. But it does mean that we do not pay attention to their party political affiliations; and only if those affliliations obtrude into programme making does anyone take note.

This attitude stems from the Board of Governors itself. They are appointed by the Government of the day, and it is something of a tribute to successive Governments that they have never tried to make the appointments political. We usually have someone who has once been a politican; and we regularly have a Trade Unionist, but more because of his expertise than because of the Trade Unions' link with the Labour Party. Beyond that, the Governors have never been overtly politically committed.

But that is not the whole reason for the non-political structure of the BBC. It has more to do, I believe, with an inherited tradition within the Board of Governors that the Board shall not be politicised. Party affiliations are something that is simply not talked about. And the same attitude holds down the line.

It is of some interest to discover how this curious tradition ever grew up in the first place. For unquestionably it stems from the time when the first Board of Governors, and the first Director General, John Reith, were appointed. It was, I believe, something of a fortunate accident. The Government of the day probably did not realise the full political potential of broadcasting, and the Press of the day were very jealous of the infant BBC, so that political news and comment was very much

restricted. The political problem, as a result, scarcely arose to begin with.

But Reith understood the problem, and from a very early stage set about creating the tradition of impartiality. So that, as step by step the restrictions were lifted, the BBC had already acquired sufficient credit for impartiality not to alarm the politicians unduly – though I say unduly because there were rows, quite serious ones, and history could easily have taken a different turn.

But by 1939 the tradition was established, thanks largely to Reith, so firmly that the BBC was never in fact taken over during the war by the Ministry of Information. It was of course very dependent on the Government for information, but with due caution it nevertheless contrived to hold on to its independence and its tradition of impartiality. Predictably, politicians argued about its political bias; and it comes as something of a surprise to discover that Winston Churchill – in the middle of the war – said privately to Reith (who was then no longer Director General) "The BBC is an enemy within the gates, doing more harm than good." But it is not recorded that he ever said so in public, and certainly he never did anything about it; so clearly the BBC's position had become secure. It is all an interesting comment on the supposedly golden age of broadcasting.

This banishing of politics from the structure of the organisation by no means keeps us out of trouble, as you all know full well. Elements of the Right, particularly when it is in power, tend to see us as dangerously Left, and elements of the Left, when it is in power, as it is now, see us as dangerously conventional and conservative. But when either Party is out of power, things look rather different, and the impartial reporting of trouble for the Government of the day acquires marked attention.

Whether the British pattern leads to less trouble with politicians than the other structures is a moot point. I suspect it

does; and I am quite clear that there are in addition two consequences of our system that are good, one external and one internal.

In the first place, whatever they may think of the end product, politicians of every shade know full well that there is no political structure within the BBC, and that the aim, if not always the result, is that everyone, whatever his personal political views, should submerge them in an ethos of impartiality. So that when things go wrong, as of course they do quite often, it becomes a question of the BBC not living up to its principles rather than of one faction having stolen a march on another. This was brought home to me only a few weeks ago when one Member of Parliament, who felt we had put on an unfair programme, and that he had been shabbily treated into the bargain, actually ended his letter saying that he was not angry, but grieved, because he knew how much trouble was actually taken to get things right.

Internally, I believe the system also has beneficent consequences, and for much the same reasons. If things go wrong, it is not because Party rivalries have failed to balance out, but because people have not lived up to a principle. And that, instead of being divisive, is something over which people can much more readily unite.

I want now to return to the two areas I touched on earlier and say a little about the terms on which they co-exist with broadcasting. Let me quote from a report to the Annan Committee on Broadcasting by a group of scientists, many of them, most of them in fact, Fellows of this Royal Society, who advise the BBC on our whole range of scientific programmes. What they say verges on the embarrassing. "The group has the highest regard for the quality of BBC science programmes and for the unique skill of the Science and Features Department. Although different members of the group are sometimes critical of individual BBC items, in general we wish to emphasise our admiration for the BBC's science output and note with

pleasure that highly regarded international awards have been received. Any criticisms in this report are simply to 'make the best better' ". By contrast, the comments on broadcasting from both sides of industry are invariably full of complaints and cricticisms. Clearly one area has come to fairly satisfactory terms with broadcasting, while the other decidedly has not. Why, one may ask, should there be such a disparity?

It has, I am clear, nothing to do with the quality of staff, but much to do with the objectivity of science as against the subjectivity of human affairs. It is highly significant, therefore, to find that the complaints we do get on scientific programmes usually arise over programmes that touch on scientific controversy, and still more over programmes that impinge on human emotions. Medicine, by definition, is such an area, and it can be difficult to present honest programmes that do not instil hopes or fears in those who watch them. In fact we go to great pains to get such programmes looked at by medical experts at an early stage to advise on the impact they are likely to make on the public. Nevertheless, from time to time, clinicians complain bitterly that we have done harm. But the balance, I believe, is greatly on the side of good, and I suspect that most doctors would agree.

Turning to industry, I am not at all sure that most employers and most Trade Union leaders would agree that the influence of broadcasting is on balance good, even though they might concede a few good programmes.

The complaints from both sides are in fact surprisingly similar, though they stem from very different assumptions; the primary complaint being, without a doubt, that we present all too often an image of conflict, with little or no emphasis on constructive cooperation.

There is something in this criticism, I do not doubt. But the fact of the matter is that Trade Unions are organisations set up to bargain for better wages and conditions with the threat of striking in the background, and bargaining is what they spend

by far the greater part of their energies on. Could the real reason why we do not put on much about Unions in relation to education or health or welfare in fact be because these things absorb rather a small fraction of their time?

And turning to another complaint, that we are apt to show militant shop stewards in preference to headquarters officials, is it not sometimes the case that the former and not the latter are calling the tune? I have no doubt that our presentation of the Union side could be better and fairer, but I am not persuaded that it is a travesty of the truth.

The industrialists' complaint stems from an altogether different attitude, the wish, often freely admitted, that Union negotiations could be conducted in private, and without all the pressures that the media bring to bear. I am afraid it is now an idle hope and I believe that employers must learn to live with the fact that their affairs, from time to time, will have to be conducted in public.

They start, of course, with some built-in disadvantages. They are usually responding to someone else's initiative; and whereas a Union leader gets where he does because of an ability to speak in public in difficult situations, the employer gets where he does for quite different reasons. But employers who take the trouble to study and work with the media rather than holding them at arm's length usually find that things get better. Companies, moreover, who are evasive with the media in one context, and all too many of them are, can scarcely complain if the media do not try very hard to find out about the good things going on quietly behind the scenes.

Implicit in all the difficulties that both sides of industry have is the peculiar nature of television itself. It is not just conveying words to the listener, but images as well. And the images by no means necessarily convey the same message as the words.

I doubt if even broadcasters are fully and consciously aware of how powerful this discrepancy can be, and I am quite sure that employers, Trade Union leaders and the general public are

scarcely aware at all. Let me give some examples, by way of advice.

If you are the boss of a large firm, and you are asked to comment on the problems of small firms, it is not wise to let yourself be televised in a Rolls Royce, smoking a cigar. No matter what you say, the picture says unsympathetic things, and contrasts with harassed little men in scrubby offices.

If you are an official of a national corporation, do not make a key speech about your Union troubles on the eve of a ballot, wearing a dinner jacket, and surrounded by others so attired, all eating and drinking. What you say may be splendid sense, but what the picture says is that you are a boss-class character living a life of luxury.

If you are a high-up Trade Union official, dealing with, shall we say, a seamen's strike, do not let yourself be televised in a comfortable land-locked office. Whatever you say, you will look irrelevant alongside seamen in the docks with their laid-up ships.

If you are a Chancellor of the Exchequer, do not, if you are to be televised, make a financial speech at a Lord Mayor's Banquet on the night before a Budget. To quote Stephen Hearst, the Controller of BBC Radio 3, who has written entertainingly and perceptively on these matters, all you will do is ensure that even non-political viewers will say to themselves "These nobs are having a good nosh up the day before we will be asked to tighten our belts", and they will react accordingly.

I have not, I should assure you, made these examples up. They are all things that have happened in recent years, and in every case the speakers' words said one thing, and the television image said quite another. Had the visual image been supportive, even though different, this might not have mattered. But in every case it was anything but supportive. And since visual images speak far more powerfully than words, the net result must have been, indeed in certain cases demonstrably was, the reverse of what was intended.

Predictably, of course, the television producer gets blamed for the overall effect; and sometimes, for all I know, he well knew what he was doing. But as a rule, I suspect he only did what came naturally. Tycoons do, in the popular imagination, and sometimes in reality, loll back in Rolls Royces, smoking cigars. National corporation officials seem at home in dinner jackets at official functions. Trade Union officials do operate in isolated offices, and Chancellors of the Exchequer often speak at grand dinners. There is nothing malicious in producers showing them in such natural hautnts.

So, if you are to be televised, give some thought not just to what you will say, but even more to how you will look. In fair measure you can set your own scene, and it will make a lot of different to people's interpretation of what you say.

So, to come back finally to the question of coming to terms with television, everyone should remember that he is not just reading out, as it were, a carefully considered letter. He is doing something much more complicated and elaborate, which conveys subtle messages that can have rather little to do with his spoken words. But these messages are powerful, and unless the speaker has some understanding of the complex nature of the whole process, he is liable to persuade people in directions he never intended. That is why, instinctively, politicians, employers, Trade Union bosses, and practically everyone else finds television a rather awesome medium – to be placated at one moment and reviled the next. Certainly, we all have yet to establish good relations with it.

LORD GOODMAN:

I am sure we are immensely indebted to Sir Michael for that absolutely fascinating discourse. I am particularly grateful to him because if what I had said at the beiginning of his lecture had in fact existed in written form, I would have suspected it had been stolen and communicated to him in order for him to lecture and establish the truth of what I had said. However, as

it did not exist in written form, it shows the remarkable perception I have in assessing the true nature of our lecturer. We have had a lecture of absolutely devastating criticism couched in terms so mild that one has to listen very critically for the slightest sound of criticism. It is a very remarkable performance and one for which we have to be very grateful.

There is time for a few questions. Who would like to start and ask Sir Michael a question?

QUESTION:

Can I ask what training is given to the staff of the BBC in order to come to terms with this problem of attempting to achieve impartiality? It is the most difficult thing in the world to create a judgment which you believe to be impartial, at the same time recognising you have thrown aside your own prejudices.

SIR MICHAEL SWANN:

It is fiendishly difficult, and I do not think anyone would pretend we are successful in it. Quite a lot of training is given. If, for instance, you are an entirely new member of staff, there is an elaborate training machinery. The Board of Governors, who spend a good deal of their time trying to make sure the public is being well served, are from time to time worried about this. I wonder sometimes, as a matter of fact, if I should not ask them to go into the News Room and produce some unbiased and impartial news themselves. That, in fact, is what the new trainees have to do. I do not suppose most people realise the magnitude of the problem. After all, even a newspaper only publishes a fraction of the news that reaches it. It is not generally realised that to read one column of, say, *The Times* takes you roughly six or seven minutes, and there are eight columns in a page of *The Times*, so to turn one page of *The Times* into a news bulletin on radio would take you one hour. Since television only gets information across at three or four times slower than radio, it would take, roughly speaking, four

days, night and day, solid, to turn the whole *Times* into a television news bulletin.

You can see there is an enormous problem of condensation. We work very hard to train people into doing this, but as a last resort it is only done by experience; some people never get there, others become very good at it. It is like the skills you need for the Press, but it is a more acute and more difficult problem simply because a greater factor of condensation has to come into it.

I will not talk about the other training mechanisms in the BBC. By comparison with the Press, I think the BBC is rather good about training, while the Press in general does all too little of it. I hope the Press who are present here will not object to that statement, but I think it is true.

QUESTION:

Sir Michael mentioned the potential troubles in the Print Room. Are there similar problems in the Cutting Room?

SIR MICHAEL SWANN:

I think one could say with a considerable sense of satisfaction, that there has been no suggestion within broadcasting – and I do not mean only in the BBC, but I think it is true also of ITV – that there has been no suggestion of any attempt to apply censorship of that sort. I suppose anything can happen in the future, and we have been keeping an eye on the problem of editors and the closed shop. But we do not think it is such an immediate problem for ourselves. I will not go into detailed reasons of why that is, but a good deal of it undoubtedly stems from the fact that implicit in broadcasting for fifty years has been the feeling that, whether you like it or not, you have got to be impartial – those are the terms on which society accepts you.

QUESTION:

I would like to ask one question, about how you see the effect on the House of Commons of being broadcast, because I have noticed since I started listening to the broadcasting of

debates from the House of Commons they seem to have become slightly more adult than they were. Could you comment on this?

SIR MICHAEL SWANN:

I think it is as much as my job would be worth if I said I thought the effect of broadcasting was to make it more adult! Certainly the broadcasting of Parliament is something the MPs have been very concerned about, and not without reason. If you had the goings on in your family circle and your kitchen broadcast to the world, you would be surprised if it did not have some effect on changing the nature of the discussion. So I have every sympathy with the MPs being a bit concerned. In practice, I believe it really has not made very much difference one way or the other, and although large numbers of people have not, as it were, rushed to listen to what goes on, we did for the very first programme of all, get a rather startling audience. Substantially more people listen to the Westminster programmes now because they can hear MPs' voices, and I think that is probably a good thing. I do not think there is really any evidence that politicians have tried to use it for their own benefit. It would, in principle, be possible for a local politician to make a speech in the House in the hope it would go out on his local radio station, when it was really only relevant and of interest to his local constituency, and so on. But on the whole we think it is a rather successful experiment, and will go on. I think there is enough interest in the audience, and in the public, that it should go on.

One of the things that undoubtedly concerns us is that radio is not wholly satisfactory as a medium – one cannot see what is happening and one gets the sound without perhaps getting the full atmosphere – and having gone thus far it would probably be a good thing to go the whole distance to television.

I think it will settle down and be a useful adjunct to people's understanding of what their MPs are doing, and it will be useful for the occasional debate, if you think of the sort of

things that Mr. Healey has been announcing tonight. When it comes to major debates on prices or debates about inflation and matters of that sort, I think it can be doing nothing but good that these should be heard, and if it leads to a better standard of debate so much the better. I thought the standard of debate always was fairly good, but then I suppose I started from hearing rather a lot of student debates!

QUESTION:

A profound philosophical point – does man communicate very differently by radio than by the written word, or the visual medium of television?

SIR MICHAEL SWANN:

This is rather complicated, but if you are reading the printed word you can read at anything between 500 and 1500 words a minute. If you are really fast you can do 1500, and if you are slow you can do about 500. A broadcast news bulletin can be read at perhaps 120 to 130 words a minute, and although people on television do doubt speak just as fast the picture comes up and you have to look at it and build up what it is about before the person starts speaking, so you put in a substantial factor of slowing down. And of course the visual mechanism can always lead a viewer to absorb all sorts of things the speaker does not intend to convey and does not wish you to absorb.

QUESTION:

The BBC World Service and its programmes, such as "From our own Foreign Correspondent", would produce their own problems, I should imagine. Would you care to comment?

SIR MICHAEL SWANN:

They do indeed. Depending on who you are, some people think the World Services do it much better than the Home Services. I think I see somewhere in the distance our Managing Director of External Services, so perhaps I should not pursue that one! But it does produce enormous difficulties. I do not know quite what sort of comment I can make about this one.

Almost whatever you do gets you into trouble somewhere, and you can rely, I suppose, on an almost basic instinctive judgment. I think it has to be said that when you have been putting news programmes together for a long time, you do almost unconsciously get a feeling for it. There was one time when I thought we had done a bad news programme, and I got hold of all the stuff that had been filtered and put together and I had a look at it and wondered if I would have put it together better, but when I had ruminated on it and realised that of course you do not have an hour to do this, you have to put it all together in about five minutes, I ended up thinking I would have done very much the same myself. But you can always criticise what has been done, and I do not know what the answer is.

I suppose the answer is, that however much they vary in political slant or whether they appeal to the masses or to the elite, the Press shows a very large degree of uniformity as to what will make the headlines, and although we make our news entirely separately from the Press it is unusual that we deviate a great deal.

There are news values, of course – the sort of ethos of journalists – and journalists have a tendency to feel these values are God-given, but they are not. Journalists are people brought up in the way that Fleet Street has gone on for years, and it may be their assumptions are wrong and it may be there is a tendency to slip in too many trivial things and sensational things, but nevertheless, when it comes to providing the sort of things people want to hear about, they become remarkably good and skilled at it. Although I find myself sometimes annoyed with what they have done, it is not often I can say I would have done something entirely different had I been in charge.

QUESTION:

Could I ask you if, as Chairman, there are any special areas which give you particularly personal cause for concern in the presentation of news or the social scene, which are really part

and parcel of this question of "coming to terms"? You have not expressed many areas of major concern. One popular one is this question of violence, and the presentation of violence. I do not know if the present society is more violent today that it was a hundred years ago. I doubt it, but I think it is widely believed, and I wonder what research the BBC are doing to evaluate this, and also whether there are some special areas of concern as far as you are concerned?

SIR MICHAEL SWANN:

The whole political area is bound to be of concern, and turning to some of the other areas, violence of course is something which must inevitably worry one. When I first became Chairman I went to some pains to read up what had been done, and I think I am now less concerned about it than I was. I believe up to a point it can be regarded as a subject where experts are less worried than they were. It is awfully difficult to do any convincing research on this – there has been an enormous amount of money spent on it, particularly in America, but to little effect, and it may be that it simply needs some brilliant idea of research to get you somewhere. The only thing I think that has emerged with any certainty is that the context in which violence appears matters very much. In Westerns, it is a bang a minute and people always biting the dust, but the conventions are so clearly understood and the context is so clearly fictional, that it does not worry anyone. On the other hand, in the newer Westerns it is still a bang a minute and red blood spurts out, and the change from black and white to colour makes it more realistic and it upsets people more. But such evidence as there is suggests that 95% of people are put off violence by this rather than encouraged by it.

But there is a small percentage of people who are in some manner or other maladjusted and who do perhaps get stirred up by violence being shown, but what do you do about that? It is very difficult indeed. If you are running a firm manufacturing drugs you are subject to very powerful Governmental regula-

tions, and you have to prove beyond any reasonable doubt that your drug can never produce any harmful results. You can never do that with television or broadcasting or books or newspapers, and the only way to be sure of doing no harm would be to never show anything violent. But if you sanitise things to such an extent that no bad thing and no violence is ever turned out, then you cease to be credible, and everyone would think you really are an "auntie" and not to be taken seriously.

We have a group within the BBC of sociologists and psychiatrists whose function it is to keep their fingers on this subject. Their opinion is that violence to the extent that we now show it is not a source of serious concern.

But you never know what will happen next. We cannot buy films to be shown until they are five years old – and the super-violent films are now about five years old. You cannot buy them singly, you have to buy them in packages, and we are going to have to buy packages of films which contain things such as "A Clockwork Orange". That shows a degree of violence way beyond what we would ever dream of allowing on to the television screen. People do not realise how much greater violence is getting inside the cinema now – so much, indeed, that I made the Board of Governors have a film showing with the censors to show what is getting out on the screens, and about which we might have to make a decision.

The most complaints we get are about bad language. I do not know whether to be worried about that or not, but there is no doubt that society at large is accepting a much greater degree of explicit language than it did a while back.

But I think the things that most concern us are in the general area of politics.

LORD GOODMAN:

I must in mercy release our speaker. He can have been in no doubt of the very sincere compliment that you have paid to him, because he, like myself, has had an opportunity of

watching your faces and seeing with what absolutely rapt attention you have been hanging on his words, and would obviously go on listening to him for another two, three, or four hours. That is why we must bring the thing to a close. We have had a most fascinating discourse.

I now ask for a vote of thanks from our trustees.

The Rt. Hon. The Lord Scarman

Lord Scarman was educated at Radley College, and Brasenose College, Oxford (of which he is now an Honorary Fellow), becoming a Harmsworth Law Scholar, Middle Temple, and a Barrister in 1936. He was appointed Queens Counsel in 1957. He served with the R.A.F.V.R. during the war and received the Russian Order of Battle Merit. Lord Justice Scarman served 12 years as a Judge of the High Court of Justice, Probate, Divorce and Admiralty Division and later the Family Division before becoming a Lord Justice of Appeal in 1973. He was made a Lord of Appeal in Ordinary in 1977.

He has served on the Council of Legal Education, was Chairman of the Law Commission from 1965–1973, Chairman of the University of London Court from 1970–81 and has served on the Statute Law Committee and the Arts Council. Currently, he is Chancellor of the University of Warwick.

'Law and Power'

delivered by

The Rt. Hon. Lord Justice Scarman

Tuesday, 18th May 1976

CHAIRMAN The Rt. Hon. The Lord Goodman C.H.

LORD GOODMAN:

My Lords, Ladies and Gentlemen, the packed hall testifies to the agreeable fact that this lecture is now becoming one of London's events. It is less difficult to become an event these days, or perhaps other events are dwindling in interest, but we have had, I think, a record of lectures over the last three years – with modesty I will not refer to the inaugural lecture – which testifies to the exceptional quality that we have been able to achieve: the willingness of speakers of great distinction to come and deliver this lecture, and obviously, the willingness of audiences of considerable distinction to come and listen to speakers of great distinction; and that, if I may say so, is a very gratifying feature.

Now this evening we have Leslie Scarman to give the lecture. I think one is obliged not to spare his blushes. I would be anxious to do so as he is an immensely modest man, but he is one of the great men of our day, perhaps better realised by lawyers than non-lawyers. Lawyers are not frightfully good at identifying their great men, and it is a special tribute to him that there is such a unanimity of the opinion of the qualities he possesses, both as a lawyer and as a man. He is – I think the

popular word is a polymath, who is a man who does a great many things. He does more things than are often realised. The first time I met him was when he became , at my invitation, a member of the Arts Council. He was an immensely valuable member of the Arts Council, with a love and appreciation of the arts which is precisely the attribute we are seeking in that very valuable body. He has a record of achievement and distinction in so many directions that it would take a lecture on its own to enumerate them all.

I am not going to do that. I am only going to say this, that this evening we have him here in his capacity as a lawyer, as a philosopher, and as a thinker. He is a rarity among lawyers, as he has been able to maintain a reforming stance without alienating the rest of the profession. How he contrives to do this I should very much like to hear from him one day, privately. The fact remains that he is one of the best loved of lawyers, but he has made no secret of the fact that there is a lot of things which need to be changed in the law. He is, of course, a Judge of outstanding distinction. He is called upon constantly by Government to discharge immensely difficult and responsible tasks where a special ability is needed, such as riots in Red Lion Square, problems in Belfast – and in respect of all these he produces reports of total clarity which somehow contrive not to outrage people who are found to be responsible and who are the subject of his measured strictures. He is a remarkable man.

He is going to talk to us about Law and Power. I must say for my part I wait with eager expectation to hear what he is going to say. I think we are all very fortunate to have him here with us to say it.

LORD JUSTICE SCARMAN:

My Lord Chairman and Ladies and Gentlemen, I shall not spend time explaining or mitigating my blushes after those opening remarks of Lord Goodman. I will get immediately to

my subject, which is "Law and Power", two contrasting and inevitable elements in all human society.

I would begin my consideration of my subject tonight by stating three propositions which I find so self-evident that I am not prepared to give reasons for my acceptance of them. I just do accept them. I do not assume them, because "assume" means they might be wrong. I accept them.

The first I put in the old Latin phrase in which it has been put for centuries, *inter arma leges silent*. I translate that into English as 'The law is helpless once the fighting has begun". Every lawyer and every thinker who believes that the law has a contribution to make towards tranquillity and order should remember this limitation upon the capacity of the law. That is my first self-evident, but necessarily accepted, proposition.

My second is a very different one. There are certain human rights, for example, personal liberty, freedom of speech and thought, equality before the law, which are so fundamental that not even a democratically-elected majority should be allowed to destroy them. This to my way of thinking is as self-evident as the first proposition. It is difficult for a democracy to accept it, but I regard it as self-evident.

Finally, there is a proposition which is not often stated. It has in fact been stated by a very distinguished Judge of the Supreme Court of the United States of America. There is in it a touch of realism which goes with my first proposition. There is no instance recorded in the history of civilised societies in which a Judge, *qua* Judge, has ever stopped a revolution.

I will just repeat these three propositions, because everything I have to say tonight proceeds upon the acceptability of them. First, "*inter arma leges silent*"; secondly, the existence of fundamental human rights, which not even a democratically-elected majority should be allowed to destroy; and thirdly, the great limitation upon the legal process that courts, *qua* courts, judges, *qua* judges, cannot stop the revolution. Within those three propositions I find the object or objects and the limits of

law and the legal process. Upon the object I find a compromise totally unacceptable. I agree with the age-old slogan *fiat justicia*, but I do not agree with the words that usually follow it, *ruat coelum*. The sky must be supported if human beings are to live in order to enjoy the benefits of justice. But I think the philosophical problem is put in these terms: how are we to support the sky so that underneath it justice may flourish?

Now, because (I think) I am a lawyer, I begin my approach to the answer to that question by considering the responsibilities of the legal profession. I think it is the duty of the legal profession of a country to persuade those who exercise power in their community that it is in their own interest, that is to say, in the interests of those who exercise power, to use the process of law as the channel for its exercise. This is undoubtedly a difficult task, because those who have the power have got to be persuaded that power unmoderated by an institutionalised system of justice will collapse into self-defeat. They have got to appreciate – and the evidence of history of course is overwhelming if only they will look at it – that those over whom power is exercised will ultimately destroy those who exercise power unless they can see that the exercise of power is just.

Put in more colloquial language, this is the selling point for the rule of law. What you have to appreciate is that the rule of law has to be sold, not to ordinary people, certainly not to the oppressed, but to the people who happen to exercise power in their community. In other words, one has to persuade the powerful that the rule of law is an attractive bargain. You have to persuade the powerful that the rule of law is needed by them just as much as by the people over whom they exercise their power. And the only way this can be done is to ram home the lesson that if they do not accept the rule of law there is ultimately and in the long term only revolution to be expected.

I have chosen to emphasise the element of bargain in the rule of law, and it is as well to reflect upon this element for a moment or so. The law might be described as a confidence

trick. It can only be enforced if it be based upon consent. One can prosecute successfully one murderer, one terrorist, but one cannot prosecute, with any social success, a million. Indeed, the principle of the law is that the legal process – by which I mean the process of resolving disputes between citizen and citizen, between Government and Government, or between Government and citizen has no inherent power at all. Its efficacy is only just as much as society chooses to permit it, and it follows that the law and the legal process can only succeed in achieving tranquillity, order and justice if they enjoy the confidence of the community. If the law and the legal process should become isolated or withdrawn from the main stream of social development, disaster beckons. Indeed, again I put it in more colloquial language; if ordinary people do not find in the legal process acceptable solutions to their problems, the problems that really trouble them, the law will be rejected.

And so, again, one comes to a general proposition which I think follows from the considerations to which I have referred, that while power is a biological sociological fact as inevitable in human society as sex, the rule of law is, like marriage, no more than an option which need not be taken up. The dilemma for civilised human beings is a harsh one. If law is to do the job that we want it to do, it must be used to curb, to restrain, the exercise of power. Yet, if those who possess the power reject the idea of legal control, the law is no better than a paper tiger. Utterly useless, a mere facade for tyranny and oppression.

I have deliberately begun my talk this evening with those general philosophical reflections. I now come to look at the United Kingdom and to seek to apply the principle running through those reflections to the current, the contemporaneous, situation, of the United Kingdom. As soon as you begin to look at the position of the law in the United Kingdom, a strange paradox arises. First, the judges and the legal profession are on the whole highly regarded and respected. And yet the function of the law in our society, if you analyse it carefully, is extremely

limited. Of course, a cynic would say that is why the judges and the legal profession are respected. It does not happen to be my view, but there is the paradox.

It is a paradox, which for reasons which I propose to elaborate, may become sinister. If the function of the law continues to be limited and confined and isolated in our society, then inevitably much that is significant in our society will escape the control of the law. Indeed, I shall attempt, not to argue fully because time will not permit it, but to indicate tonight the outline of an argument for developing the function of the law and the legal process in our society, and I shall certainly suggest that this can be done without losing the high respect and the confidence which the judicial process at present enjoys. Of course, the timid will say you cannot bring the law into the arena of so-called political controversy without damaging the reputation of the judges. Maybe, but I hope, when you have heard me out, you will see that the risk has to be taken. My own view is that it is a minimal risk, and I will give you my reasons later, but, whether it be minimal or more than minimal, the risk has to be taken, if the law and the rule of law are to be made relevant as methods of control over those problems which really are important to the great mass of our fellow citizens.

Now for a historical digression. I ask myself this question. Why, in British society, is the practice of the law so self-contained, so isolated from the main stream of the public life of our community? As you would expect in a British context, the answer to the question is a purely historical one. The present pattern of our legal system was determined when the power of the Stuart kings collapsed at the end of the 17th century. In 1688 there was the Bill of Rights; in 1700 the Act of Settlement; and in 1707 the Act of Union of England and Scotland. Those three enactments still govern the whole pattern of British public life and the legal systems – there are three of them – today. And those enactments ensured two things of immense

value. First, the sovereignty of Parliament; secondly, the independence of the judges – and I think it is worth quoting some of the words of the Bill of Rights. The sovereignty of Parliament was secured by the Bill of Rights of 1688 which contained amongst other things these provisions: that "the pretended power of suspending of all laws or the execution of laws without the consent of Parliament is illegal". There you have in a sentence the legislative supremacy of the Parliament. Then it provided that for the redress of all grievances and for the amending, strengthening and preserving the laws of Parliaments ought to be held frequently. There you have the basis of Parliament's duty to redress grievances. Those of course are the two main duties of Parliament even today — legislation, a watch on the executive to prevent the dispensing or suspending power, and the redress of grievances of individuals.

But the other important part of the settlement was that for the first time the power of the King to remove a judge was curtailed. From then on, the King could remove a judge only on an address of both Houses of Parliament. This set the English pattern under which we still live and by the Act of Union of 1707 it became the Scottish pattern; and of course, the Act of Union contained that badge of Scottish independence which they have never lost and which reinforced the English Bill of Rights, namely, the independence of their own legal system.

I would say in passing that, if anyone is about to amend the Act of Union, they had better look first at what they are losing before they decide on what they are getting!

Now, that is the theoretical distribution of power in the United Kingdom. Unfortunately it is becoming less and less in touch with the practical realities of power in the United Kingdom. It may be doubted whether Members of Parliament ever really did possess the power that the Bill of Rights sought to confer upon their assembly. But, whether that is so or not, the truth today is that Parliamentary power is exercised, not, save in the rare emergency, by Members of Parliament in their

assembly, but by the Government of the day which commands the majority. So subject to elections at periodical intervals, the Government of the day, controlled by the party from which it is drawn, exercises the sovereignty of Parliament.

But this sovereignty, particularly in its legislative aspect, is now threatened by trends and developments which were never cosnsidered by those who drafted the 17th Century Bill of Rights and Act of Settlement. The competitors for power emerge in very strange places, and all of them are animated by the best of intentions. We are not discussing evil men; we are not discussing people who have set up a wicked tyranny; we are discussing men and institutions that have developed in the last fifty years for the best of reasons and with the best of intentions; and yet they are a menace unless they are subjected to some form of coherent and consistent control and restraint.

Where are these rivals to the sovereignty of Parliament, and who are they? First of all, the Government departments themselves. As the requirements of society become more complex, as it becomes more and more necessary that not the hair on the head of the most inadequate person should suffer in our community, and we accept that that is right, so does it become necessary to build a complex administrative and bureaucratic structure to handle these complexities.

There is nothing wrong about bureaucracy. There is nothing wrong about a complex administrative structure, but it poses problems for civilised men. That is one developing source of power which for reasons which are obvious to all of you Parliament cannot hope to control. Of course, spasmodically it can do something about it, and it can lay down, if you like, general principles – but control, supervision: these are the problems.

Then – and really, I am only stressing the obvious – surely the Trade Unions and the multi-national industrial and commercial corporations are both manifestations of the increasing complexity and importance of industrial relations. They are

both of them largely outside the control of Parliament and the courts. They are real centres of power. Can society allow these centres of power such as the Government departments, the Trade Unions, multi-national corporations, to develop and to exercise their power unrestrained and unguided by law? That is the problem. The constitutional settlement of 1688 under which we still live offers absolutely no solution.

And then, there are the institutions of the new Europe. There is the Common Market, which affects only one limited aspect of the activities of our society, but a very important one — trade, commerce, and the taxation of mercantile transactions. Here we have, now recognised by law, under the European Communities Act of 1972, a source of legislative power which not only escapes the scrutiny, very largely, of Parliament and the control or supervision of the courts, but is in theory, as well as in practice, independent of both of them. The law-making source is to be found in the European Court of Justice in Luxembourg. Here again, although very different in character, is a challenge to the sovereignty of Parliament and the independence of the courts, as understood by those who drafted the 17th century Constitutional settlement under which we seek to run a late 20th century society.

Those three features that I have mentioned, departmental power, the power of the Trade Unions and the big corporations, the power of the Common Market, (and coupled with it, the power of the Human Rights movement deriving as it does from the Council of Europe at Strasbourg, which I have not yet described in any detail), here are the basic elements of the modern revolution in our society which really does make it necessary to re-think that ancient settlement under which we live. Of course, it represents a *de facto* though not *de jure* diminution of the power of Parliament and the courts. It represents the development of new centres of power, not fully recognised or precisely defined by such constitutional documents as we possess. It is not surprising, therefore, that the rule

of law and the legal process are now in a very critical condition.

As the power of Parliament and the courts slips, how is the vacuum thereby created to be filled? I would ask a detailed question. Is there a case for the introduction of a measure of judicial review in the public sector of our affairs, to assist Parliament in the control, in the restraint, of these new centres of power. My argument will be, so that you may know where I am going, that there is a very powerful case for the introduction of such a measure. But first of all, let me look at the facts. It is so easy to talk about this subject in generalisations.

Inevitably I am guilty of a measure of generalisation in a talk which can only last an hour., but I will do what I can to condescend to the particular. First of all, let us look at the power of Government departments. The best illustration of this power, a power which certainly requires control and guidance, is the Welfare State itself. If you will bear with me for a moment or so I will look at our system of supplementary benefit, and I will hope to be able to show to you that under that system as it is indeed practised – and I am not concerned with the theory of it – we see operating first, the dispensing and suspending power of the laws, which has been illegal since 1688, and secondly, a lack of power or ability in either Parliament or the courts to redress grievances arising in the administration of supplementary benefit.

I choose supplementary benefit, as this affects millions of your fellow citizens; it is far more important than the ordinary business transacted in the High Court of Justice. Let me say a word or two about it. Supplementary benefit has proved to be a basic safety net for those of our fellow citizens who, for one reason or another, cannot support themselves or their families. The law is contained in the Supplementary Benefits Act of 1966. If you read that statute, you will have a glow of pride, because it is extremely well drafted. You will see that every citizen has a right to supplementary benefit if he needs it. There

is no doubt about it; Parliament has said "This is a right". But how does it work in practice? Very, very different. It is, of course, administered upon the basis of need as assessed by Government officers. If you are dissastisfied with the assessment of the Government officer, you can get an administrative review of your case by a more senior officer. If you are still dissatisfied, you may appeal to what the Act happily calls "the Appeal Tribunal". That itself is a complete misnomer. There are in fact 120 different Supplementary Benefit Appeal Tribunals. They sit in private, they administer their very important form of justice largely according to an administrative instruction which is not published, and at the end of the day the agency which controls the whole of this for the Government, the Supplementary Benefit Commission, can reverse their decision.

Well, the language of the law is to be found in the outline I have given you: but *de facto* legal control is elsewhere. This means that something of immense importance to our fellow citizens is really being administered, not according to the way Parliament has said it should be, not according to the way the judges say is fair, but as best they can by high minded but not necessarily always terribly wise civil servants, exercising an administrative discretion in accordance with an administrative instruction. This will in the end lead to trouble, because it will create grievance.

So that you may appreciate the size of the problem, let me give you some figures. I have brought with me the figures for 1971. There are no doubt more recent figures, but I have not looked them up. 1971 is good enough. You may be sure that today the figures are heavier than those I give you. In 1971 there were between six and seven million claims in the United Kingdom for supplementary benefit. There were 22,434 appeals. Two million retired citizens had to have recourse to supplementary benefit in order to secure a minimum subsistence level. A quarter of a million unemployed had to look

exclusively to supplementary benefit for their support. In addition to these figures there were 300,000 sick and disabled persons living on supplementary benefit. There is the size of the problem. In a matter of this gravity and of this complexity a just society surely requires that somehow and somewhere the rule of law should be introduced into it so that the reality , i.e. the exercise of power by Government officers, can be seen to comply with the requirements of justice.

Now take a look at devolution. I am not concerned tonight with the politics of devolution, but we are witnessing the most extraordinary public spectacle. Here is an issue which is obviously a threat to the 1688 settlement of Parliament and the courts, but very few voices have been raised in public requiring us to look to the legal implications of devolution. Indeed, there seems to have been almost a public conspiracy not to mention the inevitable problems that will arise, if devolution comes, as between the new legislative assemblies and the United Kingdom Parliament. It appears to be though that, when disputes arise, as inevitably they will arise, as to the legislative powers of the new assemblies, or indeed of the United Kingdom Parliament, they can be dealt with on an administrative or political level. It is not for me to say that is wrong. But how is it that nobody has discussed the possibility of judicial review as the way to take the heat out of those inevitable controversies, to reduce them to a low key, to restrain them to a level which is what is needed if you are going to make something akin to a Federal system work?

Here again is a problem of emerging power, and nobody, at any rate so far as one can judge from public utterances, has yet worked out the implications of this emerging power and how one is going to restrain it in the interests of tranquillity, order, and justice.

Then there is the Human Rights picture. This again is an emerging development which we have got to face. We already know that minorities, e.g. racial minorities, women, religious

groups, and many others, have got to be accommodated. We have accepted, rightly, the responsibilities arising from the minorities in our midst. We have accepted, rightly, the obligation of the European Convention. But we have not taken more than a miniscule step towards incorporating all this into our system of law.

The factors which I have been describing represent a challenge to the rule of law, and a challenge for which the rule of law will have to be modified, as we understand it, if it is to cope. The one thing that the legal profession and the courts must not do, I would suggest, is to run for quarantine. We must accept the risk of infection. If we isolate, or continue to isolate, the legal system and the legal profession from this main stream of social development for fear of infection, if we attempt to steer a passage in mid-stream, then I cannot see any future for the rule of law. Since for the philosophical reasons I gave you at the beginning of this talk I believe, and I think most of my fellow citizens believe, the rule of law is an essential to the civilised society, this could be a disaster.

Now the suggestion that I wish to leave with you tonight – and it is only a suggestion, because it has got to be thought out and discussed – is that we need to re-think the legal basis of our constitutional settlement; that the 1707 Settlement is no longer able to cope with the developments of the 20th century. I suggest we should give consideration to the following: the introduction of a measure of judicial review, a written Constitution, entrenched provisions in that Constitution – i.e., provisions which the bare majority of Parliament cannot overturn, though the ultimate authority must remain, subject to safeguards, with the democratically-elected Parliament.

This is not starry-eyed theoretical stuff. If devolution comes, we will need a written Constitution. If we are to give effect to our international obligations in respect of human rights and the Common Market, we cannot avoid a written Constitution: neither in any of those cases will it be possible to avoid a

measure of judicial review. So the argument in favour of introducing into our Constitutional picture a measure of judicial review is very strong, and it is possible to say, as a legal scientist, that it cannot be resisted. But there are objections. Just let me look at the objections shortly.

The first and the most fundamental objection is that it puts at risk the reputation of the judges by involving them in politics. This argument just does not stand up. I am prepared to say it is nonsense. In a society governed by a written Constitution which is ultimately the creation of Parliament, which contains a measure, a strictly limited measure, of judicial review, the judges, it is said, will be forced into the political arena. But they already are in the political arena. The fallacy is to conclude that they will be required to make political decisions. They will only be asked to make legal decisions – that is to say, to act judicially in interpreting and applying the Constitution. Lawyers outside our island have been doing this successfully for a very long time. Irish judges administer an admirable constitution, and find no embarrassment. They do not find themselves accused of being politically activated. The Supreme Court of the United States of America has made itself famous for the legal and jurisprudential quality of its work. German judges do the job day in, day out, to the entire satisfaction of the German people without any trouble at all. It really is a chimera that our judges would lose their non-political character and would be thought to be making political decisions if they were given the task, which I am suggesting they should be given, of judicial review of a Constitution.

Of course, the strength of our current Constitution – and this is something which must not be lost in any reform that may come about – is the independence of judges. That can be as well secured by the Act of Settlement of 270-odd years ago. But there are other difficulties.

The first difficulty is the nature of English law. English law is essentially private law and criminal law. By private law I mean

contract tort, or delict if you live in Scotland, family law, commercial law, the disputes of citizen and citizen. Criminal law needs no explanation, and it is said, and said with some force, that common law is a private law system, and it would require a good deal of re-writing of the substance of our law to introduce into it that which I suggest is badly needed, an element of public law. I think this is right, and I think it is one of the main problems which have to be solved if the rule of law is to be extended from the sphere where it was sufficient in the past to spheres where it is required in the present and the future.

Then it is said, "Oh, but if you go over to a written Constitution, if you go over to a public law element, you are going to have to re-model the drafting of your Statute law". Well, again this is right. Since the 19th century we have followed a course of statutory drafting that has led to more and more complexities. It has made the law more and more difficult, not only for ordinary people, but for lawyers to understand, and I was interested to see, in a recent decision of the Court of Appeal, Lord Denning declaring that it would be very difficult to introduce the European Convention into English law because it is drafted in a Continental way, full of vague generalities. I would have thought Lord Denning was too good a legal historian to have fallen into that fallacy. Of course, it is true since about the middle of the 19th century that we have been drafting statutes in this very complex way, but we did not always. If we go back to the basic instruments of English law – Magna Carta, the Bill of Rights – you will find that in those days English lawyers were not frightened of the broad generalisations.

Let me quote you one section of the Bill of Rights. I am sure, if I had not told you it was in our Bill of Rights, you would have thought I was quoting either the American Constitution or the European Cnvention, but I am not. I am quoting an existing provision of English Statute law. The Bill of Rights

declared that "excessive bail ought not to be required, nor excessive fines imposed, nor cruel and unusual punishments inflicted". You could not have anything more general than that. If we could be as general as that in 1688, what is wrong in attempting a few declarations of general principle in 1976? Nevertheless, as a working lawyer I recognise there are great difficulties in remodelling English law so that we can deal with the emergence of power in the new centres to which I have referred, and I think we have got to remodel it along the general lines I have suggested, and again I put it forward really for public discussion. We need a measure of judicial control.

You can only get a measure of judicial control which is acceptable, if you have a written Constitution which gives the judges the necessary legal guidance. Untrammelled judicial discretion is as bad as any other discretion, administrative or otherwise, but, granted a written Constitution, then you can have a measure of judicial control, that is of judicial review, of the acts of the legislature. Ultimately the legislature must be sovereign, but only ultimately – i.e. in the last resort. It is not so difficult to envisage a measure of judicial control over the executive. But it requires considerable effort to extend it to the other centres of power that I have mentioned, the multinational corporations, the Common Market and the Trade Unions. But judicial review will not work, unless there is a truly comprehensive network of legal aid and advice. I believe that is feasible, not at the drop of a hat tomorrow, but if we are prepared to devote time, thought and effort to getting it, I think if we do not go that far then the new centres of power, and others that will undoubtedly emerge that we are not discussing tonight because we do not yet know what they are, will present a challenge to the rule of law that could destroy it. If you destroy the rule of law, ultimately – bloody revolution.

You may say "Well, this is intoxicating stuff. But we need a new breed of lawyer to advise us and to operate it". This I

think is an important question which certainly should be asked. Inevitably it drives attention back to the importance of legal education. I cannot say much about legal education tonight because time is short, save that I regard it as absolutely essential to the health of the Commonwealth, and having been interested in legal education for a number of years I will just indicate very shortly a few of the essentials.

First of all, we must see that our lawyers possess the ancient skills of the lawyer. The negotiating skill, the skill of advocacy, the skill in drafting documents: these skills can only be acquired if the young student is subjected to the drudgery of sound learning and technical mastery of his subject. These are as difficult for the 19-year-old as the three R's are for the 5-year-old, but just as essential. Without them you do not get anywhere. Then, of course, there is the necessity, inevitably, of integrity. But legal education needs more than the inculcation of these ancient skills, although these ancient skills care indispensable. We have somehow to educate our lawyers so that they are socially and politically alert.

In the old wicked days when only the children of the wealthy could go into the law, this was achieved by the wealth of their parents; and, before one sniffs contemptuously at the contribution of property to our society, remember that those who did have property chose to educate their children in a liberal way so that they could become liberal lawyers, doctors, politicians, and leaders. Now, for reasons which we all accept, the property qualification is not to be tolerated. Casting away, as we will and must, the property qualification, we still have got to see that those who are coming forward from all classes of our society for legal education get the same sort of liberal education that 100 years ago or more parents were willing to pay their own money to see their children had.

The other thing they have to acquire is a critical approach to the law itself. If we are prepared to spend money and devote effort to a legal education combining the encouragement of the

liberal outlook and the inculcation of the legal skills, then I would hope we would develop a new breed of lawyer who would be able to watch for social trends and developments, who would be able to look at the law and see whether the law was satisfactory as a restraint and curb upon power. But at the end of the day, remember the limitations of the legal process. No judge has ever stopped the revolution. In the clash of arms the law is silent. These are truths that must never, never be forgotten.

The real contribution of the legal process is to ensure that disputes will be handled in a low-key way, that their resolution will be a routine business, that controversy will be kept within limits and handled without passion. Somehow, these immense advantages – which are not, of course, the answer to all the problems of society – which already exist in our criminal law, and in our private law, have got to be extended to the public sector, because the public sector has become so important. It is in that sector that Government departments administer the Welfare State. It is in that sector that the Common Market is raising its head. It is in that sector that Parliament operates, and it is in that sector that the Trade Unions and the multi-national sections have to be restrained and guided. I am not saying that you may not reach heaven by another route, but, if you want to have a reasonable time before you go to heaven, then think of the rule of law.

LORD GOODMAN:

I will not try to comment on that immensely exciting lecture, delivered, if I may say so, in measured and calm tones and conveying a very passionate message. All I will say is that we have been fortunate to be here this evening to hear this timely lecture, and if I may say so without striking too pessimistic a note, that it is in time. This is one of the very important considerations that we should all weigh. Whether in fact it is a plea for us to defend the ground we all regard as an invincible

home, or a plea to us to recover the ground or some of the ground which has already been lost, at any event those are the matters upon which we must all reflect.

We now have a brief opportunity for those of you here who feel the necessity to say something, or to ask a question, to do so, and you are cordially invited to do this for a very brief period before I call for a vote of thanks. I believe the lecturer would like to have some comments, observations or suggestions if you would care to make them.

LORD GOODMAN:

I wonder if everybody heard? Perhaps the very distinguished questioner (Lord Stow Hill) would not mind if I told the audience what his question was. It was whether Mr. Healey's policy of effectively leaving income tax to be determined by Trade Union consultations was consistent with the notion that we were governed by the rule of law. I think, in a word, that was what the question was!

LORD JUSTICE SCARMAN:

It will not surprise the audience to hear that as a working Judge I am not prepared to comment! But looking at it theoretically, I myself can see abolutely no objection to a consultation outside Parliament before legislation. Indeed, when I was Chairman of the Law Commission – which I was for seven years – I was always anxious that there should be consultation outside as well as inside Parliament before there was legislation. Therefore, without commenting on the political implications of the question, which are not for me, I can see nothing necessarily unconstitutional, or necessarily contrary to the principles I was attempting to declare, in a Chancellor of the Exchequer consulting before he presents legislation to the Houses of Parliament.

QUESTION:

May I ask a scientist's question and reveal my ignorance of the law? Did not Sir John Simon's pronouncements stop a General Strike? Is that not almost stopping a revolution?

LORD JUSTICE SCARMAN:

I think the important word is "almost"!

MR. H. WALSH:

There is a certain conflict between the two propositions presented to us at the beginning of this meeting. The one was that Government by the consent of the majority is essential, and secondly, that certain tenets are so fundamental that they are in special fields; therefore I should be glad if what I see as the incompatibility of these two can be reconciled.

LORD JUSTICE SCARMAN:

They cannot be reconciled; there is an incompatibility. There are some values for which, if need be, one dies; there are some values about which you can legislate.

SIR MICHAEL SWANN:

I do not want to ask a question, but I do want to ask for the speaker's comment. He has in a variety of ways throughout his lecture stressed the sense that unless there is a broad public consent to the law, and this is something which has been put to me recently and I wonder to what extent he will agree or not agree with this – one of the ways we are getting into difficulty is that our legislation (and this is not political, the Conservatives have done it as much as the Labour Party) has moved away from the areas of public consent. The Tories did it with their Industrial Relations Act, the Labour Party have perhaps done it with their Race Relations act, and the Sex Discrimination laws and so on. How much are we bringing the law into disrepute because we have moved too far away from what either vast majorities or small minorities actually think they want?

LORD JUSTICE SCARMAN:

I think this is a very very difficult question. I think, myself, if the law moves sufficiently far away from the main stream of public opinion it will be rejected; but that does not mean there is no room for alterations in our society. Of course, a leader's job, whether he sits on the bench, in Parliament, or in a Trade

Union or in the Church, is to lead into new fields. But he has got to keep in touch with the main body of those he is leading. I think this is the whole point of leadership in human society. All that I would say for the law is that, keen as many of us are, for instance, to get this or that reform introduced, we have to accept that the law, like politics, is the art of the expedient, and you cannot go so fast that you run away from society. On the other hand, no leader may abdicate his responsibility for leadership by saying "I am going to remain in the middle of the group and never move from it". I think this is immensely difficult.

A very good illustration is, of course, the issue of Capital Punishment. We are told, I do not know with what truth, that the majority of the people in this country are in favour of capital punishment. I know that the majority of judges, including myself, are against it. Does one say "Well, we must keep in touch and bring it back", or does one say "One must maintain one's view and seek by practice and argument to persuade others that one is right". This is an illustration of the non-legal basis to a legal issue in our society. At the end of the day, it is not for judges to tell the public that there must or must not be capital punishment. It is for society, through its democratically elected institutions, to make the decision. There it is. The rule of law will be ultimately what society wishes it to be. On issues of this sort, legal, political and social, leaders can go ahead of public opinion, but they must never lose touch with it. This is a really difficult problem, and I do not think it is a purely legal problem.

LORD GOODMAN:

If there is nothing else anyone wishes to ask, there is one question I would like to ask Sir Leslie myself, which I think is an important question because he has urged, as he has before, that we ought to have a written Constitution and a Bill of Rights. Subject to the ultimate authority of Parliament, there should be certain rights so fundamental that they cannot be

abrogated. What I want to ask him is this. Is this a sensible moment to go after such a written Constitution? In 1776 when the Americans obtained it, there were a number of perfectly moral men, simple, but imbued with the feeling that they had just destroyed a despotism, and they were united in the determination not to have further despotism, and to underline and bring into relief the vital rights they thought necessary for civilised rights. That was the atmosphere in the country at the time when they wrote that marvellous Constitution. Does that atmosphere pervade our country at the moment? Would it be sensible to invite a legislature, split almost down the middle, divided between firm determination that there should be domination in industrial terms, which is a perfectly legitimate philosophy on one side, and a number of people believe that fundamental rights transcend that determination. Would this be a wise moment to try to get a written Constitution? Might we not end up with something very strange, possibly undesirable, very much at variance with what we ultimately want? Should we not wait until matters settle a bit? I think that is an important question to which I would very much like an answer.

LORD JUSTICE SCARMAN:

I do not think this is the best moment to seek a written Constitution, but we all know the old military maxim, that the best is the enemy of the good. If we wait for the right moment, it may never come, and there are reasons which I attempted to indicate, why I think we must begin now. I think devolution is one reason. I think Europe is another. I think the Welfare State is another. These are pressing problems, and what I fear is if we wait then we shall get a new order forced upon us by the development of events without having thought out what it is we want. We shall get, if you like, a Constitution by accident. Whereas what I think we want is a Constitution achieved after years of study and discussion. I cannot foresee any time when we are not going to be riven by political and social controversy.

I just think those happen to be the stormy waters in which we have to sail and make our way. Very well, if the sea is not going to be calm, we have to do what is necessary when the sea is rough. We have to think it out and plan it and design it rather than wait for a better moment and run the risk of all we have done being overcome by the development of events.

LORD GOODMAN:

We could obviously continue this fascinating discussion for hours, but many of you must be getting hungry, and we will conclude the proceedings by asking Mr. Richard Thorpe to offer a vote of thanks.

Professor Sir Martin Roth, M.D., F.R.C.P., F.R.C.Psych.
Professor of Psychiatry, University of Cambridge

After qualifying in medicine in 1941, Professor Sir Martin Roth trained in Neurology as a pupil of the late Lord Brain and in Psychiatry at The Maudsley Hospital. He directed the clinical research at Graylingwell Hospital for a 5 year period, then spent a year as Assistant Professor of Psychiatry at McGill University before his appointment to the Chair of Psychological Medicine at the University of Newcastle upon Tyne in 1956. After serving 21 years in this post he was recently elected to the first Chair of Psychiatry at the University of Cambridge. He has served as a scientific member of the Medical Research Council and Clinical Research Board and has undertaken various missions for the World Health Organisation. He has been a Visiting Professor at Universities in Australia and Scandinavia and was the first Andrew Woods Visiting Professor at the University of Iowa. He was elected the first President of the Royal College of Psychiatrists in 1971 and held this office until 1975. His interests have been in the different aspects of mental disorder in late life and the nature and origins of depressive and related disorders. He is one of the authors of the standard text 'Clinical Psychiatry' which has been translated into many languages and some years ago published with Richard Ball a monograph on the problems of intersex.

'Sexual Pornography and Society – a Psychiatric View'

delivered by

Professor Sir Martin Roth

M.D., F.R.C.P., F.R.C.Psych.

Tuesday, 24th May, 1977

CHAIRMAN Sir Michael Swann. F.R.S.

SIR MICHAEL SWANN:

Mr President, Sir Martin, ladies and gentlemen: you will have seen from the Notice put round on your chairs that Lord Goodman, who has chaired all the Goodman lectures except the first one, which he gave himself, unfortunately has been ill and is not well enough to be here with us this evening, and for a variety of reasons I have been prevailed upon to take his place. Now, filling the space left by Lord Goodman, whether in physical or psychological terms, is not really altogether easy. Indeed, of all people who fill space and need all three dimensions if not a fourth, of course Arnold Goodman is the foremost exemplar.

So I feel rather uneasy. I feel all the more uneasy, in that the sort of things which he would have said, for reasons which I should explain, I do not think I can say. I can say some of them of course, but our efficient hosts have put some of them down in print for you. I could, and would like to, indeed, say

something about the Aitchison Memorial Trust which took the extremely enlightened step of setting up the lectureship, which is different from all the lectureships I know about; but it is all set out there. And I really cannot say very much about my friend, Professor Sir Martin Roth, because that is all set out there. I could tell you about Arnold Goodman, but again, that is set out.

I suppose Arnold Goodman would also be thanking the Royal Society for letting him hold forth in this Hall, but as a Fellow of that August body I feel found to say that they could do no other, and I see no reason why we should thank them for it. (*Laughter*)

And then I could expatiate on the splendidly distinguished people who have given former Goodman lectures, but I feel rather uneasy about that, having done the third one of those lectures myself. So I really turn immediately to Sir Martin Roth and the lecture that he is going to give this evening. As Chairman of the BBC, when I first saw this title some months ago I felt a certain *frisson* because his title is in fact "Sexual Pornography and Society – a Psychiatric View". If you are anything to do with the BBC, that sort of title makes you feel a little uneasy, and indeed, as I looked at it I had the feeling that somehow or other it would combine to fix all the previous Goodman lectures; that it would indeed provoke a scandal which would immediately require Lord Goodman himself to be called in to advise (*Laughter*); the whole business would be exacerbated on my behalf by the BBC and other bits of the media; the matter would finally come for trial before the last Goodman lecturer, Lord Justice Scarman; and the matter would be recorded for posterity by that distinguished historian, the second Goodman lecturer, Asa, now Lord Briggs.

But then of course I realised that it was all going to take place in front of, I believe, such figures as Lord Longford and Mrs Whitehouse, but nevertheless within the portals of the Royal Society; and moreover, the lecturer himself was the

Professor of Psychiatry at the University of Cambridge, and I need hardly say that on both those scores we can look forward to a lecture which is distinguished, provocative, and scholarly; so without more ado, may I call on your lecturer, Martin Roth. (*Applause*)

PROFESSOR SIR MARTIN ROTH:

Sir Michael, Trustees of the Aitchison Trust, ladies and gentlemen, it is with some trepidation that I commence this lecture, having regard to the remarks of our Chairman and the illustrious list of previous lecturers. I must start with an apology, after expressing my deep regret that Lord Goodman cannot be with us. The word of apology consists merely in the fact that the original title, as I think Sir Michael will confirm, was "Mental Health in Middle and Late life". (*Laughter*) This was the spontaneous choice I made. It is a field in which I am most interested. It was in the course of a session in Arnold Goodman's flat with a number of people whom I shall not name that I found myself, through a variety of influences, converted to adopting some other title. Not until I saw this in print did I realise how far I had moved on the one hand and how many links there were between the titles on the other.

I have divided this subject up into a number of sections and I will try to remember to mention when I pass from one to the next. I shall begin with history, and I have entitled this section:

Pornography Past and Present

The literal meaning of pornography is the delineation of the life of prostitutes. But in current usage it denotes literary or graphic representation of sexual conduct whose deliberate intention is to arouse sexual desire and to facilitate its expression. Pornography is judged by this contrived design to be sharply distinct from works of art, which may engender sexual excitement but are removed from the realm of the pornographic through their embodiment of a new personal vision or

insight the artistic stamp of creation.

While a valid distinction might be conceded, in any attempt to evaluate the psychological and social effects of pornography sharply drawn demarcation lines between the two worlds would entail arbitrary judgments and circular arguments. For not only have creations judged as pornographic yesterday, reputedly gained acceptance as art and often inspired the revolutionary and original art of today, but numerous examples of this process in reverse can be cited.

In 1863 Manet exhibited a painting which portrayed the artist and his friends taking lunch in a state of harmonious communion with each other and their surroundings, engaged in pleasures delicate and civilized, which are liable nowadays to engender feelings of nostalgia. But there was a naked woman among the handsome, fully clad young men. The painting immediately caused a sensation of scandal and outrage, and was rejected by the jury for the French Royal Academy. But in a few decades Manet and his fellow Impressionists were to transfigure the vision of the most gifted and influential painters of that period, and to change the manner in which ordinary people perceived the world around them.

Now the crowds who indignantly brandished their fists and sticks and umbrellas at "Luncheon in the Grass" and later at "Olympia" could not have been aware an art form which had dealt in a far more free and explicit manner with sexual love had flourished in Japan for centuries, and remained active at the time in question. To our eyes, these prints again capture the essence of deep and delicate feelings by their spontaneity and movement, their natural balance of vigour and restraint – but the openly erotic examples used to be quietly excluded from scholarly works and were judged coarse and vulgar by cultivated Japanese of the period. For they were pornographic in the strict sense of the term, having dealt almost entirely with the life of courtesans.

Examples of the opposite tendency, rejection or relegation of

the erotic art of one era to the limbo of the pornographic in the subsequent one are readily found. The pillow books that were given to newly-married Chinese couples, and the Kama Sutra, were originally written as instruction manuals, but would be classed as pornography in many countries at the present time. One has to give a special gratuity to be allowed access to certain frescoes in Pompeii, and ladies are liable to be looked at askance. Certain scholarly works which give a comprehensive account of the arts of classical Greece which dealt in bold and uninhibited ways with hetrosexual and homosexual love are locked away in great libraries and made available only to persons with special permission.

Some Lessons from the Past

What lessons can we learn from the past? I would like to extract four conclusions, which I shall take up and develop in later sections. First, erotic art or pornography – and after the passage of centuries the distinction does become a matter of subjective preference or caprice – has been produced in abundance in every historic epoch and culture. Secondly, erotica and pornographic art appears always to have been produced in the main by males for the consumption of males. This remains conspicuously so in our own day, and I believe this one-sidedness to be rooted in certain biological Achilles heels that are peculiar to the male sex. The third point has an important bearing on the central issue of pornography's influence upon behaviour. For history teaches that there is an enormous range of variation in the pattern of sexual behaviour as portrayed by erotica that have survived from different cultures throughout the ages.

For example, among other lines of evidence, according to Professor Kenneth Dover, homosexual acts are first represented in the Greek vase paintings about the 6th Century BC, although the pattern of sexual love between men was markedly different from that with which we are familiar. The Homeic

poems contain no allusion to sexual relationships of this kind. To take a quite different culture homosexuality appears to be entirely absent in any form, according to Hoyle, from the extensive body of erotic art created by the Incas of Peru, although an astonishing variety of sexual acts is depicted. Japanese erotica are quite different again. Now the time intervals between these two civilisations are far too short for heredity to have played any appreciable part in creating the differences. Hence there is some measure of corroboration from these sources for a great deal of other evidence, that sexual behaviour in man is shaped, conditioned and conjoined with patterns of conduct that have no necessary connection with it, though unlearning in adult life is liable to prove far from easy.

Fourthly, the ubiquity down the ages of those forms of pornography that are limited to the uninhibited representation of sexual love makes it possible to reduce this lecture to manageable proportions. No purpose would be served by going back to Adam. Here I shall therefore be mainly concerned with violent pornography; with those ingredients of pornography that are relatively new, and about which the past has little in the way of lessons to offer. I refer to the sadistic violence, abasement and degradation which so often overshadow or wholly displaces the sexual act in current pornography. For it has become increasingly plain that flagellation, fetishistic masochism, symbols derived from the Nazi era, its gaolers, torturers and graveyards, appear alongside or are interwoven with erotic descriptions. Above all, it is fear and hatred, the humiliation, torture, and exploitation of women rather than the love of women that predominates.

The Maleness of Pornography

I would like then to begin with the predominant maleness of pornography. The imbalance in the pornographic activity of the sexes has been redressed to some extent by recent develop-

ments, but the situation has changed less than sometimes appears. We may take the example of the masochistic theme of bondage, which accounts for a high proportion of space in pornographic journals, and seemingly appeals to a very large clientele. It is men who are generally depicted as manacled by the hands or feet, encased in tight-fitting suits of latex rubber, helmeted, gagged, suspended from horizontal bars by leather thongs. which end as a tight collar round the neck and can cause asphyxiation at the slightest movement. The female pornographic variations on such themes are muted, and once again found mainly in publications specifically designed or mainly intended for men.

The private enactment of these fantasies sometimes has a fatal end, through failure of the elaborate chain of precautions needed to arrest the process just before asphyxiation. And it is this point just short of asphyxiation that such individuals try to reach in order to achieve sexual orgasm. The victims of this particular deviation are invariably male. And the verdict of suicide often pronounced in coroners' courts is erroneous, for it is accidental death that usually occurred during the enactment of a bizarre form of displacement of sexual desire from its normal channel of expression in a relationship with another human being.

Such individuals, as I have said, are invariably male. The main question arises, of course, is whether the propensity for minor masochistic deviations of this genre, which are common, is in any way enhanced by providing additions to the repertoire and practices of those whose skills before exposure were limited.

In the past, the male monopoly of pornography has been explained in terms of male chauvinsism and dominance. In recent years, women's struggle for liberation has begun to redress the balance, and a small price has had to be paid in the form of susceptibility to disorders to which women had formerly been relatively immune. These include a rising in

prevalence of alcoholism, smoking and maladies associated with it, and higher rates of crime and suicide, though these do not approach the rates found among men. It used to be said 20 years ago that Danish women commit suicide because they smoke cigars. Well, both were of course related to other factors. Danish women were also relatively emancipated. Such facts in no way argue against women's liberation but psychological questions of great interest are posed by the cluster of disorders to which women have become more susceptible. It is not women alone; all emancipated groups suffer a similar fate for a period. But I cannot go into such questions here.

A parallel development has been the proliferation of Lesbian pornography and literature. It is interesting that in much of the pornography with Lesbian themes that has reached a six figure readership, the central female character commonly evinces unmistakable contempt for, or revulsion from her own sex. It is a long way removed from "The Well of Loneliness". The women brutalise and degrade their partners, and their aspirations for the male gender role are manifest in their behaviour in sexual intercourse and the attitudes they adopt in their relationships both to men and women.

Some Features of Contemporary Erotic Literature and Pornography

What, then, are the features in more detail of contemporary pornography and erotic literature? We have travelled a very long distance from the Casanovas and Don Juans who for all their vainglorious boasting, their conquests, and their scalp-hunting, loved women in their own fashion. They did not asphyxiate them by painting them over in gold, nor did they project missiles at their victims with cigarettes – a touch which incidentally Freud would have appreciated.

What were the starting points and origins of the new development? Well, it had been coming for some decades. But George Orwell who saw so much, and must have been about

five hundred years old when he died in 1958 aged 47 – detected a turning point in "No Orchids for Miss Blandish" by James Hadley Chase, which enjoyed great popularity during the Battle of Britain. Orwell contrasted it with previous crime stories and those in particular in which Raffles, the gentleman burglar, figured as hero-villain.

In what follows I shall draw upon Orwell's characteristically terse, clinical summary. Miss Blandish the daughter of a millionaire is kidnapped by some gangsters, who are killed off by a larger and better-organised gang. They hold her to ransom to extract half a million dollars from her father. Their original plan had been to kill her as soon as the ransom money was received, but a chance keeps her alive. Amongst the gang is a young man named Slim, whose pleasures in life include driving knives into people's bellies, and cutting up animals with pairs of rusty scissors. Slim is sexually impotent, but takes a kind of fancy to Miss Blandish. Now Slim's mother, who is the real brain behind the gang, sees this as a chance of curing her son's sexual problems and tries to keep Miss Blandish in custody until Slim should have succeeded in raping her. After many efforts and much persuasion, including the flogging of Miss Blandish, the rape is achieved. Meanwhile, Miss Blandish's father has hired a private detective and by means of bribery and torture, he and the police manage to round up and exterminate the whole gang. Slim escapes with Miss Blandish, and is killed after a final rape. The detective prepares to restore Miss Blandish to her family. By this time, however, she has developed such a taste for Slim's caresses that, unable to live without him, she jumps out of the window of a skyscraper.

Now the book has eight murders, numerous killings and woundings, an exhumation with a careful description of the stench, the flogging of Miss Blandish, the torture of another woman with red-hot cigarette ends, a strip-tease act and a third degree scene. There is one episode in which a gangster has an orgasm while being knifed. Orwell's conclusions are of in-

terest. Comparing the schoolboy atmosphere of Raffles books with the cruelty and corruption of "No Orchids" he reflects, "One is driven to feel that snobbishness, like hypocrisy, is a check upon behaviour whose value from a social point of view has been under-rated."

There are so many perceptive insights that one is led to wonder whether the book was not written by a psychiatric gangster using a *nom de plume*. The cure of Slim achieved with the collusion of the dominant mother who has an emotional strangle-hold carried strong homosexual overtones. And the brutal beating into submission of Miss Blandish whose superior intelligence and social status would in a normal encounter have rendered Slim helpless – has a compelling clinical authenticity.

Now it is usual to make a distinction between material whose declared purpose is to stimulate commonplace erotic ideas and fantasies, or, "soft" pornography and what has come to be classed as "true" or "hard" pornography, in which all the constraints of reality are removed and the standards of the prevalent culture violated. Some evidence does exist to suggest that normally-adjusted individuals tend to reject certain kinds of "hard" pornography. Yet "No Orchids" had been read by half a million people in 1945 when Orwell was writing. And vast sales are being achieved at the present time by some novels which are indistinguishable from "hard" pornography.

For example, a recent work by a distinguished author of science fiction, written in a fast moving brilliant style, has the motor car as a sacrificial altar for bleeding and dismembered figures who find in mutilation and death among the jagged masses of twisted steel an inevitable climax for their passionless and acrobatic sexual acts. Moreover, the ordinary erotic magazines are interlarded with images of torture and images of submission. The total readership of novels and magazines of this complexion runs into millions and disposes of psychological normality of consumers as the basis of distinction between

"hard" and "soft" pornography. However, a broad distinction is valid and the pictures shown to witnesses of murders in the Linda Lovelace trial would be generally classed as "hard" pornography. Let me quote some examples.

In one, a female in chains is seen tied up by a naked man pointing a sword at the woman's genitals. In another, a man with a cat o' nine tails is striking a woman on her vulva. Yet another – a girl with distress on her face and her arms manacled – is cut, a man with a bayonet is inflicting the cuts. All these were described by expert medical witnesses as beneficial because of their value in promoting masturbation.

Now it is insufficiently known that the last two or three decades have seen the proliferation to an increasing extent of pictures of wardresses, inflicting tortures in concentration camps, vivisection experiments on women performed by Swastika laden Nazis, and even mounds of corpses from Auschwitz. Young girls in their teens are flogged, tortured and raped. They are whipped while exposed to sexual assault with red-hot implements. Scantily-clad and jack-booted Nazi women are shown branding, whipping and disembowelling their victims. Recent sado-masochistic pornography has therefore acquired a new dimension. And there can be no doubt that both the availability and consumption of such material in general is vastly greater than it was, say, half a century ago.

If we pose questions about the causes for this steep escalation, satisfactory answers elude us. We can, of course, inculpate the violence of the age but this would be evading the issue. But some more simple explanations, particularly germane for this lecture, merit consideration. The Marquis de Sade and Sacher-Masoch did not of course invent the sexual deviations they described, but the eponymous attributions were fully deserved for in their gruesome way both men were writers with remarkable gifts. And one cannot exclude the possibility that their nightmarish fantasies of human torture and degradation could have served, in some measure, to enlarge and to dissemi-

nate the available repertoire of violent sexual practices.

The Weaker Sex

The truth of the matter is that "hard" porgnography deals in its grisly aspects with indubitably morbid forms of sexual adaptation, and it depicts and panders to others that have, in their fully-fledged and exclusive form, to be regarded similarly. Deviations of every kind studied have proved to be substantially commoner among the males of the human species in every culture investigated. This has proved to be true of sadism, masochism, exhibitionism, transvestism and trans-sexualism, fetishism, bestiality, necrophilia, homosexuality, both of the exclusive and the bivalent kind.

The much-flaunted virility of the male which has been celebrated down the ages is one long whistle in the dark. It is he who is liable to incapacity in the sexual act through guilt or anxiety, whereas the woman, whether or not she is aroused, remains sexually competent in the majority of cases. And with a minimum of skill can act as if she was fully competent if not highly gifted. It is the male sex which is the impotent one with an organ that is far less well integrated than the feminine one, and as Slater has pointed out with a sexual organ that is relatively anaesthetic and all too often paralytic. (*Laughter*)

This contrast between the sexes has biological, social and psychological aspects. The woman has a far greater investment in the sexual act. The consequences for her in pregnancy and childbirth and the rearing of children and the sacrifices demanded extend over the years. Nature has therefore taken great care to ensure the competence of the woman in the act, and has in addition provided her with a special bonus. Because the sexual orgasm which she experiences at the culmination of the act is a uniquely human phenomenon not found among other higher animals.

In contrast, for the male the risk of death or other adversity from sexual intercourse is negligible. His investment in the

sexual act is much smaller, and Nature has therefore equipped him with a more fragile sexual equipment. Sexual behaviour in the human male, as well as in the higher animals, proves more difficult to acquire, more liable to disorder and disruption, and the disabilities that develop through grave deprivation or deficiency in the formative years have proved much more difficult to surmount among men than among women. Here again, experiments among higher animals appear to yield similar results.

Moreover, Nature's predisposition is to produce females. In the absence of certain hormonal substances ("Androgens") the developing infant with a male hereditary constitution will have the outward appearance of the female, but the converse is not true. If the ovaries are absent and the hormones which they produce are lacking, normal female internal and external organs will develop, although such an individual will of course be infertile.

In fact, Nature appears to have treated the male as if he were altogther more dispensable than his female partner. He has a higher mortality rate at all stages of the life span, and with few exceptions has a greater susceptibility to illnesses and a greater liability to die from them.

From birth onwards he is less capable than the female of responding with anti-bodies to certain infections. Through the possession of a second X chromosome females are provided with protective isoalleles or paired genes that enable them to escape a whole range of hereditary diseases which are found in full blown form almost entirely in the male sex. They therefore remain largely immune from haemophilia, nephrogenic diabetes insipidus, some drug-induced anaemias and deficiency of the para-thyroid glands. They are the exempt carriers of diseases for which men have an almost exclusive monopoly. And with a substantially longer life span they have a far better chance of an uneventful passage through middle life into old age.

In describing the female as a castrated male with a strong unconscious motivation to compensate for this deficiency, Freud surely got it all wrong. The boot is literally on the other foot. Women may have a higher prevalence of neurosis, but alcoholism, drug dependence, murder, violent crime, consummated suicide, dangerous driving, as well as sexual deviations of every kind are specialities of the male of the species. He may be the greater warrior and hero and all that, and more often a musical or mathematical genius. But perhaps he has greater need to sublimate. The truth must out at last. Both in regard to physical or psycho-sexual robustness, it is the male which is the weaker sex. Blessed are those with two X chromosomes, for they shall inherit the earth! (*Laughter*)

One significant difference between the sexes has probably contributed to this asymmetry. Over many thousands of generations, in fact up till about a century ago, childbirth carried a considerable mortality. Women must therefore have been exposed to a much more fierce pressure from natural selection. And it is perhaps this which has been partly responsible for their lesser mortality, greater longevity, and perhaps their greater robustness and stability as sexual beings.

Sexual Vicissitudes of the Male

The predicament of the male has some of its origins in emotional conflicts which constitute an ineluctable part of the human condition, for it is to be found everywhere. The Paradise of sexual bliss, fearless, guiltless, shameless, is largely mythical.

It follows that modern "hard" pornography falsifies the truth when it ignores all constraints, because there is no culture where all sexuality has been given completely free rein to express itself at random. The taboo on incest, for example, is universal. And this entails inhibition in circumstances where the emotional bond is strong though as Freud and others have taught, there are often powerful undercurrents of sexual desire to be curbed and rechannelled.

Moreover, society's attitudes are ambiguously poised. Chastity is approved, virility is admired, promiscuity is frowned upon, though envied, impotence ridiculed. Such contradictions could not have been better contrived if one were setting out deliberately to engender conflict and neurosis. The situation was not essentially different, in "Ancient Greece" as Professor Kenneth Dover has pointed out. For young men (as well as women) when wooed were expected to assume the role of modest virgins. If they displayed or described actual pleasure in the sexual act they were reviled and repudiated.

We are getting closer to the same insight into the reasons for the special propensity of the male to deviate in his sexual behaviour in ways that provide the central themes of pornography. The sexual act and the human relationship it celebrates, demand highly developed emotional qualities, psychological attributes, and physical skills which have to be learned by the man in particular. As the activity is conflict-laden some anxiety is inevitable. But it is the male who is most at risk in the stages of exploration – when he seeks to define his needs and identity – of failure and humiliation. A fear laden aversion may be surmounted in some but well-learned in others so that neurosis and deviation become firmly ingrained. So it is that other channels less hedged around with taboos and offering less resistance may be chosen.

In place of an emotional relationship with a real woman, the fetishist will find outlets in her furs, her high heeled shoes, her hair, or her underclothes. Or guilt may be subdued in masochistic submission which may in runaway fashion, reach extremes of self-abasement and humiliation such as flagellation and torture, surrender to menial tasks, the licking of shoes, or the cleaning of lavatories. Or the feared object is conquered or mastered by exposing her to humiliation and violence as in sadism.

Continuing in this over-simplified way, the transvestite assumes the woman's outer identity. Thus attired, he may be

sexually competent. In one form of exclusive homosexuality the man seeks a partner of his own sex for similar reasons. And the trans-sexualist goes the whole distance: he wants a surgeon to remove his hated genitalia and transform him into a glamorous female seductively attractive to men. In erotic display as in his eye for fashion he may prove more royalist than the Queen.

Pornography panders to all this. Whether we deal with hard pornography or with James Bond fiction or with "No Orchids for Miss Blandish" or with displays available in most large cities of the Western World, peering beneath the thin camouflage it is fear, envy, hatred, and the desire for the humiliation of women rather than the love of women we find.

Now some recent contributors have tried to remove the whole area of sexual deviation from the realms of disorder or disease, holding that the spurious label of medical pathology is responsible for much of the intolerance and suffering. One definition that stems from the American Psychiatric Association, has it that unless there is subjective suffering or social maladjustment, a behaviour pattern has no kinship with disease. If we accept this, whipping by women in high-heeled boots is an innocent charade in fancy dress and not masochism, exhibitionism is a feeble form of streaking, necrophilia is a logical extension of the philosopy of organ transplantation, while bestiality harms neither man or beast.

But this happens to be wholly out of keeping with the findings of psychiatry and psycho-analysis. This is what Freud had to say on the subject: "If perversion instead of merely appearing alongside the normal sexual act and object, and only when circumstances are unfavourable to them and favourable to it – if instead of this it ousts them completely and takes their place in all circumstances – if in short perversion has the characteristics of exclusive fixation, then we shall usually be justified in regarding it as a pathological symptom." Moreover, it is implicit in his teaching, that the sadist and masochist suffer

from a stunting of character and spirit which is not confined to their sexual acts alone. Any influence exerted by pornography in catering for such tendencies will not be confined, if this theory has any truth in it, to private acts without any bearing on social conduct and social well-being.

Pornography and Sexual Behaviour

At this point, we may take a look at the evidence, regarding the effects of pornography on sexual crimes. This is a complicated subject, and I can touch only upon certain of the lines of evidence. The relationship between the prevalence of sexual crimes and pornography has been fully discussed recently in many publications, and I shall confine myself to certain points. Much has been made of the purported decline of the prevalence of sexual crimes witnessed following introduction and dissemination of pornography in Denmark in the "sixties". However, as Professor Court of Adelaide has made clear, the evidence is contradictory and complex. If one accepts that some decline in the number of reported offences has occurred, and some analyses show a tendency of exactly the opposite kind, many correlated factors might well have contributed. Changes in the law had deleted some offences, reporting rates had changed and the population of Copenhagen from which the figures are mainly drawn has declined by demolition of the old high-density quarters. Moreover, the changes had begun some years before the pornography movement was initiated.

An analysis of trends in a number of different countries by Dr Court has produced evidence at least as convincing as that extracted from the figures for Copenhagen. In short, starting from a level which had been maintained at a steady rate for many years, there has been in a number of countries *first* an upward trend coinciding with or shortly following the increased availability of pornography in the community, *second*, an upward trend in sex crimes; and, *thirdly*, this trend was not observed in one area for which figures were available. This was

Singapore, where strict control over portnography had been exercised.

Now such findings are notoriously difficult to interpret. As Dr Court concedes, no causal connection can be read into such figures. Some writers elaborate on these qualifications to such an extent that one would imagine that the positive correlation could be construed as signifying that pornography could not have had an effect. This is certainly not warranted. A causal connection is not established, but it is not excluded either.

What light is shed by the evidence from sex crimes? A considerable amount of observation has been placed upon record on sex criminals who have been investigated to ascertain to what extent they had been exposed to sexual pornography, either of the "hard" or "soft" variety. The findings certainly do not substantiate any large influence by pornography on the prevalence of sexual crimes. But information obtained from individuals about their own past is notoriously subject to retrospective falsification, and this tendency is bound to be reinforced in contradictory and confusing ways, in the groups of subjects charged with different types of criminal offences who had served as the basis for comparison.

It has been reported, for example, that sex offenders exhibit less sexual response to pornographic material than controls, and are also first exposed to it at a higher age than is normal for controls. However, the claim by the sex offenders that they had been exposed to pictures of bestiality, oral sex and homosexuality before they had set eyes on pictures of normal intercourse must shed serious doubt on the validity of the methods employed.

One wonders also, how much credence can be given to the finding by Cook and Goldstein that while normal controls report an increased frequency of sexual intercourse after exposure to pornography, sex offenders describe only more frequent masturbation. Again, either the finding that sex offenders do not differ significantly from non-sex-offenders or

non-offenders in the extent of their exposure and preoccupation with erotic material, or the claim by nearly two-fifths of these offenders that pornography had played some part in compelling them to commit sexual crimes could be true. Or both might merely reflect retrospective colouring or attempted self-exculpation or self-extenuation.

There is no evidence whatever in favour of the safety-valve theory, for the published evidence lends little credence to the belief that abreaction is promoted and dangerous tendencies side-tracked into the safer channels of private fantasies. In relation to violence, the best scientific evidence is unequivocally clear. Children exposed to scenes of aggressive and violent conduct exhibit an increase in such behaviour as compared with those not so exposed. The experiments were conducted over relatively limited periods of time, but this does not affect the significance of this body of factual observation. Testimony about the effects on sexual behaviour is bound to be restricted.

It is claimed by some psychologists that pornographic material does promote sexual arousal, but this is sharply limited by a filtering process, which sifts out all those forms of sexual behaviour which happen to suit the individual's previously-formed predilections in sexual behaviour. I shall cite certain lines of evidence which throw doubt on such conclusions.

The first is that when individuals are exposed to scenes of sexual sadism on television programmes, the circumstances in which de-sensitisation from phobic and other neurotic symptoms is undertaken in the clinic are being closely replicated. Secondly, it has been demonstrated by a group of workers that changes in sexual behaviour can be promoted by such methods. Thirdly, a sexual fetish for boots has in fact been created, and thereafter extinguished, in a series of experiments. And films, photographs, and similar materials with exclusive sexual themes are being regularly employed in counselling and in the treatment of sexual disorders. There is therefore much

evidence that within limits sexual responses and behaviour can be shaped and conditioned.

Finally, the sexual conduct of whole populations has been radically altered within relatively short periods of historical time. It is a transmutation of this nature that must have taken place in Greece round about the sixth century BC, because prior to this, according to Professor Dover, vase paintings betrayed no evidence of homosexual behaviour of the kind very clearly depicted in what were at one time called "wrestling" vases. Social and psychological influences must have been the main agents. And the evidence that such factors play the predominant role in the formative years, in shaping the pattern of response in each of the sexes and innate factors a less important one (in the generality of people) can hardly be contested.

Nor is it reasonable to assume that there is a hard and fast line which sharply separates those inherently predisposed to responding to pornography with morbid sexual conduct from the majority of human beings in whom satiety and boredom are the only results. A small minority will be largely immune, and an equally small one strongly predisposed. But there will be every shade of variation in between.

I therefore share the view of Professor Eysenck (1972) and I quote: "If television advertising is effective, and there is little doubt that it is, why should television be less effective when it advertises lax morals, cruelty and violence, promiscuity, permissive behaviour generally?" As he points out, it is not the amount of sexual activity, but the conjunction with it of emotions such as aggression, hostility, cruelty, fear, anxiety and contempt which may be expected to separate sexual behaviour from love and tenderness.

Now Mr Anthony Burgess has thrown scorn upon the view that life may mimic Art. In the written and filmed versions of his novel "A Clockwork Orange" the youthful hero commits repeated acts of sexual violence, sadistic assault and brutality

in ways that breach all constraints, standards and inhibitions. But in Mr Burgess's words: "Let me say at once that no evidence has ever been adduced in a court of law to prove beyond doubt that a work of art can stimulate anti-social behaviour, or for that matter can promote altruism and the other Christian virtues."

It so happens that such evidence as there is, is almost entirely against him. The publication of Goethe's "Werther" generated an epidemic of suicides in Germany. The publication of Murger's novel "Scenes de la Vie Boheme" set a pattern for a way of life among young artists who wanted to register a protest against the vulgar materialism, sybaritic self-indulgence and meretricious bourgeois standards, which they detected during the second half of the nineteenth century in France. There were, of course, other forces working in the same direction. But it would be myopic to ignore the fashions that can be so set, by artists of genius or a discerning eye. The rugged dissolute tuberculous romantic look caught on. But this and the spitting of a few drops of artificial blood on the piano keys was harmless in comparison with any vogue that may be helped on its way by Mr Burgess's Noble Savage.

Aggression and Sex: The Dissemination of a Myth?

The pornographic conjugation of sexual love with sadism and violence would not perhaps have obtained such extensive currency if there were not such a deeply ingrained belief in our culture in an innate association between aggressiveness and sexual desirability in the male. The belief is reinforced each day from many sources. The traditional hero of fiction is violent, adventurous, and when he finally carries off his heroine it is implicit that sexual bliss reigns forever after. The Napoleonic legend which echoed down the nineteenth century and remains alive now in our time was compounded by women vanquished as well as armies conquered. But judging from the evidence that became available after Napoleon's death, many of the

ladies vanquished may have been sadly disappointed.

The remark attributed to Henry Kissinger, "Power is the supreme aphrodisiac", may have been apocryphal, but it had a stamp of authenticity and was widely attributed to him. It has not been so in all societies. China, according to Maurice Bowra, registered its remarkable achievements without the help of myths from a "Heroic Age". It is interesting, also, there was very little in the way of a cult of romantic love in Ancient China. Soldiers were held in low esteem, and one old proverb had it that "Great men are a public nuisance." They have now changed all that.

Many psycho-analysts and biologists would give support to the view which conceives sex and aggressiveness to be closely related. Indeed, Konrad Lorenz had suggested that aggressiveness is an essential pre-condition for establishing lasting bonds of love and friendship. But as Robert Hinde has pointed out, the arguments adduced in favour of such views are vague and circular. Marked aggressiveness interferes with mating instead of assisting it. And even if limited evidence favouring such an association in certain species can be cited it may be largely or entirely irrelevant for human psychology and sociology. What may have been valuable for man's Protohomonid ancestors may be mal-adaptive and undesirable in the light of his current social and biological and moral needs. These have become, and ought increasingly to be employed, as the influences that shape his future evolution.

If, then, there is no neccessary connection, we have to ask how it is that marked aggressiveness and male sexuality have come to be conceived as closely entwined in a manner reflected in the bizarre parodies of contemporary pornography. It is the fact that the myth has been with us so long that perhaps engendered the belief in its innateness. But geneticists suggest another possible explanation. Dr Dawkins' book "The Selfish Gene" is mainly devoted to the thesis that we are temporary and disposable repositories for the genes we carry. But he

devotes his final chapter to a brilliant exposition of the view that a lot of fads or ideas, not only attractive tunes or arresting fashions but whole complex systems of belief may be propagated from person to person and one brain to the next. If they prove successful, they will be transmitted down the generations in a manner that will bear a close resemblance to the transmission of traits by genes. Indeed, the propagation and transmission of ideas and fashions may occur with greater rapidity and place a more indelible stamp on the ways of thinking and behaving of men than will the traits determined by the genetic endowment of any one person.

So it is that the contributions of Socrates, Shakespeare, Isaac Newton, Michelangelo, and Bach and Mozart, are still with us, though the genes for which they were temporary repositories have long ago vanished into the general gene pool of humanity. Dawkins suggests that ideas may arise in a random manner through mere whim or chance. However, as they are also subject to something akin to natural selection, this seems on the face of it rather improbable. Three groups of factors suggest themselves as liable to endow new fashions and fads with survival value.

The first is novelty. In the short term the success of an arresting new pop song or fashion may lead to its dissemination in a manner similar to the spread of an infection in a population lacking the defences of immunity or experience against it. The analogy is not precise, but it is something of this nature that caused aboriginal peoples to be decimated by alcoholism, tuberculosis and ways of thinking unsuited to them. Secondly, an innovator with brilliant gifts of communication may prove a powerful catalyst.

So it was that Salvador Dali could convert fetishes into fashions and gain acceptance for his necrophilic images of mannequins rotting in taxicabs, of sodomies of skulls upon grand pianos. Thirdly, ripeness of time helps. In Dali's case, as Orwell has said, every capital of Europe was full of aristocrats

who had abandoned politics and sport for patronage of the arts. If you threw dead donkeys at them they threw money back. To a limited extent, Sade and Masoch might have played a similar role. Fourthly, dissemination would be assisted when the idea fulfils some unsatisfied human need or craving, or an unresolved fear or hatred.

Now fear, resentment and humiliation of women is not a new phenomenon. As Eliot pointed out in his Vickers lecture, one is bound to be struck by the ferocity with which the disparagement, denigration and vilification of women has been conducted in the past and to which they have been submitted through the ages in the cultures with which we are more familiar.

The explanation may be found in envy. Envy of a partner who is free from the deficiencies liable to reduce the male to a state of helplessness. It is in the very place where he has exhibited his greatest pride and glory that he finds himself feebly endowed in comparison with his partner. It is the male that is the jealous sex, and the forms of murderous morbid jealousy which present themselves in Courts of Law are an almost exclusively male phenomenon.

The aggressive male virility cult may therefore owe its long survival to the fact it deals vicariously with fears and uncertainties to which the male of the species is particularly susceptible. We know from the example of cigarette smoking how easy it is to implant a pattern of behaviour and spread it far and wide as a fashion, by coupling it through propaganda with virility, and how appallingly difficult it is to eradicate it, even when the effects are exactly the opposite to those sought after. This fact has to be linked with evidence that sexual responses can be readily conditioned and shaped.

Now the resemblance between the tolerance and escalation witnessed during states of drug dependence, and the increasingly brutal and sexually deviant character of pornography is superficial and devoid of physiological foundation. But

escalation is an indubitable trend. Hitchcock's "Psycho" which froze the blood of audiences 15 years ago is demoted to Black Comedy. The under-the-counter pornography of yesterday becomes the commonplace of today in magazines like *Playboy*, *Mayfair*, *Men Only* and the smart gossip columns. The fast sports car becomes a virility symbol. "Drive it like you hate it", reads one advertisement, "It is cheaper than psychiatry". (*Laughter*)

Throughout this lecture I have been more concerned with the possible effects on ordinary people rather than the tiny minorities specially predisposed to violent sexual crimes, although we cannot afford to ignore the evidence I have cited about this. It is probable, from what we know about the ways in which behaviour patterns are learned and modified, that such patterns of violence provide safety outlets. At the least they promote acceptance and numb the sensibility that enables us to empathise with suffering. At the worst, they may condition enjoyment and perhaps infliction of pain by individuals in whom, had it not been for exposure to pornography, such propensities might have remained dormant.

What is to be done?

One thing is certain. The legitimate aims of those who struggle for the liberation of women are incompatible with the ever-widening proliferation of pornographic creations of which they are subjected to degradation and torture, or given roles that are an obvious inversion of such deviations. In a more equal partnership with clear acknowledgement of what each sex is able to contribute, men may be purged of their envy and women of the desire to emulate the behaviour patterns of those who have in the past caused their subjection.

The first need, therefore, is to strip the subject clean of its encrustations of self-deceptive myth and face the problems with fresh understanding. We should also make more widely known those factors which are known to contribute to sexual

misery and frustration, and their vicarious forms of expression.

Censorship and the law relating to obscenity would require a separate lecture, and I shall confine myself to one comment. It is anomalous that there should be legislation which makes it a crime to engender racial hatred while the dissemination of literature in which women are violated and dehumanised is subject to no restrictions. Yet evidence that the latter influences overt behaviour is at least as strong as the evidence which testifies pornography to an effect by the former on conduct.

There is need, also, to distinguish between eroticism on the one hand and pornography which, either by implication or otherwise, normalises sexual sadism and humiliation on the other. And if we want a definition of corruption, the task might well commence with the example of young children submitted in their formative years to flagellation and oral intercourse. It is well known that at least one of that rare group of child murderers had a prostitute as a mother and had listened, to, and possibly witnessed, the flagellation of her clients.

If the stereotype of the aggressive predatory male has emerged somehow as a fashion or cult at some point in history, we have to take thought as to how new fashions that displace the traditional ones might be generated. This is not inherently impossible. One example is provided by Japan. After some centuries of development in which Ukiyo-e prints depicted sexual love with naturalism and delicacy, there was an abrupt change. I am indebted to a work by Evans drawn to my attention by Mr Chamberlain of Fitzwilliam Museum in Cambridge for this evidence. Towards the middle of the 19th century blood and violence were inter-fused and there was an increasing brutality in the treatment of erotic prints. Public displays of women having sexual intercourse with animals are described. As such themes had previously been absent, Western influences had very likely contributed. A fashion had emerged and spread, which then waned and vanished.

Let me point out two possible consequences that might

follow if the runaway trends are not halted. If extreme aggressiveness is depicted as an essential trait of the sexually attractive male, young men will vie and compete more and more with one another. They will try to prove themselves by feats of violence and daring in schools and football grounds, and in aggressive and anti-social acts towards others. I do not apologise for the element of conjecture. There are bound to be victors and vanquished, each with their fears and hatreds. This may be one of the ways in which violence is being exacerbated in a vicious circle, or positive feedback fashion at the present time.

And such a stereotype with its traits of violence could set a pattern and be disseminated more rapidly than if it had been genetically determined. The young and impressionable, those in flight from homes in which violence and brutality are compounded by alcoholism will be particularly liable to conform to the stereotype. Now the lives of the markedly aggressive are liable to prove chaotic and their personal relationships to prove unstable. Their life expectation is shortened by violence, accident proneness, and impulsiveness. Their children are more likely than those of others to be abandoned, deprived, battered or orphaned. The number of one-parent families already stands at hundreds of thousands, and will under such influences expand, as will the numbers of boys brought up by mothers alone. It is largely the mothers who are left holding the baby. I have described the manner in which the same common forms of arrested emotional development arise, for it should be a major purpose of social policy to create the conditions in which the greatest possible number can mature as individuals.

For all its fuzziness, "maturity" in this sense is an important psychiatric concept. Rather than try to discuss or define it I shall quote from a letter by Chekov, a man for all seasons who in simple, imperishable words displayed a deep and delicate thought into human relationships. He addressed this letter to a

drunken and dissolute older brother who behaved in a coarse and brutal manner towards his mistress. The tone of moral exhortation nowadays strikes a quaint and archaic note. He was trying to define the characteristics of what he called "the well-bred" or as we would say "mature" person. This is what he said: "they respect individuals are therefore always indulgent, gentle, polite, and compliant. Their compassion extends beyond beggars and cats . . .

"They are candid and fear lies like the plague. They do not lie even about the most trivial matters. They do not belittle themselves merely to arouse sympathy . . .

They cultivate their aesthetic sensibilities. They, and especially the artists amongst them, require spontaneity, elegance and compassion. They try their best to tame and ennoble their sexual instincts to endure her logic, and never stray from her . . .".

It would have been very illuminating to have him expand on this "ennobling sexual instinct". For there was nothing in him of the prig or puritan. There was in fact a good deal of obscenity in his letters, kept in its place by an unfailing instinct. He was protesting in his letter against the brutal sexual exploitation of a woman. In his writings he always fought the never-weary arm of terror and he would surely have joined hands with those who seek to make aggression and violence maladaptive and inappropriate, and seek therefore to prevent their psychological conjugation with the most powerful of human urges. It was only 1886, but his letter continued: "You must work at it constantly day and night; you must never stop reading and studying and exercising your will. Every hour is precious." (*Applause*)

SIR MICHAEL SWANN:

I am sure, ladies and gentlemen, that many of you will have questions that you would want to ask Sir Martin Roth. Supper in fact awaits us, and I suggest that you should perhaps do that

downstairs. So it only remains for me to do two things: and the first is on your behalf to thank most warmly the Aitchison Memorial Trustees for setting up this series of lectures; for inviting us to hear a most striking lecture this evening, and for inviting us to supper afterwards. And finally, can I call upon the Chairman of the Trust, Richard Thorpe, on my right, who is going to say some words of thanks to Sir Martin Roth. (*Applause*)

The Rt. Hon. The Lord Snow C.B.E.

Lord Snow was born in Leicester in 1905 and educated at a secondary school. He started his career as a professional scientist, though writing was always his ultimate aim. He won a research scholarship to Cambridge, worked on molecular physics, and became a Fellow of his college in 1930. He continued in academic life in Cambridge until the beginning of the war, when, because of his human and scientific knowledge, he was engaged in selecting scientific personnel. Since the war he has worked in industry, has been a Civil Service commissioner for which he recieved a knighthood in 1957, and was Parliamentary Secretary to the Minister of Technology from 1964 to 1966.

Lord Snow's academic honours included the Rede Lectureship at Cambridge, and the Godkin Lecutureship at Harvard, in which he first put forward his celebrated theory of *The Two Cultures and the Scientific Revolution*, The Regents' Professorship at the University of California at Berkeley, the Rectorship of St. Andrew's University, and many honorary degrees from universities in Europe, America and the Soviet Union. Lord Snow is also an Extraordinary Fellow of Churchill College, Cambridge, a Foreign Honorary member of the American Academy of Arts and Sciences and a Fellow of the Royal Society of Literature. He became a Life Peer in 1964.

His many publications include:

Death Under Sail
New Lives For Old
The Search
Science and Government
Variety of Men
Public Affairs
In Their Wisdom
and the *'Strangers and Friends'* sequence:
which included
Strangers and Brothers
The Affair and
Corridors of Power

Lord Snow was also the author of six successful plays including 'View over the Park', and 'The Masters'.

The Trustees of the Aitchison Memorial Fund are grateful to Lord Snow's literary executor for permission to publish his Goodman Lecture.

'Coming to Terms with Elitism.'

delivered by

The Rt. Hon. Lord Snow C.B.E.

Wednesday, 13th June, 1978

CHAIRMAN The Rt. Hon. Lord Goodman C.H.

LORD GOODMAN:

Lord Snow, Ladies and Gentlemen, this is the sixth lecture which I have been honoured by having named after me.

It would be quite wrong of me to keep you from Lord Snow a moment more than is necessary. I have known him now for a good many years. I first came to know him properly when he accepted an invitation to join the Arts Council. He was a quite exceptionally valuable member of the Council, a little taciturn, which made him more valuable in an assembly where on the whole taciturnity was not a feature of the day, but a man whose judgment and support were on almost all issues that I can remember immensely valuable. One of the reasons why I esteem him so highly is I cannot think of a single issue that arose in those days on which I did not find myself in agreement with him; even better, perhaps, on which he did not find himself in agreement with me. I developed a respect and affection for him that I shall retain for the rest of my days. He is, as I say, an immensely distinguished author. I do not think perhaps that his reputation is quite as high as it might be because he is so eminently readable. It is extremely difficult to establish an outstanding reputation as an author if you can be

read as readily and as easily and with as much pleasure as he. People always consider that a man who can be read as easily as this must in some way fail to attain the highest and most lofty peaks of intellectual distinction. You have only to read Lord Snow to see what a falsehood this is. I think his readability to some extent has detracted from the reputation he possesses, which, enormous as it is, would be heaven high if it were found more difficult to read him.

The skill with which he writes and the pleasure that he gives has been demonstrated by one fact which I do not think has been pointed out. So many of his novels have been converted so readily into plays. A number of you will have seen a number of his plays; I do not know how many there are; I certainly have seen five or six of them. They all contain absolutely splendid and exciting stories, and the ones I have seen have all been derived from novels. I think I am right in saying that nothing demonstrates his skill as a story teller and his ready ability at devising a plot that holds people than his ability to convert these novels into plays which have had an enormous success.

I think that this lecture in many ways embodies a lot of the philosophy of Lord Snow. He stands in this country principally and almost uniquely as a man who has synthesised the sciences and the humanities and who has come to recognise that the two are not incompatible. I do not think we could have had a more appropriate lecturer than Lord Snow for this occasion. I shall not keep you from him for a moment more.

THE RT. HON. THE LORD SNOW:

My Lord Chairman, Ladies and Gentlemen, it is a great pleasure and honour to be with you tonight. It is an honour because this is a distinguished series. It is a pleasure because it is in celebration of you, Sir, who to my mind fills a place in this country which is unique. I have never known anything like it in my lifetime. So I have struggled back from America in a state of some collapse, for which you will have to forgive me, because

nothing would have stopped me from speaking tonight.

Let me let you into a secret. Novelists tend to be ghouls; they prey on the living and the dead. They do not usually – though sometimes they do, I must be honest – try to give portraits of the persons whom they know, love, hate, etc. But it would be absurd to think that they do not draw on their human experiences for their starting off points for characters. Any novelist who tells you that is a liar.

In the course of this occupation there is one difficulty which almost all novelists know, certainly all decent ones. It is one which makes Lord Goodman totally exempt from the attentions of professionals. It is as near impossible as makes no matter to try to represent in fiction with any reality a good man. If you think for a moment of the longish history of the novel, there are extraordinarily few examples of novelists who have come anywhere near credibility, readability, anything you like, in portraying a good man. One or two good women have managed to find their way into fiction. The only good man I can think of you will find in the pages of Dostoievsky, who did this not only with consummate literary skill but with psychological ingenuity. It would be even harder in fiction to represent a good man who is fun. So that Lord Goodman is quite safe. As he is as much fun as any man in London, and simultaneously a very good man, as anyone who knows him will testify, he is unlikely in my view to find a place in the fiction of his time. The good turns he has done, usually invisible, are innumerable. I have had direct experience of one or two. At pains to himself – he is always pressed; he is always over-worked – he will take infinite trouble over quite a minor concern except to the person who is suffering it. We all know that; we shall all remember it. This will be in the historical record but not on the literary one.

Having said that, I think I have said the only good tempered thing I am going to say tonight, for I am going to talk with some harshness and some scorn of one of the sillier conventions or stereotypes of our time and one, though it spreads

round the western world, is probably more destructive in this country than in any.

Let me start with a word. We now use the word "elite" purely as a cliche, a slogan, a fighting word, a word of abuse. It has become so quite recently, so far as I can remember not earlier than about ten or fifteen years ago. But we are quite used to it. It is an English habit to get foreign words wrong. One of my pet aversions, which is not so serious, certainly not so destructive, is the way we use the harmless word "expertise". It does not mean in French in the least what we are bombarded with every day of the week, ripping off in every speech we ever hear, in almost every article we read, produced with an air of profound cosmopolitan knowledge. "Expertise" does not mean a skill: it means an act. If you want to get a picture valued, you go to someone who can do it and he performs an expertise. He does this on account of the qualities, the experience, he has possessed and acquired. But the English for that is "expertness", a perfectly good word; we did not need another. Why we have adopted this ridiculous babu French I have never understood. I have inveighed against it for a long time without the slightest succcess.

"Elite" though is a different cup of tea. "Elite" has become a curse word, a word of abuse, a fashionable word of libertarian conformity. It means, of course, nothing of the kind. It means a group chosen, no more than that, no less. "Elite" is "chosen". "Elite" is a group, a section, a particular body, which is chosen for a particular purpose. A football team is an elite body or an elite group. No one in his sense would think of having a non-elite football team, though now I come to think of it that may have been one of our national troubles in recent times. Yet this word "elite" has come to take on a pejorative significance.

The idea that any body of people ought to be deliberately chosen on the grounds of excellence seems to strike a peculiarly discordant note in our society. It is here, of course, that the trouble arises. With our typical habit – which is not confined to

this country, it belongs also to the whole of the western world – the idea of such an elite has come to be attached to money. That is, if there is a body chosen, then it must be due to the fact that they are richer than anybody else. Nothing could be more fallacious. Elites are usually chosen because of a skill or because of a talent. That talent should be, and usually is, more or less independent of the money or even the practical advantages from which the possessions start. It is true that they do start with the advantage of having a talent. If, then, you are objecting to an elite, you are objecting to the idea that any person or body may possess a talent, a skill, a quality, which is not common to everyone else. If that is the truth, then we are on what in my view is a suicide course. To feel that this kind of privilege, the privilege of having a talent, is bad in itself; it should not be encouraged; it should be actively discouraged – a society which feels that is on a slippery slope.

It is possible that one is reading the signs too grimly. I wish I could believe that. All the indications are that this is not the case.

Not so long ago, this country, in a sort of rough and ready, slap happy, amateurish way, was quite good at thinking that certain persons ought to have distinction and ought to be cheered on as a credit to us all. How far does that remain with us now? Probably very little. One thinks of the kind of persons to whom social recognition actually goes; the social response is curious. It does not go to the people who possess the talents of a valuable elite. It goes to pop singers, to television comedians, to an extent to certain kinds of games players. There is very little real response to anyone else.

I was moved only a year or two ago when a couple of extremely eminent people got the highest civic honour which this country can bestow. They were Lord Todd, the President of the Royal Society, and one of the best organic chemists in the world. The other was J.B. Priestley, who after an exceptionally long honourable fighting career at last was given

official recognition. This made no impact on the public. At one time it would have made a little more. Certainly it would have made much more impact in the quality press, on the various organs of publicity, the B.B.C., etc. It passed almost unnoticed. I remember looking at this with more than my usual gloom. At the same time and in the same Honours' List some moderately minor television comedians got something near the most minor civic honour which this country can bestow. That was in every quality paper, with grinning pictures of those men. I have nothing against television comedians so long as I am not asked to spend my time watching them. But these were the people who appeared in the quality papers, in successions of news programmes, and so on. That seemed to me a portent, and it still seems to me so.

More seriously, a number of us, colleagues of mine, or at least allies of mine in this particular cause, have tried to persuade successive governments that mathematics is a rather worthy thing to encourage, a particularly special talent requiring a particularly special elite. We have tried to persuade governments to take appropriate steps which are very simple – I shall come to that later and revert to it again – to see that our supply is sufficient. In mathematics in past years we have not been specially prominent in the world but we have been good enough. In trying to persuade governments that we ought to cultivate this elite what answer do we get?

One produces the argument that they are perfectly prepared to make special arrangements for musicians and dancers. They say: "Yes, we don't mind doing that because those talents can be spotted very early." One then says – I have said it myself in Parliament and I have said it in print and so have various people far more qualified than I to do so – this is precisely true of mathematics. We know a great deal about the life history of eminent mathematicians. With extremely few exceptions their talents have been visible and perceptible at an age at least as early as those at which have enabled these people one is

confronting to pick out dancers and musicians. They lie. I am afraid I have no kinder word. They say "There is considerable disagreement in educational circles about whether we can pick them out early." That is first of all not a factual truth. Much more, it conceals the real reason why they won't do it.

Once I got this much more sharply in Sweden, where people tended to be more honest. I pursued exactly the same argument with politicians in Sweden where they behave exactly as we do: they pick out their musicians and dancers early but will not move a step for anyone with any kind of mathematical – or any other kind of – intellectual distinction. I have gone through all the rigmarole once more. Their argument is the honest one: "I am afraid we could not do this. Our people would not regard this as democratic." That is a very strange use of the word "democratic", but I am sure it is the truth. This is the invisible truth behind all our pretences: either to refuse to recognise that elites exist at all or that they can be encouraged or that such encouragement is a social good. In fact, the invisible truth is that to encourage such elites would be a social evil. This is really serious. I will come later in my talk to what other societies of different kinds are doing, and finally I would like to say what I think we could do, you and I, fellow citizens. Because I believe this happens to be one of the few problems which are to an extent within our own control, intention, and will.

We know a great deal about the encouragement of intellectual elites, how they can be trained, how they should be trained. Granted that it is a good thing to do so, granted that this is what a spirited society needs, granted this is what the society in the end is as likely to be judged by as anything else, then the way is wide open.

In our own curious, haphazard, and as I said before slap happy and rough and ready way, we have been moderately good at this for a very long time. Our record at producing people of high excellence in most of the sciences and in most of

the arts stands comparison with nearly any other country, certainly with any other country of our size. That still remains. It is one of the things where the traditions and the procedures have lingered on, though now they are threatened. We have done remarkably well – on the whole better than very much bigger and richer countries. In my view, we owe a lot of our standing to just this success.

I remember speculating once about the University of Cambridge between, say, 1890 and 1925, 35 years, not very long. During that time, this university, which at no stage had as many as 4,000 undergraduates: the faculty, whom we call dons, was well under 1,000, probably something like 500 to 600. In that small community lived Rutherford and J.J. Thomson, two of the great experimental physicists of the world; Hardy and Littlewood, two of the great pure mathematicians of the world; young Dirac just coming on, by 1925 now by world standards the most eminent living Englishman; Hopkins, the father of biochemistry; Maynard Keynes, endowing practical economics with a touch of genius; a quiverful of historians, George Trevelyan among them; G.E. Moore whose influence dominated English philosophy; Russell: the list could be prolonged. I doubt if any small university in the world has ever had so many gifted people collected at the same time. I doubt very much whether it will ever happen again.

That testifies that we have not been at all bad at producing elites, by whatever random process we did it. Anyone who thinks that that was done by money and that these people were privileged by birth simply does not know the circumstances in which they were born. About half those I have mentioned were born poor, not working class, except perhaps for Rutherford, but certainly on the fringes of the lower middle class. Few of them ever had or ever made money. They had just emerged from our own strange academic process. I have forgotten perhaps the most dramatic example of all. That is the Indian mathematician Ramanujan who was born into a penniless

family in Madras and who, because we were then good at selecting talent, was brought to England and there gave us the fruits of his genius, too. If it had not been for another great mathematician he would have been totally lost. At the time he was brought out, he was earning £20 per year as a clerk in Madras and had had no serious education at all.

We have no reason to be ashamed of these results nor in my view of the processes which produced them. For the real secret, it seems to me, is that if a society really wants to encourage such talent, that is more decisive than almost anything else in the world. I agree that we were skilled, and we are still skilled, at educating our bright young in a peculiarly intense way, which is strange to most of the world, in my view too specialised in its early stages but having many advantages.

The chief advantage is that clever boys and girls educate each other; they become a kind of critical mass. If such a group is too much diluted, the advantages of concentration begin to disappear. Further, if such a group is too much diluted, you get too much of the pressure of society. Society in the bulk does not understand and does not approve of – and above all passionately envies – people of high talent. That is really the advantage of the selective process in English education, which in many ways, for benevolent reasons often, we are cheerfully, benevolently, with every expression of goodwill, throwing away in front of our eyes and with sounds of approval from large numbers of our fellow citizens.

Knowing how talent and elites can be encouraged, we can, if we have the will, enough obstinancy, and enough indifference to climates of thought, set about keeping this particular advantage for our bright young for a generation or two. It is asking a lot of those who try. It is asking them to be unpopular, but any man of spirit is willing to face that. It is asking something harder – to accept that kind intentions can lead to bad consequences.

We know how to select and encourage a mathematical elite.

We are dealing with a very rare gift, rarer than I used to think, and, unfortunately, an obstacle to one of my other pet concerns, that is, that people should on the whole be familiar with both the arts and sciences of their time: I still believe that. But if I were introducing that topic again, I should have to make a qualification. If we are going to educate a lot of people in the sciences as well as the arts, we should have to accept as a fact of life that a great many highly intelligent people find mathematics not so much difficult but impossible – impossible, that is, at any sort of serious level. It is a thing which we have all shut our eyes to, another of these harsh and bleak truths of human nature. The more one examines the problem, the more one meets brilliantly intelligent people to whom, however we set about it, whatever new and ingenious methods of inducing abstract thought we can devise, somehow it does not take.

I studied quite recently for some professional purposes the lives of the eight or nine novelists I most admire. With one exception, Stendhal, who was quite a good mathematician, all the rest were not only mathematically ordinary, that is, about the level of the ordinary intelligent person in mathematics, but mathematically stupid. They found the symbolic language of mathematics utterly incomprehensible. Some of them had strong reasons for not doing so. Dostoievsky, for instance, was trained as an engineering officer, where you had to do some trigonometry. He could not do it at all. He was quite hard working; he was poor; he was ambitious; but this he found absolutely beyond him. Until he was rescued by premature literary success he was set down at a drawing board in the old military drawing office in St. Petersburg, which he did not find congenial. The same applies to the other very great novelists – Proust, one of the cleverest men who ever lived, was utterly incompetent at mathematics, and so was Tolstoy.

One has to learn from the facts of life. So one has to say there is that negative side. But the positive side is quite easy. We know very well; we have done it for generations; we have

produced very good mathematicians and we can go on doing it. But if so, we have got to set about it and think they are rather special creatures. Let them have the stimulus of their own company. Good teaching helps, in my view, but not as much as the stimulus of associates somewhere near their own degree of talent. Above all – and this I revert to because it is the key to the whole business – they have to feel that the outside world approves of them and thinks their talent is worth working at. It may be not quite as good as being a television comedian, but it is a fairly decent thing to do. Unless we get that degree of social approval, this particular kind of talent will diminish, not too dramatically, but relatively fast in the lifetime of some of the younger people present in this room.

The same applies to most forms of conceptual science. We know how to cope; we have the techniques of selection and encouragement; the techniques are easy. The battle against outside pressures is far more difficult.

I suspect that very much the same applies to the teaching of languages at their highest level. Skill in languages is not such a specific gift as mathematics but it involves three totally different gifts, which give it a peculiar difficulty. One of the three is memory. You cannot learn languages without a really good computer memory. You cannot learn languages well without a kind of puzzle solving instinct. You can give a good linguist the Hungarian translation of a novel and ask him how long will it take to work out the text. The usual answer is about six months; with Japanese, a good deal longer. The third is ear. It is not much use learning languages unless you can speak them.

Those disparate gifts probably need very much the same special attention *in toto* as the specific gift of mathematics or other forms of conceptual thought.

I should not welcome the same argument applied to selective processes in things like the creative arts. I am sure it does not in literature. The best thing you can do for a potential writer is to get him away from literary things as rapidly and as far as

possible. If I had all the money in the world, I should be endowing scholarships for writers of promise to become doctors, engineers, lawyers, functionaries of various kinds. That would be much more valuable than any literary education they are likely to get; they will pick that up anyway. Nearly all the best writers have had that kind of non-literary education.

I suspect again the same applies to the visual arts, but not music, which is as specific and as unusual as mathematics. We know a great deal about the training of these elite qualities. What do we not know?

I am going to lead you a little further before I come back to where I think our weakness lies and where our imperative must be found.

Other countries in the western industrialised world are in substantially the same position as we are but not quite so sharply. As I mentioned at the beginning, I am just back from the United States. I have been discussing these problems with a lot of my closer friends in the intellectual world there. Being Americans, they are rather more active in their response than we are. They are less prepared to sit back and let life take its course; that is one of their strengths. They are worried. They have so many resources that they think in some way they will come through, though their great increase of strength in science through the last Jewish immigration is now losing its force. They would agree, at least the educationalists I know, with nearly all I am saying. They are worried. They cannot get the values in the right place. The social values of their society are very much the same as ours – they are not the values of a spirited society, not the values of a society which has to live in the same world as harder ones, more resolute ones, and ones which see these simple truths which I am talking about tonight with a clarity not given to us.

France used to have what for functional puroposes was the best elite education in the world; the *grande ecole* was a wonderful invention where they could train people from any

kind of provenance though once within the system they became some of the best marriage partners in France, which was a nice inducement. They have produced, since they started in Napoleonic times, a kind of functional class which could switch between government administration, academic life, and the creative arts at the drop of a hat. I often wish I had had that kind of education myself. That is being nibbled away by very much the same influences as are afflicting us. "Elite" is a French word, and it is now beginning to be used in just the same pejorative and abusive sense as we use it ourselves. The same is roughly true of the whole of the industrial west, though not in Japan where, with an intellectual and moral athleticism, which I might shy from in recommending to others, they are producing elites of all kinds. Elites of a kind of competence which is going to drive the west out of business, not only in industrial terms, unless we take a very hard, cold look at ourselves.

They pay a price. There is a price for almost any human effort. Do not think that the kind of education I believe to be a necessity to a spirited society does not exact sacrifices, does not impose misfortunes, and heart-break. Because if you are having this sort of value placed on supreme excellence, then many people, good people, nice people, will want to achieve it and will not be able to reach it. You will find that in almost any kind of specialist or elite education. That is a price you have to pay. Gentleness is a virtue. Gentleness carried to extreme limits can be very destructive. I am afraid that life is a hard and unforgiving business. That we have to accept.

What then of the great Communist societies? There the picture is very different from ours. As most people in this room will know, the Soviet Union have spent a great deal of money on education, first of all with very much the kind of spirit and empahasis which is now fashionable here, which for a long time was fashionable in America, and which is becoming fashionable all over the west. That is, everybody is potentially

capable of doing anything. You had everyone educated. Classes were not divided according to ability; they were what we call mixed ability classes; and in the long run from this great social effort your elites would come. The trouble was they did not.

Russia has a long intellectual tradition and a very good one, certainly in literature and to a considerable extent in science as well. Some of the scientists took the initiative into their own hands. They said it is true that their population was now totally literate, and that was a great feat. People are reading books who would never have thought what a book was like before the Revolution. But, they said, we are not getting anything like the products which the west in its crude way is still getting. People who knew this country, for instance like my old friend Kapitsa, said this passionately and violently to the Soviet Accademy: somehow the system is not doing all we need, and, at the highest level, what we most need. So several people said "We will do it ourselves." A mathematician at a university in Siberia and another in Moscow decided to set up their own special schools, a rather difficult thing to do in Russia. They got encouragement; people were beginning to get worried. This was the beginning of a whole set of schools, usually about 400 in size, almost always very close to or attached to universities, students selected by an old fashioned method which most of you have heard of called competitive examination. Places were passionately competed for. Russians will do almost anything to get their children on the academic or intellectual ladder. These special schools have now been going for a number of years, with startling success. They are very impressive, rather like the top forms of St. Paul's or Westminster. They are bi-sexual, with boys and girls of very high ability, very earnest, very serious, passionately eager to succeed. They have one immediate prize which stiffens the nerve. That is, anyone who is pretty successful has automatic entry to a good university. In Russia you do not just walk into a university, and this is a real prize.

The idea that any Russian in his senses would think that this was anti-democratic is just grotesque. They still have a veneration for the higher flights of intellectual life, which here, as I have suggested, has deserted us. To be an academician in Russia is to carry an aura which ought to be attached to a Fellow of the Royal Society, but isn't. I have never seen people regard Fellows of the Royal Society with almost religious respect; I should rather like to see it, but I do not. In Russia you will see it given to their academicians. I have never seen a writer in the west to whom everybody in the street touched his cap. I have seen that happen in Moscow. Writers are important there; writers have always been important. There are certain risks involved, of course.

But they are giving us a simple lesson which our 19th century ancestors would have understood very well, which to most of our fellow countrymen now would seem repugnant or almost beyond belief.

About China my knowledge is not first hand but is good second hand. I gather that since the new regime the Chinese are setting about their own elite education in almost exactly the same way as the Soviet Union. The Chinese have a very long history, 1,500 years, of competitive examinations; they know all about it. They know all about civil service administration. One of their great advantages over the Soviet Union is they had that background, the background of a commercial, administrative civilisation before they had even begun to start to industrialise; that is a great help. They have roots in the intellectual life and the values are essential to a decent and spirited society. After an interregnum, the idea that intellectuals should be put to work in the fields they now regard as one of the absurdities of the Gang of Four. Intellectuals are going to do the work which they are made for, and they are going to be given every reasonable opportunity to do so.

So the two great Communist societies are now doing what we once did, and they will do it very well. The Chinese will also

have another model, the model of Japan, not very far from them. That will also be an incentive and something to learn from; and the Chinese will learn.

I do not think I need over-stress this point. If this is what the west is going to live with, it is high time the west thought about what its own values could and should be.

Now I come to the end of all this. We know the position or we should know it; there is no excuse for not knowing it. We know the techniques if we want to improve on our present mindless lethargy, our sitting back without the slightest resistance to the climate around us. Here, I think we in this room ought to reproach ourselves. Some of what is happening to us, some of what is happening to our country in particular, is beyond our control; we are at the mercy of very large world forces. That is, economic forces we do not understand; and if we did understand, we could not do very much about them.

Yet I have been impressed – I am sure many people here have been impressed too – by how utterly passive people like ourselves have been. We see all manner of follies all round us. Follies sometimes do not matter. Sometimes follies are suicidal. Not many of us scarcely lifted a voice; I refer to people who know better and who know it all very well indeed. Nevertheless, to struggle against the current or to kick against the pricks does not come easy to many people; they certainly do not come easy to me; and we have not resisted. I have decided I am now much too old to be discreet. I do not propose to be discreet any longer.

We have to give some kind of stiffening, moral and intellectual, to what parts of this society where we might have a little effect. If we say that the country is making a complete mess of a very important slice of our mental life and our mental training, we shall get into trouble; we shall be extremely unpopular; but what does that matter? We might do a finite amount of good. I believe there are just enough spicules of good sense and resolution around us which only need stirring. I suggest to you

that this has to be done. If it is not done, we shall be leaving a worse world than we were born to. Anyway, it is better to resist than just to let the tide wash over us.

LORD GOODMAN:

We have had a very remarkable demonstration of the art of unscripted and spontaneous instruction. If I may say so, one needed to listen and watch very carefully to observe the immense storehouse of erudition that was deployed for our benefit; you needed to notice this rather carefully. It was done so naturally and so effortlessly that one would not observe that we were benefiting from the wisdom of a lifetime. We are extremely fortunate to have heard this remarkable lecture. Whether we all agree or disagree with it is another matter. Whether we regard the conclusions as a shade too pessimistic is another matter on which you may express your views.

Lord Snow has kindly agreed to answer any question that you may care to address to him on the theme of his lecture. Hence I would invite those of you who would like to ask him anything to do so now while you have the opportunity.

While you are thinking about questions, perhaps I might ask him whether he would not agree that Pierre in "War and Peace" was a good man?

THE RT. HON. THE LORD SNOW:

Yes; I think that is fair comment.

SIR MICHAEL SWANN:

I wonder if Lord Snow would care to reflect on whether at other times in history or in other countries there have been people, as he would put it, and as I would put it, as uncaring about their elites?

THE RT. HON. THE LORD SNOW:

I think that was true certainly in Venice in its decline, when they lived like us extremely comfortably, when their painting was just surviving in the work of the last Tiepolo, pretty but not first class, when intellectual life which had never been deep

rooted in Venice was not cared for at all. Although I know much less about this, it was probably similar to the last phases of the Byzantine Empire. I cannot vouch for the theological discussions, but they seem to have done precious little elsewhere, including cherishing a military elite, which they badly needed. That, in their case, was very serious. I think that is true. I have thought about this, too.

MR. FARR:

I agree with you in principle about choosing people to establish an elite, but one still has doubts about the method of choice. The Chinese, you say, have had 1,500 years' experience of conducting such examinations; but one knows that their greatest poet Tu Fu failed to pass these examinations and lived a very invisible life, although being remembered as their greatest poet.

THE RT. HON. THE LORD SNOW:

No system of examination is fool-proof. They were examining on a strictly literary curriculum. Tu Fu had a remarkable taste for the bottle. I doubt if Dylan Thomas would have made a very effective mandarin. He might very well have just scraped through the first stages of the imperial examination. By and large, their mandarinate was a very successful meritocracy for a very long time. Rather like the French civil service in the last 50 years it kept China afloat in circumstances which were very hard to keep any country afloat in. We know a fair amount about those methods; we have got better, but better with some reserves. Our present method of selection to our civil service I think has some virtues, but it tends to have a squashing effect. That is, there is almost no one who gets in like Tu Fu, who would be no good for our purposes. But I suspect at the other extreme it may keep out people who may be very valuable. I can think of a few very eminent civil servants who would not get in through the present techniques.

SIR. J. BAKER:

I think Lord Snow is being a scaremonger. It seems to me

that if he went back to Cambridge where he has obtained most of his experience he would find that the method of selection is exactly as he describes it.

THE RT. HON. THE LORD SNOW:

I am very glad to hear that. I have been accused of being a scaremonger before; I was accused of being a scaremonger in 1938. I am not very moved by that kind of accusation. It is perfectly true that the standard of admission to Cambridge and other universities is still high. People must have the stimulus behind them to go on with what is a very arduous and in many ways unrewarding life to belong to the elite. That is not at all easy. If you get more tempting lives or less exciting lives, which society is tending to approve of more and more, I will bet you will find good people sliding out. I do not mean they are necessarily going on the street, but they will not strain themselves as hard as the best people ought to strain themselves. I do keep fairly closely in touch with Cambridge, and I see certain indications of this.

MRS MARIE LOCKE:

I would like to ask Lord Snow if he would comment on whether the attitude of young people to learning is at all different today? Are they as keen and anxious to learn?

THE RT. HON. THE LORD SNOW:

I would have thought that what you might call professional families probably still maintain a fairly high standard. What I think is undoubtedly true is the incentive to learn among people who have not got an immediate example in front of them is a good deal less than it was 30 to 40 years ago. The casual pickings of society are now so great you have to be a fairly strong character to set yourself to some kind of minor hardships for quite a number of years.

LORD GOODMAN:

As Lord Snow has come here with some degree of indisposition, I shall be merciful and kind and draw the proceedings to a close, and ask someone to propose a Vote of Thanks.

Sir George Porter F.R.S.

Sir George Porter has been Director and Fullerian professor of Chemistry of the Royal Institution and Director of the Davy Faraday Research Laboratory since 1966. He was born in 1920 and educated at Thorne Grammar School, Leeds University and Emmanuel College, Cambridge. Between 1941 and 1945 he served as Radar Officer in the Royal Navy. On completion of his doctorate degree he spent a further five years in the Physical Chemistry Department of the University of Cambridge. He was appointed Professor of Physical Chemistry in the University of Sheffield in 1955. He is an Honorary Fellow of Emmanuel College, Cambridge, and Visiting Professor in University College London and Imperial College London. In 1960 he was elected a Fellow of the Royal Society and shared the Nobel Prize for Chemistry in 1967. He was knighted in 1972 and has received many honours and awards in recognition of his work, including the Davy and Rumford Medals of the Royal Society. In 1978 he gave the Romanes Lecture in Oxford and has lectured widely at home and abroad.

His research interests are in the field of fast reactions, photochemistry, photobiology and solar energy. He is also interested in scientific education and the presentation of science to non-specialists and was elected the first President of the National Association for Gifted Children in 1975. He has given many lectures and taken part in numerous debates on television and his Royal Institute Christmas Lectures on *Time Machines* and *The Natural History of a Sunbeam* were recorded by BBC.

'Evolution under the sun – has it a future?'

delivered by

Sir George Porter F.R.S

Tuesday, 12th June, 1979

CHAIRMAN The Rt. Hon. Lord Goodman C.H.

LORD GOODMAN:

Ladies and Gentlemen, but for one slightly unfortunate selection in the choice of the first lecturer, I think I should be able to claim that this is one of the most distinguished series of lectures that this country possesses. If you have a little look at the back of the programme, to see the extraordinary range of lecturers who have embarked on this lecture, and their very special distinction, you will see what I mean, and, if I may say so, this evening we only add to that distinction.

It is quite right that this lecture should have been established and that each year it should attract an audience of this size and distinction. This evening we are to have a lecture by a very distinguished scientist. My own qualifications to introduce this scientist are absolutely nil, and those of you who came ito the first lecture will remember in what a sorry fashion I proceeded to recite my ignorance, because the title of my lecture was "Coming to Terms with Science". I think I established that if there was one person who was never coming to terms with it, it was the lecturer!

That does not detract from the excitement with which I will listen to the very distinguished chemist who is going to give us

this lecture tonight. His career again I think represents the very best we have in English academic and scientific life. He is an immensely distinguished academic. He has a range of qualifications, distinctions and honours that fill a large proportion of *Who's Who*. At the same time it is clear that he has been able to harness that quite exceptional knowledge to immensely profitable and valuable practical use. That combination is very rare – not unique – but very rare, and we have therefore the good fortune to have an exceptionally rare and if not unique person addressing us tonight, and it is a great honour to have him.

May I say that I was rather apprehensive that I might see a number of people scribbling vigorously on the backs of their programmes, working out what their saving of tax would be set against the additional VAT. It is, I think, a high tribute to the drawing power of our lecturer and the fact that people intend to concentrate on the lecture that I do not perceive a single person engaged in that particular activity!

Without another word I will call on our very distinguished lecturer to address us. Thank you.

SIR GEORGE PORTER:

Lord Goodman, Ladies and Gentlemen, I am honoured to have been invited by the Aitchison Memorial Trust to deliver this Seventh Goodman Lecture. Equally, I am somewhat overawed by those who have delivered the previous six lectures, not least of course by yourself Lord Chairman, who delivered the first, and in spite of your referring to it as an aberration, your modesty is quite unfounded. I remember how, holding a large brief, to which you apparently never referred, you spoke authoritatively and entertainingly on "Coming to Terms with Science". I remember also thinking that few scientists have been equally successful in coming to terms with the law.

In any case, I know that I shall have to choose my words carefully because of the authorities on many – indeed, almost

every – subject whom one knows to be in the audience, and even more so because of those one does not know.

For example, two years ago the Goodman Lecture was delivered by Sir Martin Roth on "Sexual Pornography and Society – a Psychiatric View". My friend, Sir Hans Kornberg, found himself sitting next to Mrs. Mary Whitehouse. Eventually, Mrs. Whitehouse turned to him and said "Young man" – Sir Hans is only 50 – "Tell me, why are you interested in pornography?" to which he promptly replied that he was not interested in the subject as such and in fact did not even have a pornograph! I think he is here again tonight and I regret that my lecture is unlikely to give him such splendid opportunities for neighbourly repartee.

Just over a century ago, in 1859, Charles Darwin wrote history on the grand scale and gave man an intellectual shock to which he has not, even today, fully adjusted himself. It was a history of how the visible shape and form of living things has been determined and changed by natural selection. How and when it all began was obscure as was the molecular mechanism by which it operates. Over the last three decades these things have been clarified and what we have learned has changed our concept of ourselves and our place in the world . . . it has put man in his context.

Rather suddenly has come to us the revelation that we are living at a time when the process of evolution which has served the world for three billion years may be about to cease, or at least to change in a profound way. The Darwinian changes occurred slowly, and unnoticed by the participants, who had little to say about the forms their descendants would take. They merely fought to survive and if they survived they had the privilege of handing on their genes. The situation has changed catastrophically in the last few years. One species, man now so dominates the earth that is is in his power to eliminate most other species if he so wishes; those which survive do so only because man finds them interesting or useful and he is busy

interfering with the natural evolution even of these. Within the species, man as well, the natural selection process has almost ceased; it is no longer only the fittest who survive to have large families. We are rightly proud of our modern medicine which, coupled to our compassion keeps alive people who would otherwise not have survived childhood but, in the words of Kenneth Mellanby we are "fossilising the gene pool".

There is, of course, still a small amount of natural selection through war and a few still incurable pestilences but all of us hope that even these scourges will soon be eliminated. It is, in any case, far from clear that a third world war would be a good method of selecting those members of the species most suitable to survive and advance the evolutionary process, if indeed there were any survivors at all.

Far greater powers to play God will soon be in our hands. Cloning of large members of genetically identical individuals, of a species such as frogs, is already possible and may soon be possible in humans. So what we see happening is a rapid transfer of the responsibility for future evolution into the hands of homo sapiens. We are no longer pawns in the game, we are not even now the Kings and Queens – we are the players.

It might be argued that evolution has passed beyond the stage of the individual but that it continues through competition between industrial companies and countries. Anybody who, on visiting another country has tried to buy some present to take home which cannot equally well be bought in Oxford Street must wonder how much competition of this kind remains. In spite of attempts to enforce some natural selection through anti-trust laws, the multinational corporations become more multinational and, as with individuals, the stronger and more successful country is now expected to give economic aid to the poorer developing ones. We are approaching the Utopia in which the cake is distributed, more or less equally, by an all-seeing, all-powerful world government of man.

I should like to look at just one of our problems in this

context of evolution. It is one which is of immediate and practical importance, where scientific and technological facts are relatively well understood and where many options are open to us. It is the problem of energy – if we cannot solve this we have little hope of finding solutions to the more complex problems such as genetic manipulation.

I do not wish to inflict upon you another technical account of the virtues and vices of the various forms of power station; rather I would like to trace the history of the evolution of life from the point of view not of shape and form but of energy. Then I shall look at where we might go from here. Whether a knowledge of history is relevant to the choices we have to make you must judge, but I think that the history is interesting.

Although the Darwinian concept of natural selection is satisfying and acceptable to most people, there is one question which often seems to present a difficulty; how can such order arise spontaneously from a chaotic world?

Until recently, and to many at the present time, life is regarded as a miracle because it is contrary to all our experience in the inanimate world. Each spring, parts of the earth which were apparently lifeless become green and vegetation appears as if from nowhere. Tiny seeds grow into vast forests and small eggs grow into animals of the most intricate design. The chemical changes which have taken place over the course of evolution are even more remarkable. A primitive planet of earth, air, fire and water, somehow spontaneously brought forth the complex and delicate chemical substances of which life is made, followed by life itself, in ever increasing complexity. The evolutionary process continues beyond the individual man, and an outside observer would have noticed how, over the last few centuries, the earth grew large cities, roads and railways, whilst machines, bigger than any bird, flew over its surface at great speed.

How does it all happen? Order is being created out of chaos and this seems to happen spontaneously. Yet we know that in

our ordinary lives this is not the way things happen and that, if we leave things to themselves, they all too easily run down, lose their order and become chaotic. It is the same with chemical reactions, they go spontaneously to a state of greater chaos. Things burn but never unburn, wood disappears as smoke into the air and we would be astounded if the opposite happened and a log of wood suddenly fell out of the sky. But is this any more remarkable than what happens when a tree is created "out of thin air"? This is a statement of common experience and it is also a statement of the second law of thermodynamics . . . a law which a previous Goodman lecturer, Lord Snow, has given as an illustration of something that should be part of the common cultural understanding of all, whether scientist or not, like Shakespeare or Beethoven. But whilst the place of Shakespeare and Beethoven in our common culture is secure, some find the second law of thermodynamics more difficult, even with the help of Flanders and Swann. Yet it is simple enough . . . it merely states that within any system or space which is left to itself, isolated from the rest of things, disorder increases spontaneously . . . things get mixed up, run down, become chaotic. The scientific measure of disorder is entropy, so the second law says that, in a closed system, entropy increases spontaneously and never decreases. The life process, the process of evolution seems at first sight to be contrary to the second law of thermodynamics and to what is really the same thing . . . common experience.

The problem is easily resolved if we look more carefully at the statement I have just made. When left to itself a system becomes disordered. *When left to itself* . . . If there is contact with the outside world, if an outside influence is at work, then order can increase, entropy can decrease. Early man, trying to understand the problem, sought for this outside influence in the human form, the form of a God as the necessary source of negative entropy. Others worshipped the sun and the sun is indeed the source of energy and of negative entropy which

makes the increasing order of evolution and continuing life possible. We live not merely in a chemical world but in a photochemical world and without that light of the first day the rest could not have happened.

Although the Descartian attempts at a purely mechanistic explanation of life had to be modified, thermodynamics is as strictly applicable to the living animal or plant as it is to the steam engine. The engines of biochemistry are driven ultimately by the furnace of the sun and calculations of the maximum efficiency of the body are possible because of the work of those pioneers whose objective was to improve the steam engine. It has been said that science owes more to the steam engine than the steam engine owes to silence.

So now let us go to the very beginning of the story of how life has evolved by using the sun as its power house. The earth was formed 46 billion years ago – 46000 million years ago (I shall use the American billion of one thousand million. The British is bigger and I suppose we should therefore be proud of it but the American is better established and more useful.) Fossil evidence was until relatively recently thought to take us back only 600 million years, to the beginning of the Cambrian period and all before this was a mystery.

In the 1950's, however, palaeontologists began to look for much smaller and more primitive forms of life in older rocks and were successful, especially by use of the electron microscope.

A series of fossils from rocks 1 billion years old were found at Bitter Springs, 40 miles from Alice Springs in Australia and identified as green algae with a nucleus at various stages of cell division.

Rocks called the Gunflint cherts in Ontario take us back another billion years. The cells are more primitive . . . they do not appear to have nuclei . . . but there are many forms, and they are almost certainly of blue-green algae type and capable of photosynthesis because chemical analysis of the organic

matter shows that hydrocarbons (characteristic of chlorophyll breakdown (prostane and phytane)) are present.

Finally, the oldest known fossil, a bacterium, was found in rocks over three billion years old in South Africa called the Fig Tree chart. It is about half a micron long and a quarter of a micron wide.

FOSSILS		*TODAY*
	RAPID EVOLUTION	
BITTER SPRINGS	EUKARYOTIC CELLS (SEXUAL REPRODUCTION) GREEN ALGAE	1
GUN FLINT	FILAMENTOUS ALGAE	2
FIG TREE	BLUE-GREEN ALGAE (AUTOTROPHS) PROKARYOTIC CELLS (HETEROTHROPHS)	3
	CHEMICAL SYNTHESIS	4
		4.6 B.B.C.

Figure 1

Figure 1 summarises this evidence of early fossils and what we can say about the development of early life. But even a primitive bacterium is quite complex. *E. coli* contains about 2500 genes in a highly ordered arrangement of about 4 million pairs of necleotides and the most primitive bacterium known today, the mycoplasmas, contain nearly a million pairs. So something more primitive and still living presumably preceded these fossils and life must have started earlier still, perhaps about 4 billion years ago or only 600 million years after the earth was formed. What happened in this 600 million years?

A few years ago the microbiologist, R.Y. Stannier, wrote "Evolutionary speculation constitutes a kind of metascience, which has the same intellectual fascination for some biologists that metaphysical speculation possessed for some mediaeval scholastics. It can be considered relatively a harmless habit, like eating peanuts, unless it assumes the form of an obsession, then it becomes a vice." Since those words were written, the study of the early stages of evolution has become quite respectable, and laboratory experiments have reproduced many of the speculative theories of how organic matter may first have appeared on earth by action of the ultra-violet radiation from the sun on our primitive atmosphere, which at that time contained no oxygen and consisted principally of methane, ammonia and water. Amino acids and the cell-like structures have been made simply by heating amino acids. Many of the other building blocks of large biological molecules have been made in the laboratory simply by shining ultra-violet light on this primitive atmosphere. So the story of evolution, in broad terms of energy source, goes something like this:

The first stage used only the ultra-violet light of the sun . . . a small fraction of the total and synthesised organic molecules from the atmospheric gases, so forming a primeval broth in which life could develop and on which it could feed, by fermentation. In the second stage, once simple life has been formed, it learned how to synthesise chlorophyll and other coloured pigments so that visible light could be used. This first green revolution was essential as oxygen began to build up in the atmosphere, forming ozone and so blanketing the earth from the ultra-violet rays of the sun.

This second stage continues to the present day. The photosynthesis of organic matter from water and carbon dioxide, through absorption of visible light by the sun, has for the last 3 billion years provided man and life in general with all its energy.

Since man appeared on the earth about a million years ago

he has used this energy store from the sun in increasingly sophisticated and recently increasingly profligate ways. Before the discovery of fire, man, and all other animals, had derived their energy from the biological combustion of organic fuels within their own bodies, the fuels being derived from plants or other animals. With the discovery of fire they learned how to increase the amount of energy available to them by carrying out this process outside their bodies, albeit in a relatively primitive way, chemically speaking. The fuel was wood, or other vegetable matter. The technology seems to have developed rather slowly . . . heating and cooking were open fire affairs until larger communities, with their much larger buildings and social organisations developed in the period which we think of as the beginnings of civilisation. Other forms of solar energy were developed at this time, wind and water power in particular, as well as the only important non-solar energy source used by early man . . . the geothermal sources of hot springs.

So, about 150 years ago we see man's civilisation developing rapidly, but still largely dependent on a slave energy of animals and servants since even the wood for heating had to be hewn and carried. Nevertheless, the intellectual evolution of man proceeded far more rapidly than the biological one. The development of civilisation, of the arts and sciences, in this period, owed little to any increase in the *average* energy available to man; it was a result of a social order where the average energy was unequally shared so that mankind as a whole could achieve much more. Just as the zebra has to spend all his life feeding rather inefficiently on grass to make it possible for the lion to enjoy his leisure, so the great majority of mankind laboured most of their lives to make possible the leisure . . . and the great intellectual achievements of the few which we like to remember – and rightly so in all fairness – as the achievements of mankind as a whole.

The next stage of energy evolution was so rapid that it is

more common to speak of the industrial revolution than industrial evolution. It was a result of inventiveness of men like Savory, Newcommen and Watt two centuries ago, but their inventiveness would have been sterile without the use of a new source of power which far surpassed all that which was available from the combustion of wood and other animal biological products. It was the power accumulated in fossil form from the decay of photosynthetic products over 3000 million years and it began to be used in large quantities only just over a century ago . . . in fact, it was not until 1850 that coal overtook wood as man's principal source of energy (see Figure 2). Oil, petroleum was discovered some years before that but it was not until 1950 that it overtook coal and became, with natural gas, man's main source of power.

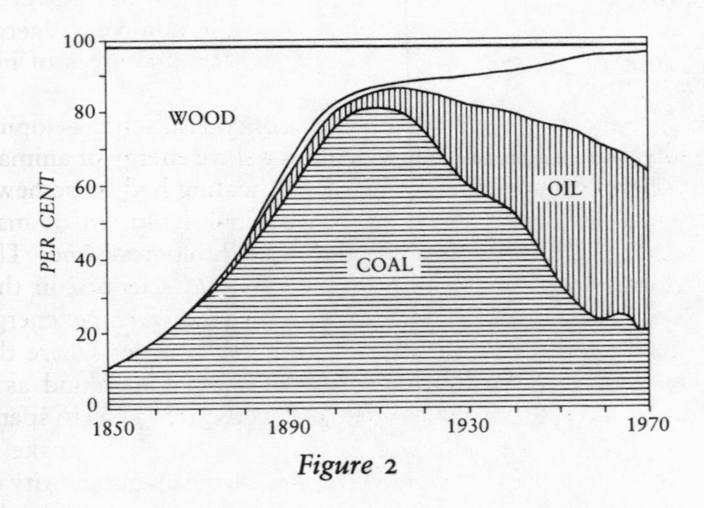

Figure 2

The technological civilisation which we enjoy – or endure – today is a product of man's ingenuity but has only been made possible by our discovery of a vast accumulated treasure trove of fossilised products of photosynthesis. Without this power,

life for many would not merely become brutal and short, it would disappear altogether because modern urban civilisations could in no way support the present large populations which depend on motorised transport to feed them, to bring their water and to remove their waste products. The electricity supply to a large city is a jugular vein and on the rare occasions when it has been severed it is not merely the well-being of its inhabitants which have been at risk but their very survival.

Let us now look at two pictures of the last century of energy evolution and the next. Figure 2 shows the changes in use of fossil fuels to which I have referred. Figure 3 shows man's use of oil and coal on a somewhat longer time scale using reasonable projections of future supply and use. On this time scale our fossil-fuel dependent civilisation is seen as a hiccup in history.

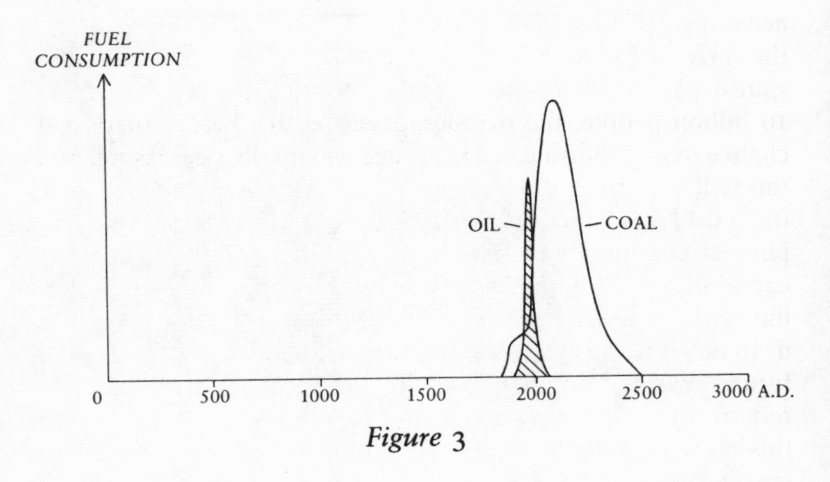

Figure 3

The future scene is black but I do not wish to be a scaremonger unnecessarily. We have oil for a few decades and coal for a few centuries and this is as long as it has taken us to adapt to our technological way of life and to increase our

population tenfold. In the time for which fossil fuels are available to us we should be able to adapt to new sources of energy and perhaps to reduce our population again. But we must recognise that the evolutionary process will not look after us automatically any more than it did for the dinosaurs . . . we are the masters of our fate now and our handling of the energy problem is something of a test case – are we able to handle our own evolution?

There are three factors which together make up the problem. First, energy supplies of the type we principally use today are limited and will run out in the foreseeable future. Second, the demand will increase because the population is increasing, and, third, the demand will increase because the people in the developing world will demand as much energy for themselves as is necessary to bring their standard of life up to that of the West. Together, these factors mean that a diminishing supply is accompanied by a demand which will increase fifteen-fold by the early part of next century. The population must increase, in spite of a falling birth rate, to about 2½ times the present one, of 10 billion people, the demographers tell us, before there is a chance of it stabilising, and perhaps eventually decreasing, and this will happen in about 50 years. The distribution of energy in the world is as unequal as that of other forms of wealth. The poorest countries have only a few per cent of the energy per capita of the developed countries and to bring all people into line with the energy consumption of a European would require us to increase the available energy by a factor of 6 . . . so for the future expected population to live at European standard will require fifteen times more energy than we consume today. If this cannot be met we can be certain of international strife and energy bargaining which will make our present conflicts about pay seem like heavenly peace.

Continuing in the spirit of this lecture I would like to explore the possibility that this problem can be resolved by continuing to use the sun as our principal source of energy, even to fulfil

the inevitable demands of the future. First, however, we should look briefly at the alternatives. There are those who say that the solution is to economise, to do with less energy, and of course we are wasteful, at least those of us who live in the United States, Europe and Japan, because we have had access to virtually free sources – just bore a hole and out it comes. But we have learned what it can do for us and henceforth we shall demand it. Market forces will make us economise but new needs for energy will arise and it is doubtful whether very large reductions in consumption are compatible with the inevitably increasing population and the demands of the Third World.

Second, there is an alternative to solar energy – nuclear energy. This is, in its present form of non-breeder reactors, not a permanent solution because the energy content of economic uranium sources is not very different from those of economic coal resources. Breeder reactors would extend this source very considerably, perhaps by a factor of fifty. In the long term, a century or two ahead, only one form of energy could be sufficient to supply the energy needs of mankind . . . nuclear fusion. There are two kinds of nuclear fusion reactor . . . those on earth, made by man, but not yet even proved possible and the one at a safe distance of 93 million miles already working well – the sun.

The problems of nuclear energy are too well known to require any discusion from me tonight. As Alvin Weinberg has pointed out, the energy requirements for the world in the year 2000 could indeed be satisfied by building one large nuclear reactor every three days starting now and continuing to do so after the year 2000, as the ones now built become obsolescent. That is a possible route for us to take, but still would not necessarily provide energy in some of the forms we need . . . storable liquid and gaseous fuels for example. And, need I say it, there are other problems.

I hope that we can rely on nuclear energy to provide most of the world's electricity supplies, in spite of these problems, and I

think that, in view of our almost insuperable energy problems, research and development and, indeed, the building of more reactors must continue. It would, however, be the height of folly, at this uncertain stage in our evolution, to put all our eggs in to the nuclear basket. One of the dangers of nuclear energy is that it is so capital intensive, and so intensive in its use of scientific and technological skills, that it may preclude the development of the alternative solar technologies.

Let me first present the euphoric case for solar energy, why it seems to attractive to many people, and then I will try to balance this by indicating some of its problems.

I have already shown how the use of solar energy is a natural extension of our evolutionary process; we have got a long way by depending on it exclusively. Furthermore, most of the energy we use today is solar energy still. This is obvious if we include the fossil fuels but it is true even excluding these. Our temperature is maintained approximately constant by the sun . . . we only use other forms of energy as a topping up process. It provides most of our light, our food, our clothing. It distils our water and raises it from the sea level to that of the land. It provides many of our raw materials such as paper and wood.

The most impressive thing about solar energy is its abundance. There is more than enough for all our needs. The solar energy falling on the earth in ten days is equivalent to all the fossil fuels on earth.

The present average energy demand of one person can be met, with a 10% efficiency of recovery, by an area of $120M^2$, i.e. a square of 11 m side, between latitudes 40N and 40S where 80% of the earth's population live and needs are greatest.

An area of 600km x 600km, at 10% efficiency would supply the whole present energy demands of mankind and 15x this, or a square of 2500km would supply the total foreseeable needs. This is 2% of the earth's land surface, one-eighth of which is useless desert.

Finally, solar energy is universally available to all people,

most of all to those who need it most. Politicians, terrorists and trade unionists cannot stop the sun shining and it is pollution free, there is not even thermal pollution. There must be a snag!

The snag is, of course, the economical one. Everything on earth is free, it just costs money to collect it. The sun's energy is particularly expensive to collect because it is spread thinly over a large area and it is intermittent and unreliable . . . it goes out when it is needed most, at night and in the winter.

It is a fact of life that, given reasonable safety, the cheapest form of energy is the one that will be adopted. The euphoric and the cynic, the environmentalist and the businessman will eventually shop around for the best value. If it is cheaper to get one's megawatts from oil than from a solar panel, oil will be used. Let us try to do a little costing of sunbeams. To do this, to be careful customers, we must first inspect the *quality* and then the *quantity* of the product.

It is important, in all energy discussions, to recognise that energy comes in various forms, which we may call high grade and low grade. In fact, the first law of thermodynamics, which is merely the law of energy conservation tells us that energy cannot be created or destroyed and if this were the whole story there would obviously be no problem of energy conseravation. Energy is always conserved – by law. What we do when we "use" energy is that we degrade it . . . we lower its quality by increasing its entropy or disorder. High grade energy such as electricity, or heat at high temperature, or mechanical work, becomes low grade heat at the temperature of its surroundings which is not of any further use.

The sun is, as I have said, a thermonuclear reactor, whose temperature at the inside is millions of degrees. On the outside, as we see it, the temperature is only 6000°C but this means that the energy is of a very high grade . . . in fact even after allowing for the fact that it fills a relatively small part of our sky, the energy we receive is 80% good stuff . . . capable of being converted into work or electricity.

But when we come to try to do this there are other restrictions. The energy of the sun is spread out over a range of I.R., visible and U.V. wavelengths. Not only do we have to absorb all this range but we have to use the energy efficiently in each region. This is impracticable and it turns out that the best we can do is use a substance which absorbs from 100 nm in the I.R. and all wavelengths below this, when we shall get an efficiency of just under 50%. It happens that silicon, the element used in solar voltaic batteries does just this. It is interesting that the leaf, evolved over a much longer time by nature, has a cut-off at 700 nm and one wonders . . . did nature make a mistake . . . can it have come up with something imperfect after all those centuries? But Professor Landsberg has pointed out that the calculations I have just given were made for a clear sky . . . if one uses instead the energy distribution typical of say, an English sky, the optimum does indeed turn out to be very near to where chlorophyll absorbs in the limit. One can only conclude that God made the green plant for the British!

Taking reflection and other losses into account, an overall efficiency of solar energy collection, as free energy – energy capable of doing useful work – of about 30% is theoretically feasible. With silicon cells 17% has actually been achieved and more than 10% is common. So we will take 10% as a reasonable expectation of collection efficiency.

Now, how much energy can be collected on our roof or our field?

Solar energy is distributed unequally but less so than is often supposed. In Britain the average, day and night, winter and summer, is about 125 w/m^2. In desert regions, it is about 250 w/m^2 and these desert areas cover ⅛th of the earth's surface.

Now to return to economics; what does this mean in $cost/m^2$ of collection? The present cost of nuclear or other power station is about $1 watt and rising rapidly. If we take an insolation of 200 w/m^2 and utilise it at 10% efficiency we shall

therefore be competitive if our collection costs \$20/m^2. This is much less than photovaltaics at present, about 100 times less, but the USA has a programme, which is probably realistic, to get within a factor of two of this figure in the 1980s. Low grade heat collectors for heating houses and water are already borderline and economic in some countries like Israel. But there is another form of solar energy which receives less attention and which I think holds out far more promise and I should like to devote the rest of my time to it.

Man needs his energy mainly in three forms . . . low grade heat and electricity problems may be met by nuclear and other forms of energy but our immediate as well as long term problem is chemical fuel . . . liquid and gas. Whatever form we eventually want for our energy, a storable chemical fuel will always be the most valuable . . . it cuts costs by load spreading. Electricity cannot be stored, heat can only be stored for short periods . . . chemical fuels are prime sources particularly when we are concerned with the sun as our source since its operation is so badly matched to our demand.

At first sight the prospects for manufacturing units which will produce gas or petroleum or their equivalent at 10% efficiency and cost less that \$20/m^2 may seem remote . . . what can you buy today at \$20/m^2? One begins to think of old newspapers, and leaves. And indeed leaves in some form or other may be the answer. The somewhat futuristic proposition I would like to consider is a world where man's two essential needs, food and fuels, are both farmed from the land.

The so-called world food problem is certainly soluble. By conservative estimates even the land now under cultivation, if farmed by presently demonstrated technology, would feed 45 billion people – more than 4x the projected maximum population. New developments in genetic engineering of crop plants, use of other arable land would provide more and, as a last resort, the giving over of some of the present grazing land to vegetable crops . . . a little less beef in our diet . . . could extend

these resources further. The problems are essentially ones of distribution and economics . . . food is, or can be made available if the poor can afford to buy it.

The earth's land surface covers about 13 billion hectares of which 1.4 billion are cultivated and about 3 billion could be cultivated. Non-cultivatable desert covers 1.7b hectares and another 2.6b hectares is rocky or arid. At 10% efficiency, and an average of 200w/m^2 we would require only ½ billion hectares, arable or otherwise, to provide the energy needs of man as projected.

Unfortunately the efficiency of photosynthesis is far less than 10%. Average best growth rates round the year rarely exceed 1% . . . sugar cane is one of the best at about 1.2% though, at the peak growing period, things are much better and as much as 5% may be achieved. Photosynthesis occurs over most parts of the earth to some degree but the overall efficiency is only 0.1%, one 50th of the best. Even with this low efficiency, the annual biomass produced has an energy about ten times greater than the world's annual total use and is about 200x our food consumption.

It is chemistry on a massive scale. All our atmospheric CO_2 is recycled through the photosynthetic system every 300 years, all the oxygen in 2000 years and even all the water every 2 million years.

The utilisation of biomass for energy is very dependent on geography at the present time. Some countries, such as Brazil, are in a very favourable position and are taking advantage of it by producing alcohol, as a substitute for petrol, from the fermentation of crops such as sugar cane and cassava (tapioca). The National Alcohol Programme (which must sound, to some, as a sort of nationalised elysium) was established in 1975 and the state of Sao Paolo is already up to 20% alcohol in its gasoline. This amount can be used without engine modification. (Sao Paolo has already over one million cars). With modification, pure alcohol can be used and Brazil is embarking

on an imaginative and very large programme to achieve this. About one-fifth of their total gasoline requirement should be met from alcohol by next year.

China is less favourably endowed with rapid growing areas than Brazil and its needs are different and less at present. It is estimated that there are over 5 million biogas plants in operation at the present time. These produce methane on a domestic scale by fermentation of domestic wastes and are very simply built, being rather similar to a septic tank.

When thinking of countries like China it is important to recognise that there are, in many parts of the world, energy problems which are quite as serious as ours, even though the quantities of energy concerned are relatively minute. Biomass is, as it always has been, the principal – even the only source of energy. Table 1 shows how important this is for a great number of people . . . even as much as one third of the world population. Their crisis is not caused by a shortage of oil but of wood increased population, and the consequent increased energy demand is leading to rapid deforestation, increased use

Table 1 consumption of fuel wood and dung as percentage of total energy consumption

Western Europe	0·7
World	6
Latin America	20
Africa	60
India	56
Rural India	93
Certain villages *	100

* Approximately 1 million villages of several hundred or thousand people each, worldwide.

of dung for heating and cooking and a vicious circle in which the fertiliser is not returned to the land and the land becomes barren.

The energy problem of the world is therefore composed of three rather separate problems. Two of these are short term, but very different depending on whether we are considering the developed high energy consumers or the developing low energy countries. The third part of the problem is the long term one.

Considering first the short term problem, in the developed countries this can probably be solved by an admixture of increased coal mining (with gasification) and increased nuclear reactors. The problem of the developing countries is more serious in the short term . . . unless they are fortunate enough to strike oil, as Mexico has done recently, and the Gulf States did long ago (and indeed as Britain has done, though there are few who would feel justified at present in classifying us as a country which is developing even with the help of our oil). At present there is no hope at all that the billion poorest people in the world can pay for the energy they need by buying oil, coal or nuclear power stations, and unless they are to depend entirely on charity from the developed countries, their self sufficiency will have to depend principally on biomass which they grow. Much can be done by using what they have more efficiently, their concepts of heat and fuel conservation are perhaps the most primitive aspects of their lives, followed closely by the inefficiency of their agriculture and particularly their silviculture. The world market price of energy from a charcoal fire or a bullock may be greater than that from an oil stove or diesel engine but if you have wood and a bullock, but no oil and no money, the market prices are of little interest.

But now what of the third, the long term problem and its solution. When we have had time to respond to the double attack of depleting fossil fuels and increasing demand, what will our Utopia be like? Well, firstly, if it is to be any sort of Utopia, all people in it will have to have enough energy to give

them a standard of life which we, in the developed world, consider to be a reasonable minimum and I have already shown that this will require about 15 times as much energy as we use at present. Where will this come from?

One thing is certain, even if unlimited nuclear energy becomes available, man's principal supply of energy will still come from the sun. The sun will always supply most of our heat and light, all our food and most of our organic raw materials. We can therefore never do without solar energy . . . whether we shall eventually do without nuclear energy is more problematic. Certainly, at the present time, it would be most unwise to assume that to do without it is compatible with a technological civilisation such as most of us envisage, and if we are honest with ourselves, wish to have.

There is no need for friction between supporters of different forms of energy supply because all forms will probably be necessary and, even with a plentiful supply, some ecological niche will probably be found for each of them, sugar alcohol in Brazil, wave power off the Western Isles, hydroelectric power in Norway, nuclear power near centres of electricity-dependent populations and solar power where unused land is plentiful.

I should like to spend the last few minutes of this lecture developing this last theme . . . solar power on a world scale from the desert areas of the world as a future option. We cannot, in considering resources such as energy, be too parochial and, in any case, those of us who have spent the last few months in England can only maintain an interest in solar energy by taking a global view. As I have already said, one third of the earth's desert areas is capable of supplying all the projected needs of the world if collected at 10% efficiency, but can this be done? How will it be done? We might collect the energy as heat, with or without mirror concentrators, or as electricty using photovoltaics which are efficient and already well developed. Each of these methods has two disadvantages, they are both very expensive and they have no long term

storage. Storage can be added, in chemical batteries for example, but this adds enormously to the already large cost. Costs are rapidly being reduced, particularly of photovoltaic cells, but the collection areas are so large that they may never be reduced to make them competitive with nuclear power stations.

Another approach would be to grow biomass in arid regions and Professor Calvin and others are investigating the possibility of using unconventional crops, such as the species euphorbia which produce rubber and similar hydrocarbons and some of which can survive in the desert. But "survive" is perhaps the word, and, to be economic, survival is not enough – it must flourish. Genetic manipulation may improve the situation but there are other difficulties always associated with living plants, such as the need for large quantities of water and fertilisers.

Can we not take just the part of this wonderful process of photosynthesis, learn from the plant how it is done, and make a leaf; one that does not have to be cosseted with fertiliser and use many times its own weight of water, which does not have to be harvested, which produces the goods . . . gas, petrol, alcohol, for example, that we want, directly without the need for chemical processing, fermentation, and so forth. In short, cannot we make a leaf more suited to our needs.

This is a serious ambition, now in several laboratories, including my own. It is a complex, and therefore a rather long term programme. To begin with we know quite a lot about how the process of photosynthesis in the leaf works but some essential parts of it are still a complete mystery so there is much to be done. Then we have to construct something which, although very much simpler than the leaf, will necessarily have to be very complex chemically because we know that there will have to be at least a dozen steps in the process and they will all have to occur in the right sequence, efficiently in sunlight. In fact, most of these separate steps have already been carried out in the laboratory and, although a final answer, a real working

leaf, is a long way off, I think it is likely to be in working order before a nuclear fusion reactor. Furthermore, although the lead times for the introduction of new forms of energy on a large scale are always long, the lead times for this sort of research to come to fruition, not to mention the cost, are likely to be less than for projects where the unit size is very large.

In the long term therefore, unless we destroy ourselves by some catastrophe, we can look forward to a world in which a stable, if large, population is supplied with all the food and energy necessary for the good life . . . whatever by that time the good life is supposed to be. In the meantime, our ambition will have to be more modest and I think that a good working ethic might be that which I heard Linus Pauling suggest recently. The greatest happiness, whether of the greatest number or merely of the few, is difficult to quantify and there is little evidence that higher technology, in the advanced countries at any rate, is leading towards such a goal. Rather, therefore, than the increase of happiness, Pauling suggests, our ambition should perhaps be to *decrease unhappiness*. In many parts of the world a few kilowatts of power, from whatever source, would go a long way towards this goal, and in the most needy parts of the world the sun is plentiful. Evolution under the sun provides the best hope for the immediate energy future of these people and a longer term hope for us all.

LORD GOODMAN:

I must say I never thought that I wanted any lecture, particularly a scientific one, to continue for as long as that, and I think we must all be extremely grateful to Sir George for that fascinating address. I do not think I have ever seen erudition carried more lightly and brilliance described more skilfully in the sense that it is presented in a totally intelligible way to people like myself who thought we would find it totally unintelligible. We are extremely grateful. Perhaps even .more than the brilliance and interest of the content was the asto-

nishing skill of the delivery. I have rarely heard a lecturer deliver a lecture so impressively and in so uncontrived a fashion. If the universities are ever wise enough to issue instructions to lecturers on how to give lectures, Sir George would have to be the first instructor and he would have to be in command at every university in the world. I congratulate him.

He has said he is prepared to answer questions, and I have a feeling that given a moment or two to recover from a slightly stunning effect of that lecture, and its enormous implications, quite a number of you will want to ask him something. If you would like to reflect for a moment, he is willing to do so for a reasonable length of time.

QUESTION:

Seawater as a single chemical entity, is the largest available substance on the globe. One ninth of this consists of hydrogen by weight. What hope is there of some breakdown process making this hydrogen available as an ideal fuel?

SIR GEORGE PORTER:

To make hydrogen from water you have to put in the energy in some way. One way you can do it is just to use your nuclear energy to make electricity and then electrolyse the water into oxygen and hydrogen but the way I was suggesting is similar to what we are doing when the plant makes sugar from carbon dioxide. We take water, shine light on it by a relatively complicated process – one has to add things to help it along – and split it into oxygen and hydrogen, but the crux is you have to put energy in and my suggestion is that that energy would be the sun, as it is in photosynthesis.

QUESTION:

You mentioned China and the use of biogas. You said 5 billion units. Are you suggesting that these are now insufficient? What is the level of technology in these units? I know China is now going into oil in a great way. Have they reached the limit of efficiency in the biogas plants or is there a technological advance that could be made here?

Sir George Porter:

I cannot speak very authoritatively on this. I have heard this figure only a few weeks ago. I am hoping to go to China in a month or two and I hope to see these, but the answer to your question is that this is very much of a village energy economy. They dig a hole in the ground. They put bricks over the top. The waste products go into this and methane gas is produced by fermentation. It is a domestic affair like a septic tank and that is why there are such a large number. You obviously cannot do this in the middle of Peking very easily and so other forms of energy have been, and are going to be, necessary for industrial China.

Question:

A year ago the estimate was 7 billion biogas plants in China. They are working now on improving the efficiency of gas production but this is compromised for the appearance of improving the health. They are also working on biogas systems with refuse from food processing factories and they are setting up training centres to train a lot of people in China in building the plants as apprentices.

Sir George Porter:

Thank you very much. I should make the point that burning dung is a terrible waste from the land point of view. It would otherwise go back to the land and be a very necessary fertiliser. The reduction of wood forests in places like India is as serious a problem to them as our depletion of oil reserves is to us. If you use the fermentation process, you still have the residue, the nitrogeneous part, and so on, as fertiliser. It is very much better than just burning it.

Question:

You mentioned that there were some hidden costs in connection with nuclear reactors, when you were doing your cost comparison. Could you give one or two examples of the kind of thing you had in mind?

SIR GEORGE PORTER:

The sort of thing I was thinking about was security over many thousands of years of the waste products and the hidden costs of the non-existent insurance for a large scale accident.

QUESTION:

One of the troubles with wave energy systems and tidal systems is, of course, the irregularity of the whole business, and I imagine the same sort of thing occurs in collecting heat by reflection in the desert, where there are dust storms. There is one place where there are no dust storms, or little irregularity, and that is way above the atmosphere in the stratosphere. If we could collect the energy there of course we could have permanently reasonable stable conditions and be able if we could only translate it from a hundred kilometres or so, back to earth. What do you think?

SIR GEORGE PORTER:

Firstly, let me say that the irregularity is of no consequence if you have storage. If the whole thing gets covered with sand that is another matter. The irregularity is a disadvantage if you are making electricity, or if you are making heat, because the supply is out of phase but, as far as making chemical fuels is concerned, it does not matter in the least any more than it matters particularly when we grow our wheat, because that is something that can be kept over at least 12 months.

On the plans for the space station which Glazer has proposed, I cannot begin to make these sums add up. In the first place, the figures I have given show that 20 dollars a square metre is what you can afford to spend on earth and in space it is only about 100 dollars. You cannot make tracking mirrors on earth for that sum. Land, even the best arable land, costs far less than the 20 dollars per square metre that we are talking of. Why put it up in space, which is bound to be more expensive?

QUESTION:

I am slightly surprised that you are so positive that nuclear energy should continue in view of your great optimism about

solar energy. I am not saying I personally do not have any strong views one way or the other. If you could explain perhaps why it would not be reasonable to at least go slow on nuclear energy for a while until we see how quickly some of these other things could be brought to fruition?

SIR GEORGE PORTER:

I have two reasons for taking that view. If everything does well, everything will be all right with both nuclear and solar energy. I would not like to hazard a guess in the long term as to which would be cheaper, solar or nuclear for the production of electricity, supposing all the hazards and all the problems are solved. Until they are, I think that we should keep all our options open, because we want to get the most convenient method and the cheapest.

I am glad you asked that as the last question because it enables me to say, and I must emphasise this, that what I have talked about in the last few minutes of my lecture is work of great hope, but there is no certainty of success at the moment. It would be extremely dangerous to rely on this just as it would be dangerous to rely on nuclear fusion. I think that both may have unforeseen problems. Even though nuclear research and the building of prototype nuclear power stations is much more expensive than the research or the building of prototype solar equipment, we must keep the option open at least until we are actually getting energy economically out of the solar plants.

If in thirty years time something goes wrong with the solar option if it does not work out, if we find ourselves with no oil, insufficient coal, inadequate water supplies and no nuclear energy, we are going to be in real trouble. It is not just that life will be less comfortable. If a city like London or New York runs out of electricity, the people are going to die. The sewers are run by electricity, the food supply has to be transported, and these places will become uninhabitable in a very short time. We have to play safe and keep all the options open.

Lord Goodman:

Obviously we could go on all night. It is now appropriate I think that I call on a very old friend, Dick Harris, to propose a vote of thanks.

The Honorable Philip M. Kaiser

Philip M. Kaiser was born in 1913. He graduated from the University of Wisconsin in 1935 and won a Rhodes Scholarship to Oxford where he was at Balliol College from 1936 to 1939. He was President of the Balliol Junior Common Room and was succeeded in that post by Edward Heath, Denis Healey and Roy Jenkins, in that order.

On his return to the United States in 1939, he joined the staff of the Board of Governors of the Federal Reserve Bank in Washington. After the outbreak of the War, he moved to the Board of Economic Warfare where he served as Chief of its Projects Operation Staff. In 1946, he joined the State Department, working in the bureau which dealt with international organizations. He was then transferred to the Office of International Labor Affais in the Department of Labor and in 1949 president Truman appointed him Assistant Secretary of Labor in charge of International Affairs. He was one of the youngest members of President Truman's sub-cabinet.

From 1949 to 1953, during his tenure as Assistant Sceretary, he was the U.S. Goverment member on the Governing Body of the International Labor Organization and Chief of the U.S Delegations to the annual International Labor Conferences. he was also a member of the top interdepartmental committees which developed the Greek-Turkish aid program and the Marshall Plan, and the U.S. Board of the Foreign Service.

There followed a period of non-diplomatic life, which coincided with the Republican Administration under President Eisenhower, during which Ambassador Kaiser was Special Assistant to Governor Averell Harriman of New York, and then Professor of International Relations at the American University in Washington D.C.

He returned to the State Department in 1961 when President Kennedy appointed him as U.S. Ambassador to the Republics of Senegal and Mauritania. In 1964, under President Johnson, he came to London, and served as American Minister and Deputy Chief of Mission to Ambassador David Bruce. He remained in the Embassy until 1969. Following the election of President Nixon, he retired from the Government once again to become Chairman and Managing Director of Encyclopaedia Britannica in the U.K..

He lived in London until 1977 when President Carter appointed him Ambassador to Hungary. During his tenure in Budapest he played an important role in the dramatic improvement in U.S Hungarian relations. He was U.S Ambassador to Austria from 1980–81.

'Woodrow Wilson and the Modern American Presidency'

delivered by

The Hon. Philip M. Kaiser, Ambassador of the United States to Austria

Monday, 16th June, 1980

CHAIRMAN The Rt. Hon. The Lord Goodman C.H.

LORD GOODMAN:

Ladies and Gentlemen, we are very honoured by the distinction of the audience here this evening. This is the eighth Goodman Lecture – although it is slightly embarrassing to describe it by that title – and I think it is fair to say that it has, given once a year, made a modest addition to the cultural life of London. You will see that, after the first lecture, they took a leap forward in quality and distinction and I think it is right to say that lecturers hitherto and up-to-date have been of quite outstanding distinction, as I say with that solitary exception.

Tonight we have a very great capture; for a London lecture, we have a most unique and unusual lecturer. We have Mr. Philip Kaiser whom I can claim to have been a friend of for many years. He has had a very distinguished career. You have in front of you the card which gives an account of his life and an account of his achievements. Having achieved the rank of Ambassador to Hungary a very short time ago, he has been promoted to be the United States Ambassador to Austria in Vienna.

He is a man of rare intellectual distinction, exceptional curiosity of mind and, as you will observe also, great modesty; and I think that we shall have a lecture of very splendid quality. There is nothing more irritating for a lecturer than to hear his chairman predicting what exceptional quality the lecture is going to possess, but on this occasion, if I may say so, I do it with very quiet confidence. Irvine Aitchison, in whose memory these lectures have been established, would I think have been especially proud to have been here this evening.

MR. PHILIP KAISER:

Thank you very much, Lord Goodman, Mr. Callaghan, ladies and gentlemen. I appreciate those warm words of introduction, which remind me of the time many years ago when my elder son, who is now a rather distinguished journalist, was about six years old and I had just been appointed Assistant Secretary of Labour by one of my favourite Presidents, Harry Truman. We were having dinner together – Hannah, our son and I – in the middle of the dinner Bob said, "Mother, do some boys grow up and become lion tamers"; and Mother said "Yes." He said, "Well, maybe I will become a lion tamer." Then a few mouthfuls later, he said, "Mother , I think maybe instead of a lion tamer I will become a fire fighter"; and mother allowed that that was a respectable career too. Then there was a long and ominous silence, at the end of which he said, "Why do some boys grow up and become nothing at all, Mother, like Daddy, for example!"

Hannah and I are delighted to be here tonight. Whenever we come to England we feel that we are coming home. I first came here as a student in 1936. A few years later we were married in Oxford on the day that the Rhodes Trustees allowed me to perform that rash act; and it is no secret that, from the beginning of 1964, we have spent twelve happy years here. There is a special pleasure in spending an evening with so many old friends.

The Eighth Goodman Lecture

Whatever other reactions you may have to my remarks tonight, I am confident you will agree that, in today's world, the American presidency is a subject of more than academic interest.

I start with Woodrow Wilson, because he was the first President to confront the great foreign, as well as domestic, problems of this century and the first to deal with the new role of the United States as a world power as well as the increased role of the Government in an industrial society; and he left a legacy of ideas and presidential style that greatly influenced succeeding presidents. In the 56 years since Wilson's death, American presidents have had to cope with the same basic issues that preoccupied him, and they have acted largely within the framework set by his successes and failures.

Herbert Hoover admired him. Franklin Roosevelt was "haunted by Wilson's ghost". Truman conceived of the presidency in Wilsonian terms. Kennedy's inaugural speech was clearly within the Wilsonian tradition. Johnson too was an authentic Wilson heir. His presidential activism made possible remarkable achievements on the domestic front, although in foreign affairs he strained constitutional practice. Nixon claimed that Wilson was one of his heroes, though Nixon's behaviour went far beyond Wilson's basic conception of the role of the American chief executive. Carter has tried to repair the damage done to the presidency by Vietnam and Watergate, while his advocacy of human rights descends directly from the moralism that permeated Wilson's domestic and foreign policies.

It is difficult to understand Wilson's contribution without some appreciation of his background. In spite of Marx's contention, individuals do make a great difference in history, and the life of Woodrow Wilson is a good example.

Wilson was born in Virginia in 1856 to a Presbyterian minister's family, whose forebears had filled Scottish pulpits for six generations. He inherited, naturally enough, a strong

Calvinistic conscience. Early in life, Wilson decided on a political career and chose Gladstone as his hero, which led Herbert Edgar to comment that, "Wilson's choice of Gladstone is appropriate, the two men being completely alike in character, in quality of mind, and in their intimate knowledge of God's hopes and plans!"

Wilson shared his father's strong faith in the teachings of the Presbyterian church and God's purposes, one of which was to make him a great man. Wilson's poor health, including occasional nervous breakdowns, presented him with severe handicaps, but his sense of mission was strong enough to overcome them all.

After finishing his undergraduate studies at Princeton, Wilson first chose the law as a route to politics, passing brilliantly the examination for the Bar in 1882. However, not very good at attracting clients and too moralistic to accept those who did not have the right obviously on their side, he abandoned law to study political science at Johns Hopkins University. His first book, his Ph.D. thesis entitled "Congressional Government", won the John Marshall prize and has become something of a classic.

In 1890, he became Professor of Jurisprudence and Political Economy at Princeton. Here, his eloquent lectures drew hundreds of students, and his public speeches, in which he attacked the power of money and the increasing concern with making it, were also warmly received by his audiences. Wilson was elected President of Princeton in 1902, chiefly because of his popularity as a professor and orator and because the retiring president thought him a safe choice, a man who would be content to preach a new gospel without making upsetting changes. Little did he know his man. Before long, Wilson was redesigning the curriculum and, through an innovative preceptor system, he brought students and faculty closer together.

However, he was defeated when he attempted to change Princeton's traditional eating clubs into democratic residents'

halls, which he saw as the salvation of Princeton and of the democratic spirit in education. It was often impossible for Wilson to separate issues from men and, when one great friend, John Hibben, tried to get him to compromise, Wilson treated him with cold contempt and never again sought his friendship. Throughout all his life, Wilson's friendships followed this pattern, particularly at critical moments in his career as Governor of New Jersey and, tragically, at the end of his career over the League of Nations.

After the defeat of the dormitory project and four years of battle with the trustees over a new graduate school, Wilson's standing at the university had reached a low point, and the governorship of New Jersey appeared as a way out, as well as a means of fulfilling his now heightened political ambitions.

Wilson's election as a reform governor in a state politically corrupt was the first of an extraordinary series of events that led to the Presidency. Ironically, Wilson was launched into national politics by a Conservative, George Harvey, the Editor of *Harper's Weekly*, and a man of influence on Wall Street. Harvey pushed Wilson as an alternative to a third term for Theodore Roosevelt and a fourth nomination, which was even more radical, of William Jennings Bryan. Harvey saw the governorship of New Jersey as the next step to the White House.

Harvey was able to convince the Democratic boss, Jim Smith, that to win the election of 1910 he had to nominate a reform candidate and Wilson was the ideal choice. Although many of the delegates had never even heard of Wilson, Smith forced the State Convention to nominate him. Smith, like President Patton of Princeton, made the mistake of regarding Wilson as safe. As Governor, Wilson showed a genius for sensing public opinion and manipulating it for his own political purposes. He broke with Smith, destroying the traditional Democratic organisation in the process, and he forced a liberal programme through the New Jersey legislature which won the

support of the progressive elements throughout the country.

By 1912, the national Progressive movement was reaching its apex and helped propel Wilson into the White House. He was a long-shot in the Democratic Party convention, but after a bitter fight won the nomination on the 46th ballot, thanks in part to the support of William Jennings Bryan, the leader of the party's Western Progressives.

The nomination would have been a dubious prize without the split in the Republican Party. The election of 1912 marked a dramatic protest against the effect of rapid industrialisation during the previous 50 years and the increasing concentration of economic power in the hands of trusts. Not only did the Democrats turn to Wilson, but ex-President Theodore Roosevelt split the Republicans by forming the Progressive Party after the conservative old guard had forced President Taft's renomination. The Republican split enabled Wilson to win with the smallest popular vote since Lincoln's tie for the three candidates in 1860. It was only the third time since 1856 that a Democrat had been elected President.

The campaign was dominated by a debate between Wilson and Roosevelt on the proper role of government in the economy. Roosevelt, who as President had gained a reputation as a trust-buster, argued now that the government should regulate monopoly and not abolish it. Wilson, however, insisted that monopoly would eventually destroy both economic and political freedom; and his "New Freedom" programme sought to destroy monopoly and restore free competition which he, like so many other Americans, saw as the epitome of the American system. Of the two approaches, Roosevelt's "New Nationalism" was the more realistic, as Wilson's own subsequent experiences showed. Both shared an underlying principle: that the government must be used as the instrument to achieve greater human welfare in the economic field. The election results proved that Wilson and Roosevelt had caught

the temper of the times. Between them, they received 70% of the popular vote.

Even before he entered politics, Wilson had strong views on the importance of an active presidency. In *Congressional Government* he had written: "The President is at liberty both in law and conscience to be as big a man as he can. The centre of power must rest in the Presidency." He vigorously and resourcefully put this belief into practice. For the first time since the second President, John Adams, Wilson delivered his messages to Congress in person. He lobbied in the Capitol for action on his Bills. He had legislation drafted in the executive branch and he developed to a fine art the use of patronage for the purpose of influencing congressmen and senators. Theodore Roosevelt had been the first President since Lincoln to assert any of the latent powers of the presidency. Wilson went far beyond in making the executive a major branch of the government, nor did Wilson hesitate to appeal to public opinion over Congressional heads.

In 1913, when his first important legislative proposal, tariff law reform, was in danger of being mutilated by special interests, Wilson publicly attacked the tariff law. "There is evidence," he said, "that money without limit is being spent to sustain this lobby and to create the appearance of pressure of public opinion. It is of serious interest to the country that the people at large should have no lobby and be voiceless in these matters, while great bodies of astute men seek to create an artificial opinion and to overscome the interests of the public for their private profit." The public responded and the Senate passed the first tariff reduction in decades. Wilson thus became the architect of the modern free trade tradition.

There followed in rapid succession the Federal Reserve Act of 1913, the Layton Anti-Trust Act, the creation of the Federal Trade Commission, and a law providing for an eight-hour day on interstate railways. All of this and more he accomplished during his first 18 months in office. Never before had the

country seen so much social and economic legislation and acted so rapidly; and only twice since, under F.D.R. and Lyndon Johnson, has anything comparable been achieved.

Paradoxically, most of Wilson's legislation had the effect of regulating rather than restructuring the economy, as he had proposed during his campaign. Wilson's failure to effect any fundamental changes in the structure of society signalled the Progressive movement's failure to reduce concentration of economic power; but his regulating reforms established important precedents later expanded by the New Deal.

The regulatory approach, however, had its limits: a business recession struck at America in 1914 and Wilson, sharing the prevailing ignorance of macro-economics, was forced to call a halt to reform. However, early in the year of 1916, with an eye to the large Progressive vote, Wilson again tackled social issues. After his courageous appointment of the progressive Louis Brandeis to the Supreme Court, Wilson pushed through Congress the Workman's Compensation Act, the Child Labour law, and other reform measures which added significantly to his domestic achievements. They were the first real attempt to use the government as an instrument for economic and social welfare, and they left important institutional precedents.

After the outbreak of war in 1914, Wilson increasingly turned his attention to world affairs. Domestically, the essence of progressivism, particularly in the hands of Wilson, was moralism. He brought the same cast of mind to foreign policy, stressing that it was American's duty to use her moral influence to promote liberty, justice and a righteous peace. He thought it was America's destiny to make her impact on the world through example rather than through involvement. At the same time, he recognised that the non-intervention precepts of Washington and Jefferson were not necessarily adequate guides for American policy.

The Mexican crisis, precipitated by the murder of the revolutionary leader Madero, posed Wilson's first major test in

foreign affairs. While Theodore Roosevelt had pursued interventionism in the Caribbean with barely concealed cynicism, Wilson's Mexican policy was motivated by idealism. "Morality and not expediency is the thing that must guide us," he said.
"The influence of the United States must be used in support of constitutionalism." In 1913, Wilson told Sir William Tyrrell, secretary to the British Ambassador in Washington: "I am going to teach the South American Republics to elect good men." The establishment and maintenance of a democratic regime in Mexico was more complicated that Wilson had foreseen. At one point, he felt compelled to land Marines at Vera Cruz. In spite of his moral motivations, Wilson was eventually forced to abandon his intervention in Mexico, after leaving a legacy of animosity that took a generation to overcome.

Wilson's first reaction to the European war was to call it "A conflict with which we have nothing to do and whose causes cannot touch us." He believed that, by remaining neutral, America could act as a mediating nation and exercise and enforce moral principles. At the same time, he insisted that America's rights as a neutral must be fully respected by all belligerents. Because German violations through submarine warfare involved loss of life, while British violations did not, and because of personal sympathy for the Allies which reflected the predominant view of America, Wilson's advocacy of neutral rights bore more heavily on Germany than on Britain. The war created acute strains on United States relations with Germany, particularly after the sinking of the "Lusitania" in May 1915.

In December 1916, following his re-election by a razor-thin majority after campaigning on the slogan, "He kept us out of the war", Wilson tried to make peace through mediation, thus avoiding direct American involvement. Neither the Allies nor the Central Powers were willing to make peace on the terms he

proposed, and the opportunity for a moderate peace settlement was lost.

In early 1917, the German government decided to resume unrestricted submarine warfare. This made United States entry almost inevitable. In April, Wilson, responding to public sentiment as well as to his own sense of mission, asked Congress for a declaration of war. Now he was determined that the war was to be fought to achieve the highest ideals rather than to satisfy selfish national interest. He had to justify his intervention in moral terms. The American public, still in the grip of progressive impulses, responded in the same spirit. In the speech before Congress, Wilson emphasised that "America was fighting for democracy, for the rights and liberties of small nations and for a universal dominion of right by such a concert of free people as shall bring peace and safety to all nations and make the world itself at last free."

The Bolshevik Revolution in 1917 ensured that the war would become an ideological struggle and forced the Allies to become more specific about their war aims. After seizing power, Lenin and Trotsky called for a just peace based on a renunciation of territorial annexations and for self-determination for subject peoples. It was no accident that Wilson's famous "Fourteen Points" speech followed in January 1918. The "Fourteen Points" included Wilson's peace aims and embodied his idealistic foreign policy programme. In addition, they were an opening salvo in a campaign against Lenin for the allegiance of the European peoples as well as a brilliant stroke of psychological warfare against the Germans. Wilson called for open diplomacy, freedom of the seas, frontiers based on national self-determination, freedom for subject peoples of the Austrian, German and Russian Empires, the establishment of a world organisation of nations and, significantly, a German withdrawal from Russia. The struggle to determine the shape of post-war Europe had begun.

Wilson' s programme related his own vision of the post-war

world to that of the non-revolutionary liberal and social-democratic forces of Europe. He had become the spokesman of progressive liberalism at home. He was now projecting this doctrine on the world scene. America, in his view, had a mission to lead mankind towards the orderly international society of the future.

Events in the autumn of 1918 set the stage for the difficult, frustrating negotiations at Versailles. The German revolution that Wilson had hoped for occurred and an armistice was negotiated largely on the basis of Wilson's Fourteen Points. At the same time, however, conservative forces in the Allied nations improved their positions. In 1918, the "Khaki" election in Britain greatly strengthened the Tories; and in America the Republicans, running largely on a platform for a punitive peace, won control over Congress after Wilson had blundered by making the peace treaty a partisan campaign issue. Later, he compounded his mistake by failing to include a Republican of stature in the American delegation to Versailles. Thus, both Wilson's and Lloyd George's freedom of action was severely curtailed during the peace treaty negotiations.

When Wilson arrived in Europe – the first President ever to leave the country while in office – to head the American delegation at the peace conference, he was acclaimed almost as a Messiah. Before long, however, his enormous popularity both at home and abroad was dissipated by his seeming failure to cope effectively with the complex negotiations.

Essentially, there were three competing visions of the post-war world when the Versailles negotiations were taking place. The first, from the Bolsheviks, envisaged a spreading workers' revolution and a victory for international communism. The second, the Wilsonian view, foresaw the spread of parliamentary democracy and reformist capitalism and a new diplomacy based on the Fourteen Points to preserve peace. The Third, advocated most effectively by the French Premier Clemenceau, favoured a punitive peace involving vast reparations and loss

of territory for Germany, the defeat of democratic socialism and the overthrow or containment of the Russian Revolution.

Wilson, hampered by illness as well as political weakness, was unable to overcome the resistance of his Allies, particularly Clemenceau and Orlando of Italy. (It was Clemenceau who made the famous remark: "Ten points were enough for God"). Wilson reacted to compromises and failures by pinning his hopes on the fourteenth point, the League of Nations. Since like most Americans he still rejected the balance of power as a peace-keeping mechanism, he failed to appreciate that leaving Russia out of the post-war order would create a substantially unbalanced situation and he looked to the League of Nations to resolve future international disputes. While hardly sympathising with the Bolsheviks, he agreed with his advisers that the American people would not support any sustained military intervention.

Thus, Wilson's hopes for a just and humane peace based on new world order were doomed by political differences at home, by the conflicting aspirations of the victors, by the impossibility of integrating the Soviets into the post-war European system, and ultimately by the very complexity of the situation. However, Clemenceau's victory was a hollow one. The French contented themselves with the illusion that the new Eastern European states would contain both Germany and Russia, a concept whose bankruptcy was dramatically realised in the Nazi-Soviet pact of 1939.

Wilson had accepted many compromises at Versailles in order to gain the acceptance of his fourteenth point, the establishment of the League. Never admitting publicly that the terms of the Treaty fell short of his expectations, he argued that the creation of a League would justify the sacrifices of the war. His obsessive rejection of senatorial amendments to the League Covenant was self-defeating. By the fall of 1919, the idealism generated by the war had eroded and public opinion was turning against him. American groups with ties to the old

world criticised Wilson for failing to satisfy the demands of Ireland, Poland and Italy. The liberals, who had been amongst Wilson's staunchest supporters, were bitter about a settlement that perpetuated the evils of the pre-war world, and provided little hope of realising his Fourteen points. They also thought that Article 10 of the League Covenant, which obliged the signatory powers to respect and preserve the territorial integrity and political independence of all members, would be used to sustain the *status quo*. And traditional isolationists, who had been silent during the war, now vigorously attacked Article 10, because it meant permanent involvement in world affairs.

The Republicans, smelling victory in 1920, spurred on by Wilson's arch-enemy Senator Lodge, were doing everything possible to turn Wilson's deteriorating position to their advantage. In the face of a situation that demanded resourcefulness, imagination and flexibility, a tired and frustrated Wilson, forgetting what he had preached and practised earlier, failed lamentably. He insisted that the Senate accept the text of the League Covenant without significant changes. When the Senate refused Wilson, against the advice of his doctors, went to the country in a frantic attempt to rally public opinion behind his own position.

Before completing his tour, Wilson suffered a stroke and he returned to Washington a desperately ill man. For nine months he was unable to carry out the responsibilities of his office; and in an extraordinary episode in American history the country was kept ignorant of the fact that Mrs. Wilson, with the help of Wilson's doctor, had assumed the government's executive functions.

Within a year after Wilson was stricken, the Senate rejected the Treaty. The election of 1920 became a plebiscite on Wilson's internationalism, and the Republicans won by a landslide. The victory of Harding's isolation movement was bitter proof that America was not yet ready for Wilson's noble experiment and had rejected his active presidency.

Developments in the 1920s seemed to reinforce the sentiments that had elected Harding. It was a decade of great American prosperity, based on an expanding national market buttressed by isolationism. There was a return to passive administration led by passive presidents, and Wilson seemed throughly discredited. In 1929, however, there was a dramatic change. The financial crash brought on the greatest depression in American history and unhinged the world economy, posing new threats to the fragile inter-war peace. It revived the need for affirmative government and the Wilson experience became the guide to presidential action and style.

When F.D.R. assumed office in 1933, he faced economic and social problems more complex and pressing than any previous president. His temperament and personality, his appreciation of the institutional legacy of the Wilson administration, in which he had served as Assistant Secretary of the Navy, and his commitment to the Wilsonian conception of the presidency helped him to meet the demands of the American public for immediate action.

Through constant personal contact with the members of Congress, effective use of patronage, executive formulation of bills and direct appeals to the public against special interests, Roosevelt pushed through a programme which greatly increased Government involvement in the economic life of the nation. In dealing with the public, Roosevelt resumed the practice of regular press conferences and made brilliant use of the radio, an instrument not available to his predecessor.

Roosevelt went beyond Wilson in trying to achieve economic and social changes within the framework of a regulated capitalism. F.D.R. made government responsible for social security, wages, housing and unemployment insurance. He was the first president who attempted to use the techniques of macro-economics to improve the performance of a nation's economy, although it is no secret that he never really understood Keynes.

This trend has continued. The Employment Act of 1946, passed by President Truman, declared full employment an objective national policy, and established a Council of Economic Advisers in the office of the President to help the government chart a course of steady economic growth. This was a radical departure from previous doctrine and practice. Although a relatively passive president, Eisenhower accepted in principle the commitment to regulate the economy. President Kennedy vigorously implemented it. His guidelines for wage settlements, his attack on the United States Steel Company for announcing price increases without first consulting the government, and his innovative tax policies added new dimensions to presidential involvement in directing the nation's economy. And even President Nixon did not hesitate to impose wage and price controls to brake inflationary trends.

Presidential economic involvement has become an established Wilsonian legacy. In spite of the rise of conservative sentiment, with its emphasis on less government, Americans still expect the chief executive to play a crucial role in maintaining the nation's prosperity. The Federal Budget is at the centre of economic management, and gives the President enormous power to determine the pattern of the country's economy. Presidents, as well as Prime Ministers, must now cope with the political consequences of John Maynard Keynes.

In dealing with international affairs, particularly the Second World War and its aftermath, Roosevelt, Truman and their successors also profited from Wilson's ideas, achievements and failures. F.D.R. had supported the League when he was running for Vice-President in 1920. However, always the politician, he was responsive to the isolationism which persisted in the 1930s. He was discouraged by the unfavourable public reaction to his famous "Quarantine the Aggressors" speech in 1937, and until the fall of France he moved cautiously on foreign affairs.

For practical balance of power as well as ideological reasons, F.D.R.'s sympathies lay with the Allies. A masterful tactician, he anticipated American involvement – indeed, he manipulated public opinion to encourage it – and took steps early to avoid Wilson's errors. Even before Pearl Harbour, he appointed two distinguished Republicans to his Cabinet as Secretary of War and Secretary of the Navy. He saw to it that Republican Congressional leaders were associated with the peace-making process in its earlier stages, and he was able to commit the United States to membership in the United Nations even before the end of hostilities.

Thus, Roosevelt was more successful than Wilson in securing a broad consensus in favour of his policies. In his attitude towards American war aims, he combined Wilsonian idealism with enlightened realism. In his early definition of these aims, and particularly in the Atlantic Charter, he resorted to flights of Wilsonian idealism in an effort to arouse support for the war. On the other hand, his belief in the possibility of co-existence with Stalinism, his attempts to prepare the American people for a less than perfect peace settlement, and his scepticism about the efficacy of the United Nations, reflected his determination to avoid the pitfalls of excessive idealism. His death foreclosed the possibility of his trying to put his mixture of idealism and realism into practice.

Within two years of Roosevelt's death, Harry S. Truman, with a somewhat different conception of the state of the world, had produced an activist foreign policy in many ways reminiscent of Wilson. He combined balance of power considerations with moral fervour and a sense of mission. In 1947, it was clear that Western Europe was economically prostrate and that the Soviet Union represented a major ideological threat to Western democracies and a military threat to the world balance of power. Truman decided that the situation called for an American commitment on a world-wide scale; and his specific goal, the containment of Soviet Communism and power, made it

possible for him to break through the barriers of isolationism where Wilson had failed.

Through his Greek-Turkish policy, through Marshall Aid and membership in NATO, Truman allied the United States to Western Europe and made it possible for her to revive economically and politically and to resist Stalin's pressures. Truman had obviously learned from Wilson how *not* to handle Congress. He got his key international legislation through a Republican controlled Congress; and then won the 1948 election by campaigning against the "Do-nothing, good-for-nothing" Eightieth Congress! (He was, of course, exploiting Congressional failure to act in the domestic field).

Mutatis mutandis Truman's successors have tried to manage foreign policy within the Wilsonian tradition: a sense of moral obligation to defend freedom anywhere in the world, plus a continuing open-ended political economic and military commitment to that objective, have been the hallmarks of that policy. The spirit of this policy reached its apogee in John F. Kennedy's inaugrural address in 1961, when he said "We shall pay any price, bear any burden, meet any hardship, support any friend, oppose any foe to assure the survival and the success of liberty."

After the nuclear missile crisis of 1963, Kennedy realised that the nature of the world had so altered that accommodation with the Soviet Union was both possible and necessary. However, by the late 1960s the Vietnam war had raised practical as well as moral questions about the basis of American policies.

Americans became aware of two fundamental facts of international relations that they had almost lost sight of at the height of the Cold War: American power to shape international relations has limits and, consequently, the means to implement policy should be carefully chosen and roughly proportionate to its ends; and, secondly, Americans were also

disturbed by the expansion of Presidential power arising from the Vietnam conflict.

On the domestic front, Johnson proved to be a brilliant disciple of Wilson and F.D.R. His extraordinary knowledge of the intricacies of Congressional behaviour and his skilful use of presidential power and prestige enabled him to push through some of the most significant social legislation of the twentieth century, including the liberalisation of immigration laws, federal aid for schools, and the famous Civil Rights Act of 1964, which transformed race relations in America. Unfortunately, however, in dealing with the Vietnam war, Johnson tended to abuse presidential power. He disregarded Congressional prerogatives, became excessively secretive and condoned the spread of misinformation. As the frustrations over Vietnam increased, he became less receptive to unsympathetic advice and less responsive to public opinion.

Under the continuous pressure of Vietnam, using national security as his rationalisation, Nixon went much further than Johnson in asserting presidential power and in upsetting the institutional balance that has always been essential to the proper functioning of the American democratic system. This is not the place to deal at any length with the Nixon presidency, but it is a fact that he so abused his presidential power as dramatized by Cambodia and Watergate, that, for the first time in our history, a President had to resign in order to avoid impeachment.

After the excesses of the Nixon administration, it was inevitable that Congress should take steps to re-assert its prerogatives and clip presidential wings. In foreign relations in particular Congress insisted on re-asserting its constitutional authority. It not only passed legislation to reinforce its prerogatives, particularly in regard to decisions of war and peace; but it also aggressively involved itself in the making of decisions heretofore considered executive responsibilities. It was determined to rein in the President.

The strong reaction of the American people and Congress to Vietnam and Watergate raised two crucial questions. Would America revert to its pre-war isolationism? Would this reaction so enfeeble the presidency as to prevent future chief executives from asserting the kind of leadership that has proved so essential to the effective functioning of the American democratic system?

Thus, the two basic tenets of the Wilsonian inheritance had been challenged: a major international role commensurate with her capabilities, and faithful to her traditions is an essential ingredient of the peacefully ordered world; and that, for domestic reasons as well as international reasons, our system requires a strong and purposeful President, but one who expounds equally strong and purposeful forms of democratic control.

At a time when criticising President Carter at home or abroad, no matter what he does or says, has become fair game, it is worth noting I suggest that he has taken important steps to repair the damage done by Vietnam and Watergate, and he has done so in a manner compatible with the American constitutional system. Our allies, as well as Americans themselves, should appreciate the persistent and enlightened manner in which President Carter has maintained United States international involvement, and not infrequently with significant success, in Panama, for example, in the Middle East, and in reinforcing the NATO alliance. As the President is trying to cope realistically with the implications of the Soviet invasion of Afghanistan, it is worth recording too that his administration has made a determined effort to reduce tensions between East and West. He pursued with vigour the Strategic Arms Limitation Talks. He proposed a series of negotiations to limit the spread of conventional armaments and to reach a treaty banning nuclear testing; and he continues to push for the success of the MBFR negotiations. Moreover, during the last three years he has worked actively and often successfully to

develop good relations with the countries of Eastern Europe. And in the best Wilsonian tradition, he has worked hard and persistently to widen the application of human rights, as well as other provisions of the Helsinki Pact.

He has not always been consistent on the issues, but which President has since the end of World War II or for that matter, which British Prime Minister? If, as Ralph Waldo Emerson said, "A foolish consistency is the hobgoblin of little minds," then two of my favourite presidents – Franklin D. Roosevelt and Harry S. Truman – must have had very large minds indeed!

President Carter has tried to re-establish the kind of relationship between the President, the bureaucracy, Congress and the people that was shattered by Vietnam and Watergate and which is so essential if current international political and economic problems are to be dealt with effectively. It is no small task to create, as we must in years ahead, a new national consensus of goals and methods in American foreign policy. It will be very difficult to do so unless the kind of presidency developed by Wilson is restored as an essential ingredient in the American political process.

If you will allow me, Mr. Chairman, I will conclude by telling you a story about one of my favourite Americans who unfortunately was never elected President. It is a true story about Adlai Stevenson. After he made a campaign speech in 1960 in support of Jack Kennedy, an elderly lady came up to him and said, "Governor, you were marvellous; that was the most superfluous speech I have ever heard." He said: "Thank you very much, my dear; in the light of what you have just said, I think I will have it published, posthumously." The lady then replied: "That's wonderful, Governor; the sooner the better!"

LORD GOODMAN:

Those of you who have been here on previous occasions,

know that our lecturers have always been generous in being willing to answer questions and I do hope that, after that fascinating lecture, you may want to ask Mr. Kaiser a question or two. In fact, perhaps I might ask him the first one. You said, Mr. Kaiser, that in your opinion Franklin Roosevelt was more successful in dealing with the peace negotiations than Wilson. Would that be because he had had a greater experience of international affairs?

MR. KAISER:

Yes, indeed. As I indicated, he was very conscious of the Wilsonian experience. He had been part of the Wilson administration during the war as Assistant Secretary of the Navy – in fact, there were a good number of members of his own administration who had received their training in the Wilson administration. F.D.R. was always haunted by the ghost of Wilson. It reflects the fact that (a) he had this experience and (b) always had a special interest in avoiding Wilson's mistakes in international affairs.

LORD GOODMAN:

If there is any other question you would like to ask, I am sure Mr Kaiser will be happy to answer, but I do not think that extends to predicting the result of the election! Short of that, I am sure he will answer any question arising directly from his lecture or otherwise.

QUESTION:

Mr. Kaiser, I thought, whenever I have read history in the past, that there was a great antagonism, or certain antagonism, between President Wilson and Mr. Lloyd George. You did not mention that at all. You did mention M. Clemenceau. Is that so, or have I mis-interpreted it?

MR. KAISER:

I think there is no doubt that Wilson was not happy about Lloyd George's performance at Versailles, but he was much more unhappy about the performance of Clemenceau and Orlando. I think a reading of history would reveal that there

was a little more sympathy for Lloyd George on the part of Wilson, but as I indicated Lloyd George was hampered by the results of the election in 1918.

QUESTION:

If you are not prepared to predict the outcome of the election, are you prepared to predict what will be the balance of power between the Presidency, Congress and Senate as it now stands?

MR. KAISER:

I think that there are the beginnings of the redressing of the balance. There is a shift away from the strong post-Vietnam and Watergate reaction. I think people are beginning to realise that Congress has overdone its act, so to speak, and there is a need to redress the balance. There is a desire for the kind of activist role that the President must play in order to make the constitutional division of power system work.

LORD GOODMAN:

In this country, we have a quite brief election campaign. The Prime Minister, at his own discretion, can dissolve Parliament and assign the date of the election. Sometimes the public are slightly misled as to what the intention may be! Would you think that is a preferable system to the system you operate of fixed dates and a very long campaign?

MR. KAISER:

I think that is a very good question, but I also think it would be very foolish of me to answer it! I suppose I can put on my diplomatic cap and say that there are plusses in each of the systems and there are also minuses in each of the systems. Your system is best for your set-up and our system is best for our set-up.

QUESTION:

Mr. Chairman, Mr. Kaiser made no reference to the implementation of political ideas of the Supreme Court. Is there any connection between the implementation of those powers and the role of the Supreme Court?

MR. KAISER:

I am not sure I follow your question. You are suggesting, I think, that the Supreme Court is a very powerful force in the way our government operates; and the answer to that would be, "Yes." The division of power between the three bodies – the legislature, the judiciary, and the excutive – has, from the very beginning, been a key factor in our history; but in recent years perhaps the Supreme Court has played an even greater role than heretofore. In the days of Wilson and the early days of F.D.R. they were a conservative force; I referred to the appointment, for example, of Justice Brandeis to the Supreme Court. Justice Brandeis was a very great figure. He was known as the "People's lawyer"; he was Jewish, and no man of Jewish extraction had ever been appointed to the Supreme Court before; and the country considered him a "flaming Liberal". Wilson's appointment of Justice Brandeis to the Supreme Court was an act, as I have indicated, of great courage and political significance.

In later history, in the early New Deal, we had a conservative Supreme Court. There were only two consistently liberal members – the same Justice Brandeis and the famous Oliver Wendell Holmes, who had been appointed by Theodore Roosevelt. They were the two who almost always voted in the minority when the then Supreme Court was throwing out some of the New Deal legislation. Subsequently, in our time or in the time of the younger people here, the Supreme Court has played a very progressive and liberal role: in race relations – for example, the famous decision in 1954 – and on other delicate political issues that Congress has had neither the courage nor the ability to face up to; so that the power of the Supreme Court today is a very considerable one. It is definitely holding up its part of our tri-partite system.

QUESTION:

Mr. Chairman, a great many of the claims that Mr. Kaiser has said stimulate one and make one want to put many

questions to him. I would like to put just one question, and that is about his central theme which is, if I understand him, that the outstanding contribution that Mr. Wilson made to the conduct of foreign affairs was to import into that conduct above all moral principle. He went on to say that no President could act successfully for the American people unless he followed that example; but is it not the case that it is this import of moral principle into the conduct of foreign affairs which, particularly since 1945, has caused major embarrassment to America's allies and great troubles short of success for the American people?

Mr. Kaiser:

First of all, it is absolutely true that this was a major contribution of Wilson, although it was in the best American tradition and followed from what earlier Presidents had said and done. It was the combination of that principle and an involvement in world affairs, that is Wilson's attempt to get the United States to play a world role, which was a break, of course, with the traditional isolationism which had become almost sacrosanct in American history. As to the second part of your question that is a crucial one and one about which we can talk for a long time. I would simply say the following: in my view, the commitment to human rights is very much in the best American tradition. It is a commitment that must be at the basis of any effective consensus of the American people in regard to foreign affairs. On the other hand, it is one that is, as you have suggested, difficult to apply in the very complicated and far from satisfactory world today. It does create problems and it is difficult always to be consistent about the application of policy of this kind. Its application sometimes runs counter to our security, at least short-term security, interests; but in the long run it combines what is right and what is practical. It is right in terms of what Americans feel they stand for and what they think they represent, and I also suggest that in the long run it serves the best interests of all peoples and the best interests of

an ordered world community.

QUESTION:

Does Mr. Kaiser think the Zimmermann letter was a factor in inducing Wilson to come into the war at that stage, or would he have come in later?

MR. KAISER:

I am sure that Zimmermann might have contributed to the sentiment and the feeling that came to a head. As I recall it, the Zimmermann letter was in 1917, after the German government decided to go ahead with its unlimited submarine warfare. The Zimmermann letter contributed to the atmosphere and the sentiment that propelled Wilson into the war, but crucial was the German decision to institute unlimited submarine warfare.

QUESTION:

Do you think there could be any circumstances under which presidents could assert any sort of party discipline in order to carry the Congress or where they have the majority in Congress? This is after all a problem to which you referred several times.

MR. KAISER:

I think that is one of the problems that there is in being a President. As we all know, there is nothing equivalent to the kind of party discipline in the United States Congress that you have in your House of Commons here. A President has to win a Senator's vote no matter what party he belongs to every time a new issue comes up for a vote. There has been, through the years, a certain amount of party loyalty which a President, if skilful, can exploit for his objectives; but in recent years there has been a loosening of even the moderate party discipline that existed before. That is the result of a whole series of institutional changes that we do not have the time to go into here.

The real point, however, is that it is more difficult today than it ever was before, I think, for a President to evoke from even his own party in Congress the kind of support he would like. If you review history, you will find that even F.D.R. – who

I suppose was the most powerful President since the end of World War I – who was elected four times to the presidency, had trouble with the Congress, which was always Democratic in his time. You may remember his war-time executive order limiting incomes to $25,000 a year for the duration of the war; that was overwhelmingly reversed by the United States Congress, and there were other similar instances as well. In short, it is very difficult for any President under any circumstances to get the consistent support of his Congress for his programme, even a Congress controlled by his party. It has become even more difficult in the contemporary world as a result of recent developments, particularly over the last ten years.

LORD GOODMAN:

Mr. Kaiser has been exceptionally generous with his time, and I think he has wholly vindicated my prediction about the quality of the lecture. I will ask Mr. Wingate to propose a vote of thanks.

The Rt. Hon. The Lord Hunter of Newington, D.L., Hon. LL.D., F.R.C.P., F.R.S.E.

Robert B. Hunter was educated at George Watson's College in Edinburgh, where he was born in 1915, and in 1938 he graduated from the University of Edinburgh MB., Ch.B.

After a short period of working at the Edinburgh Royal Infirmary he joined the Royal Army Medical Corps in 1940 and was discharged 6 years later. His military service included 2½ years in the Blood Transfusion Service in the Middle East and 18 months as personal physician to Field-Marshal Lord Montgomery in the forward areas in Germany.

At the end of the war, Dr. Hunter, as he then was, was appointed Lecturer in Therapeutics at the University of St. Andrews when he accepted the Chair of Materia Medica, Pharmacology and Therapeutics. He subsequently held the same Chair in the University of Dundee and during this period was Consultant Physician to Maryfield Hospital, Dundee, and the Dundee General Hospitals. From 1958 to 1962 he was Dean of the Faculty of Medicine in the University of St. Andrews.

He has always taken a keen interest in postgraduate medical education and as well as being Director of Postgraduate Medical Education in the University of St. Andrews he was secretary of the Scottish Postgraduate Medical Association and adviser to the World Health Organisation on postgraduate medical education in Europe.

The College of Physicians and Surgeons of Norway awarded him the Malthe Foundation Prize in 1958, and the American College of Physicians the Purdue Frederick Medical Achievement Award in the same year.

From 1960 to 1964 he was a member of the Medical Research Council Clinical Research Board and from 1964 to 1968 a member of the University Grants Committee, chairing its Medical Sub-Committee from 1966 to 1968.

In 1968 he moved to Birmingham as Vice-Chancellor of the University of Birmingham and held the post until 1981.

Over the years he has been a member of a number of Goverment committees. In particular, from 1970 to 1972 he was Chairman of the Deparment of Health and Social Security Working Party on Medical Administrators in the Health Service and from 1973 to 1980 Chairman of the Department of Health and Social Security Independent Scientific Committee on Smoking and Health.

He is associated with many distinguished bodies – Fellow of the Royal Colleges of Physicians of London and Edinburgh, Honorary Fellow of the American College of Physicians, Fellow of the Royal Society of Edinburgh, Fellow of the Insitute of Biology and Honorary Fellow of the Faculty of Community Medicine. He has been awarded the honorary degree of LL.D. by the Universities of Dundee and Birmingham.

He was knighted in 1977 and created a life peer in 1978 as the Lord Hunter of Newington.

'The National Health Service – what Prospects?'

delivered by

The Rt. Hon. The Lord Hunter of Newington

D.L., Hon. LL.D., F.R.C.P. F.R.S.E. Vice-Chancellor and Principal,
The University of Birmingham

Wednesday 10th June, 1981

CHAIRMAN The Rt. Hon. The Lord Goodman C.H.

LORD GOODMAN:

May I welcome you all to the ninth of this what I may with due modesty call a very distinguished series of lectures. Except for one lamentable mistake at the outset, the other lecturers were people of very exceptional distinction, and this evening we have someone who very appropriately matches their distinction. We are most indebted to Lord Hunter for coming to give this lecture. He has selected a topic of very great and immediate interest, and his claim to speak on the subject is more than demonstrated as you will find from the biographical details with which I think most of you have been supplied.

We have succeeded in establishing a series of lectures that now has become a very important part of the cultural life of the country. There is only one a year, but it is one of the most important lectures given, and the size of this audience late in the evening, resisting the other attractions available in London, indicates the popularity of the lectures and their claim to be

regarded as a significant feature, as I have said , in our cultural life.

Lord Hunter is a doctor and a scientist, and a research worker of very, very great eminence and distinction. We are very fortunate to have him, and I will not delay you from hearing him for another moment, but will ask him to give his address to us on this exceptionally exciting and interesting subject. Thank you very much. (*Applause*).

LORD HUNTER:

Lord Goodman, Ladies and Gentlemen: "The National Health Service – What Prospects?".

In 1937, The Political and Economic Planning Unit published a report on the British Health Service which was welcomed as one of the most comprehensive and important surveys of the subject ever made. The report emphasised the inadequacy of many of the country's environmental services, including sewerage, refuse collection, water supply, control of noise and atmospheric pollution and housing. It is now recognised that improvement of these services had a major impact on the health of the British people, and attention has been drawn to them by Prof. McKeown in his book *The Role of Medicine*. With regard to the Health Service itself, there has been produced a coordination that never existed before – no matter now imperfect it is – and there has been maintained a kind of balance between public health, family doctor and hospital services which contrasts with the unbalanced changes which have taken place in some other countries.

"We are," said Lord Horder in 1938, "bad planners by temperament. The practical expression of our unplanned energies are often cumbersome and wasteful." How right he was, and so it continues to be.

In 1975 the Central Policy Review staff drew attention to the poor coordination between government departments in the field of social policy. Was it better and more effective than in

1939, when health, housing, sanitation and pollution were all under a single department, the Ministry of Health? In 1968 it was stripped of many of these and at the same time became that big spender, the Department of Health and Social Security.

An example of vision for the future was the Dawson of Penn Report of 1920 which proposed the establishment of health centres as part of a comprehensive programme of community and personal health services, as did a consultative committee of the Welsh Board of Health. In 1979 in the West Midlands there was £2,500,000 waiting to be spent on health centres. The doctors are not enamoured of them. The Dawson of Penn Report defined medical services as those which are domiciliary as distinct from institutional, and those which are individual as distinct from communal. The domiciliary services should include doctors, dentists, pharmacists, nurses, midwives and health visitors who would constitute the periphery of the scheme, the remainder of which would be institutional. These domiciliary services would be based on the primary health centre which would provide medical, surgical and maternity wards, out-patient clinics with accommodation for treatment, investigation, and communal and ancillary services. It would be conducted by general practitioners of a district with the aid of consultants. The secondary health centres, the Report suggests, would be more specialist in character and would include facilities for cases requiring highly specialised diagnosis and treatment. They would be staffed by consultants and specialists. Wherever possible, they suggested, every secondary health centre should be brought into relation with a teaching hospital which would guide collective investigation, post-graduate study and research. In this work health centres and the doctors connected with them would play an important part.

They recommended – and this is 1920 – that there should be a single health authority to supervise local administration of all allied services, whether curative or preventive, with representa-

tion from the medical profession on each authority. Local Medical Advisory Councils should be established. So suggested Dawson of Penn in 1920.

In 1938, after forty years in public life, Lord Horder claimed that it was "not very difficult" to define the needs of an ideal health service. These were: "Firstly, we must help the fit to remain fit. Secondly, we must raise the general standard of fitness (health) by correcting certain tendencies towards lowering it inherent in modern life. Thirdly, we must do our utmost to control diseases due to preventable agents. Fourthly, we must cure or alleviate disease when it occurs. These are our needs," said Lord Horder, "and they should be considered in that order, more and more in that order as civilisation progresses and as the grosser infections come under control." So that Lord Horder put health first, together with the health-creating services which were seen to be those that provided better food, housing and recreation.

It seems that the path was clearly marked and the priorities required for the nation's health identified long before a National Health Service came into being. Both these proposals required the creation of national and regional agencies concerned with a whole range of health and related services, but as we will see it did not happen.

Circumstances have radically altered since 1930. There have been technical changes, economic problems and fundamental changes in social attitudes which have contributed to this. There have been in addition a series of battles and compromises, many political, some of which surrounded the introduction of the Health Service and which have been the cause of difficulties and strife over many years. Some of the most intractable involve the medical profession which, for its own good reasons, brings professional freedom out of the bag when almost any change is proposed and has consistently declined to involve itself in comprehensive forward planning of the National Health Service while at the same time demanding a

satisfactory career structure for its members.

The Ministry of Health was founded after World War One and was created because of the concern of the Local Government Board with the field of environmental health, infectious diseases including tuberculosis, child welfare and the maternity programme, which were the growing hospital developments out of older institutions. Little, if anything, was done about the proposals of Dawson of Penn and Lord Horder. The time was not ripe.

The year 1938 brought the planning for the war and the organisation of emergency hospital provision and the coordination of local hospitals and medical services through the Emergency Medical Service. The war-time service proved to be an effective instrument for the utilisation of all types of hospitals, and Meidical Officers of Health played an important part in it. Consultants from the voluntary hospitals visited local authority hospitals, or the new EMS hospitals, and there was a massive step forward in communication between the different parts of the hospital service which had lived in relative isolation with different responsibilities for so many years.

During this time, of course, the general practitioner service and the Medical Officer of Health services continued along established lines, but even during the war time with all the extra work, ARP, evacuees, the lot, the Medical Officers of Health made substantial developments in the field of nutrition, prevention of infectious diseases, and many others.

If one remembers this war-time experience, the plans for the National Health Service as it emerged in 1947 were not surprising. The main feature was to extend the hospital changes to which I have referred and bring all hospitals under state ownership, though this was not the issue that was publicly debated. There was to be a continuation of Medical Officer of Health services and general practitioner services, a tri-partite division of services with different and disconnected responsibilities within one National Health Service but not

unified. The Ministry of Health found its territory much widened to include all hospital services. The Medical Officers of Health lost the responsibility for local government hospitals but gained new responsibilities in preventive and allied social fields.

We now enter the period 1948 to 1968, the time when attempts at rationalisation of hospital services were extended and when voluntary and ex-local authority hospitals came under the Regional Hospital Boards and the Boards of Governors' systems. It is for consideration whether this monopoly system was good or bad, but it had to happen, because the voluntary hospitals were bankrupt. A complicated relationship grew up, particularly in medical teaching centres, between Boards of Governors and Regional Hospital Boards. In Birmingham relations were happy. This was the period of major capital investment in hospital medicine which inevitably set the stage for the developments in the 1980s, in spite of the recent attempts to change direction. Expenditure by Regional Hospital Boards and Boards of Governors on capital works was very modest in the first seven or eight years of the new service and did not in fact exceed £10 million a year in 1955.

In the late 1950s and early 1960s there was a rapid acceleration in accordance with a Hospital Plan for each region published in 1962. Shades of the then Minister of Health, Enoch Powell.

In 1968-69 expenditure had increased to £94 million a year. The interesting thing is the delay for a decade after 1948 before capital building got under way and, having been concerned with some of these things, one realises how difficult it was to get it started. Planning took five to eight years. This poses very serious problems, ladies and gentlemen, if you want to change course, particularly if the foundation of change is tied up with capital building. It is impossible to do it quickly. Between March 1948 and March 1966 £37 million was spent in the West Midlands, but by 1974 it was £124 million. The hospital

building programme was accelerating rapidly. This was the time of planning the thousand-bed hospital and the district general hospitals. It seemed as though the stage was set to create a massive range of new hospitals across the length and breadth of the land. They would be the lynch-pin of the new service. Scant attention was paid to the first priority of Dawson of Penn, education and prevention.

However, by the late 1960s other factors were beginning to impinge on the concept of the hospital sickness service. On the one hand the reorganisation of local government was planned, and inevitably changes in social services. Secondly, the Department of Health and Social Security was established in 1968, this replacing the old Ministry of Health. Medical work, medical care, was now to become part of the social network. The merger of health and social services in practice was only a gradual process of cross-departmental discussion and policy-making, and for a number of years co-operation was not very close. The effect on the Health Service of having a Secretary of State who also had to argue in the Cabinet for the needs of the social services is a very important matter, but one suspects not much discussed. It would not be unfair to say that the interests of Dick Crossman and his successor – and also David Ennals – were probably more in the social services than in health. One naturally becomes anxious as to whether the wide-ranging responsibilities of the Secretary of State would have an adverse influence on the expenditure on health. When the volume of public expenditure is expressed at constant 1976 prices the 1971-72 social budget appears to have been 54% of the total public expenditure, rising to 59% in 1976-77. Although in volume terms the share of health in the social budget seems to fall, I am assured that the health share of the total public expenditure remains unchanged. The position is a complicated one affected substantially by the increase in the numbers of unemployed, but the evidence would seem to be that the Secretary of State's social services role has not had an adverse

effect on health expenditure. Perhaps it could be argued that health may have done better than it might otherwise have done by having a single Cabinet Minister in charge, even with a wider span of responsibilities.

But perhaps what is most relevant in the run-up period to reorganisation is the effect of the conflicting philosophies which formed the background to reorganisation in 1974. There are a number of factors, some important and some less so, which should be examined. There is the deceptively simple political belief that everybody should participate in government and management. The fact was that local government was still smarting from the realisation that it had lost control of its hospitals in 1948. Preventive medicine until 1974 stayed in the control of local government and had begun to develop the closest links with the social services. This was now to be changed and put into the new service.

The hospital service, as we have seen, received a massive capital injection which in fact decided the future, and the general practitioner services were substantially run in isolation, though the regional hospital boards had developed important contacts with them and with the preventive services. But most striking of all this and the key to the puzzle is the massive investment in the hospital part of the sickness services. Major expenditure was controlled by the Department through the capital development programme and its recurrent costs. The magnitude of the change of events and the focus of major change is also illustrated by the staff changes which occurred in England. Between 1949 and 1969 the population increased from 43.8 million to 48.8 million, but the number of general practitioners fell somewhat. The number of hospital consultants practically doubled. The number of registrars and senior house officers increased four-fold, a reflection of the major investment in the hospital services.

In the period between 1948 and 1974 the tri-partite structure maintained the gulf between the divisions of the Health

Service, and those who thought about the whole complicated business of the delivery of medical care to the people of this country were very few, apart from Sir George Godber, the Chief Medical Officer, and his staff. It was Sir George's vision, I believe, which finally produced the plan to bring them together. The new Department of Health and Social Security under his professional guidance led to the developments which culminated in the 1974 Health Services Act amalgamating medical practice, health education, preventive medicine, hospitals and general practitioner services in one organisation embedded as they now were as the smallest spending part of the social service department and increasingly dominated, politically and practically, by new philosophies.

So the socio-political background to the 1974 Act was very different from 1948. Now we had strong political guidance linked with a concept of the welfare state, the social services, preventive medicine and curative medicine. The government was advised by a firm of management consultants, who were used to capitalist, profit-making enterprises. The complicated business of medical care when the pacemakers, the practical decision makers and the spenders are on the ward floor and not in the boardroom was perhaps something that they did not fully appreciate. What has however become clear out of all this experience is that there are natural tensions between political and social philosophies on the one hand and the demands of medical care and therapeutic services on the other. These conflicts and tensions will have to be resolved to the greater good of the health service provided for the people of this country.

Resources are distributed by Boards. The resources are spent by doctors guided by different rules and until recently little concerned with the resource allocation and management problems. As we will see, the tensions of this debate have crystallised around resource allocation, but it is right that we should recognise from the beginning that without the legitimate

tensions of this situation we will not get the best health service and the best methods of delivery of medical care.

During this period, 1948 to 1974, as some people here may remember very vividly, there were revolutionary changes taking place and they were taking place in society, in government, in the attitude of people to sickness and health. To the doctors and their professional associations the most exciting changes were taking place in the hospitals. This was because of rapid scientific changes – the development of a new, effective range of treatments from penicillin to cardiac by-pass. It is well understood that the 1948 Britain had fallen behind in medical discovery because of the war, but in the next twenty years we developed a whole host of new specialities based on scientific discoveries. The places where this happened – in fact the only places which in the 1940s and 1950s were geared to receive these ideas and exploit them – were the London and civic university hospitals, which were trained and equipped for reseach as well as for medical care. No one really appreciated the magnitude and cost of this scientific development, going on at the same time as the socio-political changes. Its cost has to be recognised as one of the factors in causing inequality of medical care in this country, but it must also be recognised that if it had not happened then British medicine as a whole would have suffered.

The student in the 1950s was brought in contact with this exciting world. He did not see very much of preventive medicine. A little private practice, perhaps a little of mental illness. He was more likely to hear of social revolutions in the University Union than in the medical schools. Modest attempts were made to correct these deficiencies by the revision of the medical curricula in the early 1960s, and particularly following Lord Todd's Royal Commission in 1968; but in spite of the scientific revolution and the medical advances to which I have referred the intriguing position in which we now find ourselves seems to be that the pacemaker of change is no longer the

hospital combined with scientific advances and therapeutic medicine, but rather medicine is being dragged along as part of an expensive social revolution within which the sickness service will have to fight for the resources that it needs.

I have mentioned some of these wider political and medical changes and changes in attitudes. What about resource allocation and management in the Health Service? As might well be imagined, the development of the voluntary hospitals often reflected the wealth of a city as well as the public interest, and these and local authority hospitals all varied in quality for a number of reasons. The consequence was that the sickness resources were unevenly distributed in Great Britain in 1948, when the Service was initiated. Inevitably as a consequence of the on-going commitment the resources which the government first provided were designed to meet the existing needs and took into account existing development plans together with an element of "development money". Between 1948 and 1970 there was a series of forward looks in resource allocation; but towards the end of that period it was becoming perfectly obvious to the new Department of Health and Social Security that "development money" was always outweighed by the vast bulk of resources attracted by existing programmes and commitments, and the growing capital programme to which I have referred, with its additional recurrent commitments – what is called RCCS.

The result was that, after twenty years, with the possible exception of Wales, there were only a few substantial developments outside the well-off areas. The poor were getting poorer. At the same time there were, as I have indicated, good practical reasons for the increased costs: the massive and costly advances in diagnosis and treatment. It was hoped, I think, that as the capital programme grew and became more substantial then the deprived parts of England would be rescued in the same way as Wales was rescued by a capital investment with

additional recurrent costs. Incidentally, I think it is true to say that Scotland was never deprived.

In 1970, the Crossman redistribution formula was introduced as an attempt to move away from what appeared to be an increasingly unsatisfactory state of affairs and the increasing awareness of the new Department about the competing claims of the social services and other health measures as well as hospitals for the sick. It was proposed to phase out the system of recurrent costs of capital schemes over a number of years, and additional monies would have to be found by the Boards by making savings. By 1975 it was quite obvious this was not working. The recurrent costs of new hospitals varied from two to five times the recurrent costs of the old hospitals which they replaced. In consequence, the Resource Allocation Working Party (RAWP), well known to some people here, was set up by Dr. David Owen, then Minister of Health. Its interim report was somewhat similar to the Crossman formula, but it rejected the bed element in that formula and introduced the dubious Standard Mortality Rate as a measure of morbidity, which it is not. Moreover, it endorsed the end of RCCS in 1976/77. In its second report it was proposed that there should be a supplementary increment for teaching, (SIFT), and attempts were made to begin to tackle the capital problem. Of course, almost at the same time, the capital programmes were drastically cut because of national economies, and in addition it became evident that there was to be very little new money for a number of years on the recurrent account.

The effect of these RAWP recommendations – theoretical and other calculations based on mortality figures – created deprived and over-provided Areas and Regions which led to an acute feeling of injustice: injustice on the part of those who realised how under-privileged they were; injustice by those in London who believed themselves to be the cream of British medicine and believed themselves to have been responsible for its excellence. There were strong emotional reactions by the

North against the South-East, but in the event, in the first year of the reallocation a very modest reallocation of resources took place. In practical terms, additional resources had to go to the Trent and North-West Regions, particularly to the new medical schools where major capital developments were taking place.

Certainly in the West Midlands the continuing pace of the capital programme already in the pipeline attracted a considerable portion of new monies. In 1976-77 of £7.8 million additional monies, £5.2 million had to be spent on recurring costs of the programmes for which capital provision had been made. The policy was still being decided by the decisions of the past.

In all this it is well to separate the political decision from the practical problem and identify the area of legitimate tension. Politically, the fair shares formula is totally acceptable. What was not and is not grasped is the cost of the revolution in diagnostic and therapeutic medicine which coincided with the first twenty years of the new service. Without the special funding of centres of excellence, which it was proposed to stop, this would have been poorer and British medicine would have become second-rate in world terms. The fact that it is not possible and may never be possible to extend such provision to all areas has to be faced and an alternative solution found. Perhaps we cannot continue to spend the medical share of the social services vote in this way.

For those who would criticise the Department of Health and Social Security for central dictation, it is perhaps well to remember that Trent, Manchester and the West Midlands failed to use their earliest opportunities in the 1950s and 1960s and therefore failed to exploit the opportunities of a capital programme made available to them. Ministers of Health in these days in their desire to avoid calling the tune, did not insist as they might have done on more productive efforts in the Regions which were lagging.

It is not my intention to discuss the details of the RAWP formula, but it is a fascinating study illustrating the interface between political decision and practical reality. RAWP specifies equality as a principle, and it is clear in the concept that results are related to calculated need, if that can be determined, and not to rights or economic value. It is concerned with the needs of administering bodies, not the patients. The needs of patients are not dealt with.

There are of course several alternatives within the notion of "equality" and the examination of an apparently simple formula leads one into some fairly difficult problems. The rate of approach towards the targets that were proposed were unrealistic and have been modified and modified again by Ministerial statement. The whole process of resource distribution must be greatly revised to get a proper distribution of resources between Areas and Districts, though the RAWP formula may well be reasonable in relation to Regions. But it is not only the cost of the sickness service and new hospitals provided in deprived areas, it is the cost of a whole gamut of social and welfare services administered by the same department which makes the mind boggle. How does one cut the cake between preventive measures of unproved worth, palliative social remedies of some value and provision for the old and mentally infirm? The whole sick-care system is now a component of the social care system, as I have indicated. In England the health share and particularly the sickness share may be declining. The services which are easily seen and evaluated and understood I would have thought would benefit most. Investment in resources for hospital-based secondary and tertiary care has at no time been sufficient to provide the technical base that the medical and allied services need for an efficient operation.

The new look in recent years has been the provision of guide lines by the DHSS to Regional and Area Authorities. An example of this is "Care in Action", and it refers to nearly 100

reports many made by professionally interested people about their own interests. These recommendations are approved by the Ministers. The weakness of this approach, as Sir Douglas Black has indicated, is the determination of each branch of the profession to do its "own thing". Some really hard professional synthesis and analysis is required.

May I quote from Sir Douglas's report "Inequalities in Health". He says: "All professions tend to become over-committed to existing practice and their receptivity to the need for change is liable to become weak. The medical, nursing and other professions are like other professions in this respect. We are pointing out the uncomfortable fact that society cannot look to the professions working within the health services for an account of illness and health which is always as detached or as full as it might be."

Political and social decisions with medical consequences, often unsuspected, are inevitably made by Ministers. The reallocation of resources for the care of the elderly is one. Five out of six of all patients over the age of 65 admitted to British hospitals required short-term care and curative or palliative procedures, and they would be the first to lose if funds now applied to acute hospital care were withdrawn to pay for amenities during long-term care or for social services in the community. The patient with blindness due to cataract requires an operation, not social support as a blind person. A wheel-chair and a sympathetic social worker are poor substitutes for surgery when an individual requires arthroplasty of the hip. There is an urgent need for proper consultation and debate on these and other issues and paradoxically, to me at least, it seems the least intensely involved in this are the medical profession. Many of their leaders do not seem to concern themselves with the complicated problems that we are discussing, and yet it is the informed, critical, professional input into the system which is in my view deficient. Doctors must be prepared to compete and argue for resources available and be

prepared to strike a realistic balance with the demands of the social services and welfare, the needs of which are so much more easily understood by laymen, because after all one can produce a politically satisfying result in months in many of the social services. The planning of complex modern hospitals may take ten years. We do not hear cogent and convincing medical arguments. What we hear are constant complaints against the Government. It is simply self-defeating to spend our efforts on demanding more.

Now a further reorganisation of the administration of the Health Service is taking place. The Area Health Authorities are to disappear and to be replaced by District Authorities with different responsibilities, as yet not clearly defined, and by Regional Authorities with functions also undefined at the moment but undoubtedly different from the past regional arrangements and likely to be the subject of future review.

While these changes in administration are going on, is it not appropriate to look at the demands for medical care and the organisation of its delivery. Would it be too bold to suggest the real need is the organisation of patient services and the administrative changes proposed should meet that need effectively as well as political and democratic aspirations. Patients first! Let us look at it broadly and consider where the need is greatest and how most effectively we can use the resources. The priorities are: health education and preventive medicine; the care of children; occupational health; the care of the elderly; and of course, at the same time, there must be an investment of resources to maintain and improve the quality of medical care, and research and development in relation to health.

The first three priorities are urgently required. They are of proven worth. They pay dividends of an immediate and obvious kind. In my Raymond Priestley Lecture [8] earlier this year I gave some consideration to health education and preventive medicine. Only a very small part of these responsibi-

lities can be discharged effectively by hospitals. There is undoubtedly much to be learned about health education – who should do it and how to influence people to avoid or prevent diseases – but the main focus must be in the education of children. They are most at risk from malnutrition, from alcohol, tobacco, and easily form habits that will go with them into adult life. One hopes the Health Education Council will increasingly find its proper role in this task. One wonders if the dental and medical care of children should not be reorganised and streamlined.

Many modern philosophies militate against success in health education. It is generally accepted that individuals have responsibilities in relation to personal health and their habits, but in some curious way any attempt to coerce them into meeting their responsibilities is an intolerable intrusion into individual freedom. Resources to meet the consequences, of course, have now to be provided without question by the State. What are the barriers to assumption of responsibilitiy for one's own health? Lack of interest; poor education programmes; perhaps until recently the general indifference of the health professions. So the reorganised Health Service must provide for health education, preventive medicine, and the care and health education of children, but it must also provide the correct environment for the work most people do and that means occupational health.

Modern scientific technology is responsible for the bewildering and increasing rate of change and the introduction of new materials and processes into industry. Perhaps 1,500 new chemical compounds a year; are any of them carcinogenic? This branch of medicine has been the Cinderella of the Health Service. Most of it was in the past done part-time by general practitioners without any special training or experience. Management, unions and employees demand change, as do the steadily increasing requirements of the Health and Safety Executive. So that the growing and developing National

Health Service must have as one of its priorities occupational health.

The fourth category was the elderly, which often means active people who, like old cars, need a little bit of care and attention and sometimes a spare part. Only a small number in this category are the infirm, the aged, the confused and the incontinent. At present the majority of the elderly sick are treated in general medical and surgical wards. Should they continue to be treated there?

It is easy now to see that in 1974 we should have built on what was good. The Regional Hospital Boards had a quarter of a century of experience behind them. Their officers had developed channels of communication with the Medical Officer of Health and his growing social services and also with the general practitioners when they could relax sufficiently not to feel threatened. The question that has to be answered *now* is: Can we get the National Health Service on an evolutionary path with sufficient flexibilities to make changes when patient needs demand? I think it is possible and that the Regional Health Authorities can do this. But they must have the correct status and authority and not face the threat of a further review. It cannot be done at District level. The Boards at District level do not have a wide enough vision to achieve this kind of balance. To achieve it nationally, apart from general guidelines, I believe it is courting disaster.

Is there in fact a need for primary and secondary care centres as envisaged sixty years ago? I do not think there needs to be the sharp division between services and specialities that we have created. The local need and other factors should decide on the degree of staffing and facilities for an area, but one thing I am clear about is this: we need better services of a modern kind outside general hospitals. There are important policy decisions to be made in the Eighties and the hospitals of the future should either be a care centre or a small, highly developed collection of specialist units.

There were parts of the Dawson Report which to me seem highly relevant today and which have not been introduced in any substantial degree. The Report suggested that the hub of the Health Service should be the secondary health centres, which should also be models of equipment and organisation, because they would have a key educational function and would be the centres of post-graduate study for doctors, nurses and others. In these centres there would be laboratories for pathology, pharmacy, radiology and so on. Such services would remove from the hospitals many cases who would inevitably be admitted there in the absence of secondary health centres. How desperately we need to have something done now. These centres would also be the focus of the community care programmes.

I was concerned, ladies and gentlemen, with the development of the National Health Service with its roots in the hospital service, and together with others (some of them present tonight) was the medical member of the University Grants Committee. I was connected in one way or another with the development of several of the new medical centres and teaching hospitals in the United Kingdom. We are now facing a dilemma that this country cannot afford to have such hospitals as the focus in delivering medical care to the population of the country, and I believe that Lord Dawson's suggestion of secondary care centres is something which urgently requires examination, together with a major degree of co-operation in the medical profession in the development of the National Health Service. But there is also a great need for co-operation with and education of the professions allied to medicine. Do we require an "Academy of Medicine" with all the professions concerned working together towards a common goal? It has been suggested before. One vitally important result could be an understanding between the professions which is so necessary to make these complicated co-operative experiments work.

When it comes to resources, are the British people happy

that we spend less on medical care than any of the industrialised Western nations? Even though the evidence that we have seems to support the fact that health has maintained its proportion of the social services vote, in fact the share of the nation's wealth spent on health is substantially less than that of our European partners. We must begin to prepare for increased expenditure as soon as this is possible, but without a sound, flexible, imaginative, new plan, the resources will undoubtedly be wasted.

What a challenge for the new Regional Health Authorities given the chance. Thank you. (*Applause*).

LORD GOODMAN:

Lord Hunter has very kindly said that he will answer any questions for a restricted period of time if anybody in the audience wants to ask some questions. Perhaps I might say one or two things. Firstly, as I am sure you will agree, the quite exceptional wisdom in the choice of lecturer this evening has been more than amply demonstrated. My own feeling is that under that very quiet and modest delivery a most perceptive and penetrating investigation into the most important of our social services has been extended to us tonight, and we have had an opportunity of thinking about things that, speaking for myself, I had not really considered in the course of the busy lives we all lead. I think we are profoundly indebted to Lord Hunter for that particular lecture.

It demonstrates also that only someone possessed of his quite exceptional qualifications and the variety of them could have delivered that lecture. He is of course a most distinguished doctor; he is also a man who is an expert in the field of medical research; and, above all, he is a university administrator and someone acquainted with the problems of administration, who has established a reputation as one of the most distinguished university administrators in the country. It is the synthesis of those three qualifications which has enabled him to deliver this

lecture tonight, and I cannot think of many people who could have delivered it. So that we have very special cause to be grateful to him.

Lord Hunter has said that he will answer any questions and by now you have had time to think of a few, and I would be very pleased to take the first of the questions that you want to ask.

QUESTION:

If we were successful in making people take greater responsibilities themselves and we remain in having the Ministry dealing with both health and social security, would we not increase life expectation and thereby drag more money through the social security system?

LORD HUNTER:

Yes!

QUESTION:

Lord Hunter mentioned the importance of health education and preventive medicine and the importance perhaps of the individual in taking some responsibility for this, but should we not also be looking to Government to assist this? Must we remain one of the few European countries still to have no legislation relating, for example, to the wearing of seat belts? Must we remain one of the few European countries to have no legislation relating to advertisements of tobacco products, which kill perhaps 50,000 people a year at least in this country?

LORD HUNTER:

I started off thinking as you did and I consulted a friend of mine who had concerned himself with the history of legislation in relation to alcohol. Many people think that the thing to do is to legislate – that the Government must do something – but if you look at alcohol problems, think of what happened to the United States and Sweden and think what happened to our own country in the Eighteenth Century and the way that legislation, under certain circumstances, is highly ineffective and under other circumstances is highly effective. It is a very

complicated business. It depends really on the will of the people if they wish it to happen. I would have thought that you would only need to go into the Underground to see the number of people who go into a non-smoking carriage in the Underground. There have been changes of that kind. I think Government must seek out areas where the public wish to have progress, but there are other areas which I am not going to discuss tonight – unless I am provoked – where if you start trying to legislate all you will do is to create a worse problem that you have got.

QUESTION:

Lord Hunter, following up these remarks of yours, are you of the opinion that the more the State does for you the less self-supporting the individual becomes, and this is not a good thing? I do not want the State to look after me from the cradle to the grave. I want to look after myself.

LORD HUNTER:

I think that there is something here that requires examination and discussion in the light of what has happened in the last ten or fifteen years, and that is what was really meant by Beveridge with the original proposals about social services, because the fundamental proposal was really to create a safety net underneath people and society so that the individuals could regain their strength and set off again and, if they are unable to do so, they would be cared for. I am not a social scientist, but there is obviously a very important area here that needs to be examined. One also needs to identify the drift situation which has taken place over the last fifteen to twenty years about the rights of people and their entitlement to benefits of different kinds. We have got into a situation which is very different from what was originally envisaged and which has become rapidly so expensive that the country cannot afford to do it on the scale that it is trying to do.

QUESTION:

Following on from that, I had expected that you might touch

on developments in private medicine. Having just come from the opening of yet another private hospital with the Minister of State pressing the partnership between the National Health Service and the private sector, I would like to ask you what your own views are. There has been a very fundamental change just within the last four or five years with respect to the development of the private sector, and I think many of us would be interested to hear your comments. Is this going to pull the Health Service down? Are there any advantages for the Health Service in the private sector? To me, these are very important questions.

LORD HUNTER:

I do not really know which question you are asking. Are you asking whether it is possible, if one joins a private health scheme, to get more personal and more immediate attention than one can do under the National Health Service as it exists at the present time?

QUESTION:

No, I am asking you if the diversion of many of the British public to the private sector is not going to be a very major factor affecting the development of the Health Service?

LORD HUNTER:

I am not trying to dodge that question, but I was at a meeting the other day where I was told by authorities from the British Medical Association that we are over-producing doctors in this country; in other words, there are more doctors being produced than we can handle. It does not happen to be my point of view. There are many short in specialties. I think that it is a competitive situation. The Health Service, and particularly the university medical centres, must be made attractive. I do not think the question is whether people go into the Health Service or private medicine; the question is whether they go to Australia or New Zealand. The emigration figures for last year of professional people leaving this country and going to Australia, New Zealand and Canada are quite

remarkable. So that I think really this challenge has got to be undertaken. It is a very difficult thing for me in a university post to start talking about private practice, because you cannot do the kind of job that full time clinical and academic staff are demanded of by their colleagues here and in other countries and do very much in the way of private practice as well. You can do consultant practice for a few patients who need your particular knowledge, but you could not possibly go into the hurly burly of private practice, where inevitably you are at the demands of the person who is paying you; but I think this business of losing good people into the private sector to me just represents a challenge.

At the time when I left Scotland the number of people who voluntarily took full time Health Service posts in the National Health Service was somewhere about 60% of the people. There were a lot of reasons for that, but people were beginning to develop a life style in the medical and professional practice which gave them a great deal of satisfaction in working for the National Health Service. What is wrong at the moment is that they take jobs in the Health Service but they do not work for it. If the people who are in the Army, the Navy or the police behaved in the way people do in the National Health Service, these organisations would not work. It requires the devotion of people to the objectives, and what we have to define if we can are the objectives.

QUESTION:

How worried should we be about the Government's schemes to merge and close down some of the centres of excellence in medical research?

LORD HUNTER:

I think we cannot afford many centres which have grown up for historical reasons and then the population and all kinds of other things change. I would have thought this kind of thing must be taken into consideration if you could only get proper professional planning. If we had a wartime situation there

would have been no difficulty, or much less difficulty, of people going from London medical schools to other places. I have often said that they should be trying to attract them to Leicester or Nottingham or other places. It is a very complicated and difficult thing, but if you followed what I said in my lecture, for what it is worth, it should be the job of the four regional authorities in London to sort this one out over the next decade. I do not think you can have quick reports as to how to resolve things of this kind, because it is the lives and careers of people that are involved on the staff side as well as the care of the patients. So I would have thought it is at least a ten-year plan that has to be evolved by a regional authority which has the responsibility for coordinating all the services in its region.

QUESTION:

Do you really think there is a realistic possibility of improving the National Health Service under the present atmosphere of financial stringency, which is likely to last for a great many years to come?

LORD HUNTER:

I do not know, but I think we are stuck with it and I think there are many people who feel that they must try to improve it. I think there are other ways of delivering medical care than what we do. If you look into business you will find that business companies change their ways of doing things. There are many jobs which perhaps nurses should be doing which doctors now do. One of the things about the private practice is that it is highly inefficient from the point of view of skills, because a doctor may be doing for a patient (because that patient is paying for his services) a whole range of things, some of which might well be done better by another professional person. It is putting the clock back in one sense, but I think we have got to try. I came back from Hong Kong feeling that the cloud was beginning to lift. We had met some people who really believed in the future and they were working together for

a common purpose. This is what is really fundamentally needed in this country and, specifically in relation to our topic tonight, people should believe that you can create a health care system. If the people doing it do not believe in what they are doing then it is not going to be any good.

LORD GOODMAN:

I wonder if I might conclude the questions by asking whether you think that the National Health Service has justified itself in terms of providing a better medical service than existed before its introduction?

LORD HUNTER:

Undoubtedly it has, yes.

LORD GOODMAN:

I will ask Mr. Wingate if he will propose the vote of thanks.

Professor John Yudkin

M.A., PH.D., M.D., F.I.Biol., F.R.S.C., F.R.C.P.

John Yudkin was born in London in 1910 and graduated at Chelsea College with a B.Sc. in Chemistry. He went on to Christ's College Cambridge, with a scholarship, and took Part II of the tripos in biochemistry two years later. he then embarked on research in biochemistry, taking his Ph.D. in 1935. Meanwhile, he began his studies in medicine, and took the M.B.,B.Chir. degrees in 1938. With these qualifications he decided to specialise in the field of nutrition and joined the Nutrition Laboratory at Cambridge. During this time he carried out research in nutrition as Benn Levy Student, Grocers' Company Scholar and Sir Hadley Stewart Research Fellow. He was supervisor in physiology and biochemistry at Christ's College, and later Director of Medical Studies.

During the Second World War he worked as a pathologist in the R.A.M.C. During this time he was in charge of a hospital laboratory in Sierra Leone, where his enthusiasm for research enabled him to undertake and solve one or two longstanding problems affecting Army personnel.

At the age of 34 he was appointed to the Chair of Physiology at London University at Queen Elizabeth College. He set about persuading the University to institute a Department of Nutrition, which was done in 1954; this was the first university department in Europe devoted to undergraduate and postgraduate teaching and to research in nutrition. In 1954 he left the Department of Physiology and took the newly-instituted Chair of Nutrition.

Professor Yudkin has always taken a very wide view of nutrition, which he considers to be as much concerned with the social sciences of economics, sociology, anthropology and psychology as with the experimental laboratory sciences of physiology and biochemistry. In recent years his own research has been concerned with the role of nutrition in western diseases such as overweight, coronary thrombosis and diabetes; he speaks of working on the problem of "the malnutrition of affluence".

Professor Yudkin has always been interested in the importance of contact between the academic scientist and the general public. He has frequently given talks to lay audiences, and taken part in programmes on radio and television. Much of his spare time has been given to writing non-specialist books and articles in newspapers and magazines, some of which have been translated into a number of foreign languages.

His research work has been published in some 300 articles in scientific and medical journals, and he has contributed to, and edited, several technical books. He retired from Queen Elizabeth College in 1971, and was appointed Emeritus Professor of Nutrition by the University of London. Since that time he has devoted himself to his research and writing.

Professor Yudkin was awarded the William Julius Mickle Fellowship for Medical Research by the University of London in 1961. He is a Fellow of the Royal College of Physicians, Fellow of the Royal Society of Chemistry and Fellow of the Institute of Biology. After his retirement he was elected Fellow of Queen Elizabeth College, the only non-administrative member of the College to have been awarded this distinction.

'Nutritional Advice – Dilemmas and Conflicts'

delivered by

Professor John Yudkin

M.A., Ph.D., M.D.,F.I.Biol., F.R.S.C., F.R.C.P.

Wednesday, 9th June, 1982

CHAIRMAN The Rt. Hon. The Lord Goodman C.H.

LORD GOODMAN:

Ladies and gentleman, may I welcome you to the tenth of what are flatteringly, perhaps over flatteringly, described as "The Goodman Lectures". When Mr Ballantine, here, and his co-trustees decided to inaugurate a lecture in honour of the late Irvine Aitchison, I do not think anyone would have appreciated that in ten years it would have become a feature, albeit a modest feature, in the social and intellectual life of London. I do not think that is too high a claim.

The nine previous lectures, marred, perhaps, by one single aberration in the first one, were delivered by some of the most distinguished intellectuals and academics in the country. One has only to look at the list of people who delivered them to see what their distinction was. There was Lord Briggs, who did the second one, there was Sir Michael Swann (now Lord Swann) who gave the third, there was Lord Justice Scarman (now Lord Scarman) – incidentally, Professor Yudkin can take heart from the fact that almost everyone who gave these lectures has either been a nobleman or promoted to the nobility – there was

Professor Sir Martin Roth – he has not gone up yet – there was Lord Snow – the only change in his case being, alas, the fact that he is deceased – there was Sir George Porter, there was Hon. Philip Kaiser – who was the American Ambassador both to Hungary and Austria – and, finally, we had Lord Hunter giving the one in 1981.

That is not only quite an exceptional list in terms of distinction, it is also quite an exceptional list in terms of the range, variety and interest in the subjects that they discussed. We can, I think, confidently expect a lecture tonight of equal quality.

There is nothing more irritating in this world, I think, than for a lecturer to hear his Chairman tell the audience how much the lecture is going to delight them. Nothing is more likely to put him off his stroke than to hear a preliminary eulogy before the lecture is delivered, so I will not indulge in that.

I would only say this. Professor Yudkin is a distinguished, indeed a world authority on nutrition and on food. There is a general belief, which he himself has aired in one of his prefaces, that this is a particular scientific skill that requires no knowledge of any kind to deploy. All I can say is that is a great mistake if you look at Professor Yudkin's qualifications. The notion that an authority on diet can double between being a fashion correspondent and a diet correspondent is, I think, slightly mistaken if you look at the immense knowledge, experience and skill deployed by Professor Yudkin. He has the very highest medical qualifications: he is a Doctor of Medicine and a Fellow of the Royal College of Physicians. Those doctors who are here will know that those are outstanding, in fact the very accolade of medical distinction. He has the highest scientific qualifications: he is an M.A. and a Doctor of Philosopy. In fact, I could go on for quite a long time telling you what he is. What he certainly is is a man of immense distinction and immense knowledge and I shall be very surprised – slightly departing from my own intention not to boost

him too much – if he does not demonstrate these facts while he is talking.

He is also a man of quite savage, brutal sadistic quality. The reason for that is this. He has enunciated the unthinkable proposition that the only way to slim is to eat less. (*Laughter*). I hope we may have some words of repentence during the course of this lecture because those members of the audience who have the slightest embonpoint, if I may use that slightly disarming word, would be against him from the very moment they heard of this doctrine, but, as I say, he has the opportunity of recantation.

We are very fortunate indeed to have Professor Yudkin as the tenth lecturer. I may say that all previous lectures are going to be published before very long and they will be able to, I hope, redeem my claim that they were of outstanding quality.

The only other thing I have to say is that at the end of the lecture Professor Yudkin has generously indicated he will be willing to answer questions. If I may venture to say so, this is not an opportunity for procuring free medical advice, but if there is a genuine question arising from his talk or arising from your general interest in the subject do not hesitate to ask him. Professor Yudkin. (*Applause*).

PROFESSOR YUDKIN:

My Lord Chairman, the reason why these lectures bear your name is that they record the many kindnesses that you showed the late Irvine Aitchison, as well as the sage advice and considerable help you gave him. It occurs to me that if all those to whom you showed similar kindness, advice and help were to found lectures bearing your name, they could not be annual lectures, since there would not be enough days in the year for the lectures to be delivered.

Before that happens, however, it is with some degree of diffidence that I join the list of distinguished speakers who have given the first nine Goodman lectures to the Aitchison Memorial Trust.

The Tenth Goodman Lecture

Nutritional Advice – Dilemmas and Conflicts

My lords, ladies and gentlemen: It has been assumed, until recently, that the occurrence of malnutrition is associated with the existence of poverty. The corollary, which was long accepted by economists, politicians and nutritionists, was that the elimination of poverty would result in the elimination of malnutrition. It is now clear, however, that the affluence that has been achieved in many Western countries has resulted in a *wide* choice of good but not necessarily in a *wise* choice of food. In these countries, a decrease in the prevalence of the classical malnutrition of poverty has coincided with an increase in the prevalence of the new malnutrition of affluence. Most physicians and medical scientists agree that, to a greater or lesser extent, the food we eat plays a part in several diseases including dental decay, overweight, coronary thrombosis and diabetes, which are becoming more and more common in the more prosperous countries.

Public concern about our diet is evident from the increasing number of health food stores, articles and books on nutrition, and of publications on nutrition by organisations such as the Department of Health and the Health Education Council. I propose today to examine the following questions: What do people in affluent countries know about the foods they eat? Where does this knowledge come from? How accurate is the information that people are given? Finally, if, as I think we shall see, much of the information is confusing, or misleading, or ineffective, can we devise a simpler, more accurate and more effective method of diminishing the prevalence of the malnutrition of affluence?

For more than two thousands years, and up to the end of the eighteenth century, individual foods were considered to be beneficial or harmful according to their effect upon the four bodily humours – blood, phlegm, black bile and yellow bile. All diseases were supposed to be caused by an imbalance of the humours, which could be improved or worsened by partaking

of particular foods. During the past one hundred years, it has become clear that the foods we eat have to supply the body with something like 50 to 60 essential materials in order that the body can grow, make good wear and tear, and so remain healthy. Apart from carbohydrate and fat, used mostly for the production of energy, the body also needs the essential nutrients comprising protein, vitamins and mineral elements, which have both to be of the correct sort and to be present in adequate amounts in the foods we eat.

But many lay people have taken these more recently established facts about nutrition, and incorporated them into beliefs that have no basis in reality. As an example, let us see what many people think about the vitamins. Their properties certainly are extraordinary, since very small amounts are able to prevent ill-health or even death. The average daily amount needed varies from 30mg. for vitamin C, down to 3 or 4 micrograms for vitamin B_{12}. Thus one ounce of vitamin C will meet the daily needs of about one thousand people, and an ounce of vitamin B_{12} the needs of ten million people. Vitamins appear even more remarkable when it is realised that such very small quantities do not simply prevent disease but can cure it. A patient with beri-beri who can be expected to die of severe heart failure within the next day or two may be given 3 or 4 milligrams of vitamin B_1 – about one ten-thousandth of an ounce – and 48 hours later may feel well enough to walk out of the hospital.

The almost magical properties with which the vitamins are endowed give rise to several sorts of misconceptions by the public. People may be taking a diet that they know is nutritionally bad, but they suppose that they have turned it into a good diet by regularly taking vitamin pills. Many breakfast cereals, the nutritional value of which has been said by an American senator to be similar to that of the packet in which they are bought, are believed to be transformed into nutritionally highly desirable foods by the manufacturers' addition

of a few vitamins and some iron.

Most dentists and doctors deplore the practice of giving babies and small children syrupy drinks, but mothers ignore the ill-effects these drinks produce if they use them to administer vitamin C. Another misconception is exploited by those who promote vitamin preparations when they imply that if a little can prevent illness, more can produce an exceptional degree of positive health. Since shortage of vitamin A leads to an impairment of night vision, it is thought that a large amount of vitamin A will enable one to see in the dark like a cat. Since shortage of vitamin E leads to sterility in a rat, it is suggested that pills with vitamin E will make one a vigorous sexual athlete. The fact is that, unless the diet is short of vitamins, which is quite unlikely in this country, taking them will do nothing to improve night vision, resistance to infection, digestion or any other bodily function.

Again, it is the aura that surrounds the word "vitamin" that was responsible for the invention of vitamin B_{17}. This was a new name given to a preparation called Laetrile, marketed in many parts of the United States of America as a cure for cancer. There is no evidence that it is effective for this purpose, and it has no known action as a vitamin or in any other way, except that it may be harmful since it can produce cyanide in the body.

These and many other misconceptions are not, however, confined to the vitamins. Many people do not seem totally to have abandoned the older view that individual foods have especially beneficial effects or especially deleterious effects. The commonest statement made about a particular food is that it is "good for you" or that it is "bad for you". Sometimes, the "good" food is supposed to owe its virtue to its richness in one or more nutrients, but often it is "good" for reasons over and above its nutrient content. Perhaps the best known of these especially good foods is honey; others are yoghourt, cider vinegar, pollen, sea salt and vegetable juices. However, the fact is that while there are foods that are harmful to the body, there

are no foods that have specific and beneficial effects on the body.

Where then do people get their nutritional information from? There are several institutes and university departments where nutritional research and teaching are undertaken. Nutrition is also taught – though usually rather grudgingly – to medical and nursing students; it is now taught too in many schools, usually as part of Home Economics. But such instruction by no means provides the only source from which lay people get their nutritional information; nor is it the most effective source. Much of what the public gets to know about nutrition comes from articles in newspapers or magazines, from popular books, or from the advertising and labelling of particular foods.

The pieces of nutritional misinformation that frequently appear in magazines are perhaps not so surprising when one realises, as our Chairman said, that they might have been written by someone who, in the last issue, was describing the new hairstyles and in the next issue will be doing a piece on how to avoid freckles. In the current issue you might well read that calcium will strengthen the nails and that lecithin tablets will mobilise the body's fat stores; neither statement is true. A very erudite cookery writer in one of the up-market Sunday newspapers enjoys including nutritional information in his articles, but often it is less than reliable. He writes that strict vegetarians (vegans) are likely to suffer from protein deficiency but not from vitamin deficiency: the opposite is in fact true. He also is quite sure that the Chinese do not eat butter or cheese because they suffer from intolerance to lactose (milk sugar); but lactose is present in the watery part of milk and is removed when cheese and butter are made.

It is chiefly newspapers and magazines that are responsible for promoting some of the more exotic faddish foods, like royal jelly or the New Zealand green-lipped mussel. People shopping in health food stores seem to be impressed when they

are told that the New Zealand green-lipped mussel contains eleven different minerals, seventeen different amino-acids, vitamins A and B, and carbohydrates and lipid. A pamphlet with this information continues: "So the mussel is bursting with essential nutrients". But one could say just as much about a piece of bread – white or brown. Simply to state that the mussel contains this or that essential nutritional component is rather like saying that you can continue to meet your regular financial commitments because you have a regular income, without observing that this income totals £10 a week.

Quantities really do matter. The royal jelly commended in many books and articles is supposed to owe its allegedly remarkable health-giving properties to a high concentration of the vitamin panthothenate. Apart from the fact that no-one ever goes short of this vitamin in their food, the tiny amount of the royal jelly that is in the available preparations might be enough to produce an effect on a bee larva, but it is certainly not enough for a human being weighing as much as several million bee larvae.

In case neither green-lipped mussels from the New Zealand seas nor tablets with royal jelly are regular items in your normal diet, let me take a more homely example: parsley. Not everybody goes along with Ogden Nash in saying that "parsley is gharsley", but anyone who has had any instruction at all in nutrition will have been told that parsley is very rich in vitamin C: 100 grams of parsley (about 3 1/2 ounces) contains some 150mg. of vitamin C, which is three times as much as in the same quantity of orange juice. But have you ever seen 100 grams of parsley? Last summer I collected, though with some difficulty, 100 grams, which occupied at least two or three litres in volume – about half a gallon. I suppose it is just about conceivable that a parsley addict, applying himself conscientiously to taking parsley with everything, could manage to get through 100 grams during a year, in which case it would contribute as much vitamin C to his average diet as would a

teaspoon or so of boiled potato each day.

When popular writers do refer to quantities, they may be ludicrously inaccurate. A recent best-selling American book on slimming says: "A water melon, very obviously a carbohydrate, contains 25% protein". The real value is about one-fifth of 1%, so the figure given by the author is wrong by a factor of more than 100; arather like ordering a pint of beer and getting a teaspoonful.

Let me now turn to advertising. The Advertising Standards Authority says that advertisements must be legal, decent, honest and truthful. They can, nevertheless, be misleading. A margarine may indeed be made from edible vegetable oils, as it says on the label, but this hides the fact that the oil has been chemically transformed by hydrogenation and, incidentally, it now resembles the hard fats that are supposed to be bad for the heart, rather than the soft fats that are supposed to be good. It could be just as true to say that the pleasant-smelling material in the small bottle on my laboratory shelf has been made from freshly-picked, sun-ripened peaches; it is unlikely that you could at once realise that I am talking of prussic acid. A drowning man would hardly be consoled if he were told that the water contains oxygen, when in fact it is hydrogenated oxygen – H_20 – that is filling his lungs.

Acceptance of a particular food that is recommended for health reasons is influenced by whether it is likely to be commercially worthwhile for a food manufacturer to produce it. The evidence that fibre is an important dietary constituent in the prevention of serious disease is really not very strong. One of the reasons why this belief is now so widespread lies, I am sure, in the vigorous marketing of such items as Kellogg's All-Bran. A year or two ago Kellogg's issued this statement: "A diet deficient in fibre makes people more prone to diseases like appendicitis, diverticular disease, cancer and heart attacks". This dogmatic assertion is certainly not endorsed by the recent report on fibre from the Royal College of Physicians.

Similarly, the view that we should give up butter in favour of soft margarine owes a great deal to the promotional activities of the manufacturers of Flora margarine. On the other hand, where dietary advice recommends reduced consumption of a food, it clearly will not be supported by those who manufacture or market that food. Most nutritionists say that we take too much sugar; it would however not be expected that the commercial interests involved in producing and using sugar would go out of their way to support the nutritionists in promoting a call for reduction in consumption.

Having criticised lay writers and food manufacturers for misleading the public about nutrition, I must, to be fair, point to some of the ways in which we professional nutritionists are less than perfect nutrition educators. It is not so much that we are wrong in the detail that we impart; but the general advice we give is often impractical, or misleading, or meaningless. It is impractical, and incidentally quite unnecessary, to tell people, as some nutritionists do, that they must eat breakfast, when there are some who are nauseated at the mere thought of eating breakfast.

It is misleading to tell people that all they need to do is to make sure that they have a varied diet. Here is an example of a very varied diet that is nutritionally appalling:

Breakfast: Toast, marmalade, sweet roll, black coffee;
Lunch: Cola drink, chocolate biscuits, ice cream;
Tea: Cake, tea;
Evening meal: Fish fingers, pickles, milk shake, tinned fruit salad;
T. V. refreshment: One pint of beer.

In terms of the number of dietary items, this is about as varied as anyone can have. In terms of nutritional desirability, it is very bad indeed. A much less varied diet, but a nutritionally far superior diet, need contain nothing but meat, cheese and fruit.

Even less useful is the advice that one needs a "balanced" diet. What foods are to be balanced against what? If it means that the diet should be balanced so as to provide all the body's needs, then this is like saying that, in order to have a good diet, you must have a good diet.

Perhaps the most common injunction is that one should eat in moderation, both as to the total amount eaten and the amount of each item. I hear this mostly in connection with our research into the ill-effects that result from the quantities of sugar that are in many of our present-day diets. Let us visualise a patient consulting his doctor in the year 1770, which is just before there was a rapid rise in sugar consumption. The doctor advises him on his diet and includes the suggestion that he take no more than a moderate amount of sugar. The average consumption at that time was about two ounces a week, and the patient and the doctor agree that he could have up to this amount. Today, we take on average about two pounds a week. quite a few people take two or even three times this amount. What then is our present conception of "moderation" in sugar consumption? If we recommend that people eat up to today's average consumption, two pounds a week, we are recommending something like 15 times as much as did the doctor of two hundred years ago.

This may be the place for me to say a word in answer to those who complain that they are very confused by what they are told they should be eating, since nutritionists are constantly changing their minds and often give advice that contradicts that which they gave only a little while ago. Sometimes this is justified criticism, but not always. Often the advice that is being changed has come not from nutritionists, but from someone who, especially today, finds he can get a large following by writing manifest nonsense if the makes it sensational enough. This is particularly true if he promises that, if you follow his advice, your arthritis will be cured or you will rapidly get rid of your overweight. It is not *bona fide* nutrition-

ists who have recommended vitamin B_6 for arthritis or cider vinegar for overweight.

A valid criticism of advice that changes, however, arises from the nature of nutrition itself. On the one hand, like all sciences, nutritional science does not have all the answers; if it did, I and all the other nutritionists would be wasting our time doing research. On the other hand, unlike most other scientists, we cannot tell people who seek our advice that we cannot answer because our knowledge is incomplete. It would not satisfy a mother who wants to feed her children in the best possible way, or the many adults who want to know how to lose weight without becoming malnourished. So we have to take the knowledge we have – which, although incomplete, is by now pretty extensive – and to it we add our judgment which depends on our personal experience and, no doubt, on our personal idiosyncrasies – prejudices, if you like.

Because of these considerations, it may well be that the advice given by different nutritionists is different. There is no general agreement about the importance of changing the amount and kind of fat as a means of reducing the risk of developing heart disease, or about the need to include a fair amount of roughage in the diet. As for changes, progress in nutritional science is responsible for the abandonment of the recommendation, common forty or fifty years ago, that doses of vitamin A will help to prevent coughs and colds and other infections.

So far I have talked almost entirely about the ways in which we are, at best, badly advised about what we should eat and, at worst, grossly deceived. Let me now say something about the rules of sensible eating that can be deduced from considerations that require no specialist knowledge about nutrition; indeed, how to be sure that you are eating wisely while concerning yourself not at all with calories or cholesterol, protein or polyunsaturates, carbohydrates or calcium.

Advice that is simple and easy to follow is particularly

important today when an increasing number of people are concerned about their nutrition. They are worried about whether their food is produced in the best possible conditions; they believe that the land on which crops are grown and animals graze is in a poor state, because of the use of artificial fertilisers; that crops and animals are treated with chemicals including hormones that are a hazard to human health and that food is processed in the factories in ways that diminish nutritional value. They seek their remedy by buying food in health food stores, or increasingly now, in special sections of supermarkets.

I think it is logical for people with these anxieties to buy their food from places that sell "organically-grown foods" that have not been treated with pesticides and hormones, although I must say at once that I do not share the view that they are better or safer than the same foods grown and treated conventionally. What I find illogical, however, is the range of items bought in the health food store by people who are so concerned about what they consider unnatural methods of food production. The majority of the goods there would be more at home in a pharmacy than in a grocery, consisting of powders, pills and elixirs producded by the most sophisticated and elaborate methods of purification, separation and modern chemcical synthesis. I still have the naive belief that nutrition is to do with eating food.

Ask yourself, then, how do all animals in their ordinary environment choose their food? Why do keepers in the zoo try to give their charges as nearly as possible the same diet as they eat in the wild? Why is it that these animals in their own habitats clearly choose the diet best suited to their own anatomy and physiology, while man needs to be taught by experts what he should eat? As a friend of mine said, a crossword enthusiast, "the gnu doesn't need a gnutritionist." All animals in their normal environment choose the right foods, avoid the wrong foods, and eat as much as they need

and no more. Modern man, by contrast, often avoids eating the right foods, even if they are available, often eats the wrong foods, and often eats significantly more than he needs.

It is axiomatic that the choice of foods by all species, including man in his hunting and food-gathering days, must have been the foods that were best suited to them. Natural selection would otherwise have ensured that the species did not survive. We can say then that when an animal chooses the food it likes, it is choosing the food it needs. Why can man no longer depend on his nutritional instinct to satisfy his nutritional needs? The answer is that he has been able to make new foods that possess the qualities he uses in choosing what to eat, but it turns out that these qualities do not include the requirement that they constitute an ideal diet.

The two most important reasons why people eat particular foods are availability and attractiveness. People eat the foods they like if they can get them. Man's present-day foods include not only new and improved species and strains of animals and plants; they also include foods that are made from extracts, mixed and compounded in a way that satisfies these two criteria of avilability and attractiveness. There is nothing, however, that ensures that the properties of such foods also include adequate nutritional value.

When we eat a bar of chocolate or jam roll with custard, or when we take a cola drink or a glass of beer, the small contribution they make to our nutritional state, other than to supply often superfluous calories, can hardly be said to be beneficial. We can no longer say that choosing the foods we like is the same as choosing the foods that we need.

The logical conclusion is that we would be choosing our diets with nutritional wisdom if our choice were limited to the foods that were available to our pre-agricultural ancestors. That, in exact detail, would not now be impossible, particularly in urbanised societies. Nevertheless, it is reasonable to say that the nearer we get to man's hunting and food-gathering

diet, the more likely we are to be well-nourished and the more we can depend on our instinctive choice. Thus, good nutrition can be assured by taking care to avoid the wrong foods rather than by taking care to eat the right foods.

If you avoid the wrong sorts of foods, it is clear that you can now choose only from the right sorts of foods. Moreover, there is a mechanism that will prevent you from confining yourself to one such food and so running the risk of going short of nutrients found only in the foods that you have not eaten. Since people soon get tired of eating one sort of food, there is a natural tendency to move on to a different sort of food. If, for example, you begin a meal with meat and spaghetti, you may eat until you do not want any more of this food, but you are now quite happy to have some fruit. In this way you get one group of nutrients from the first course and a different, though perhaps overlapping, group of nutrients from the second course.

There is some experimental evidence, as well as common sense, to support my contention that you will be sure to eat the right foods in the right amounts if you simply avoid eating the wrong foods. We have given rats a special diet that will keep them alive if they are not also offered sugar, which we know they like. When, however, we allow them access to sugar, they eat it, become ill and die; surviving longer if they eat small amounts at intervals, and dying sooner if they eat larger amounts and more frequently. And here are the results of another experiment. Rats will thrive if given a well-designed diet, and remain healthy, sleek and lithe for up to three years. If, however, they are allowed to choose, in addition to this good diet, from a range of manufactured foods such as cornflakes, cake and biscuits, they overeat and become fat – just as you and I do.

I know of only one relevant experiment with human beings. This was with babies from six months of age, who were allowed to choose their own diet from a wide range of foods,

and to eat as much as they wished. Over several years of observation, the babies grew as well as babies fed conventionally; they were not fat, and they were, if anything, healthier. The clue to this was not only that they were offered a range of "good" foods, but that they were not offered made-up foods such as cakes, soft drinks, desserts and confectionery.

I have, I hope, shown you why you do not need to be a nutritionist in order to know how to eat wisely. Certainly you would do well not to accept too readily the advice given to you by beauty editors, or the advertisers, or even those who write in the Sunday heavies. If you follow the simple rules I have given you, you can do very well as your own nutritionist, and you could put the professional nutritionist out of business – including your 10th Goodman lecturer. (*Applause*).

LORD GOODMAN:

Before you rush home to throw away your parsley, cornflakes, All-bran and whatever else it is that has been condemned this evening – I am not sure what there is left to eat – I ought to tell you there is, after this lecture, to those of you who have the courage to partake, some refreshments downstairs and we hope you will stay and participate in them.

May I just say this. I said Professor Yudkin was a very remarkable man. I think one of the most remarkable features of this lecture, which several of you, I am sure, will have noticed, was the elegance and simplicity of its delivery. This is the rarest of qualities and I was immensely impressed by it. As to the validity of what he says, I do not think I will be an especially good testimonial so I will refrain from commending him, but it was obviously a lecture of immense distinction and I think, in some ways – I hesitate to say this – the most entertaining of the Goodman lectures that have been delivered. We have all, I think, cause for great gratitude to him.

I said at the outset that he is prepared to answer questions. I

would like to invite those members of the audience who would like to ask him a question to do so. Would you please stand up, give your name and, perhaps, if you have some professional concern in the matter, you would state that as well.

MRS. BALLANTINE:

What about saccharine instead of sugar?

PROFESSOR YUDKIN:

May I give a double answer: The ideal thing, I am sure, is gradually to wean yourself from wanting something sweet, otherwise one is always attracted to taking sugary things in circumstances where you cannot find your saccharine, but faute de mieux if you really have to choose between the two then saccharine, certainly, is better than sugar.

LORD SWANN:

Can I ask you this. You gave us a little glimpse of what the advising doctor would have been saying in 1770. I wonder if you would like to enlarge on good and bad advice 200 years ago, 400 years ago and 600 years ago.

PROFESSOR YUDKIN:

I have a suspicion that Lord Swann does not really expect me to answer that question. I think that in medicine, in so far as it is scientific – and it is not wholly scientific for the reasons I gave about nutrition, you have to provide answers sometimes which you do not have – as in other sciences, we are slowly approaching this asymptote where we know most of what there is to know about medicine which means the further back you go the less reliable medicine was, except of course that up until about 300 years ago there was no difference between medicine then taught and practised from the medicine taught 2,000 years ago; it was still medicine based on the teaching of Hippocrates, whoever he was and the way in which you decided what treatment to give was to look up what was said by Hippocrates and other ancient writers. You did that in 1600 or even later just as well as you did in 600 or at the time of Jesus. So there was not much change in those times. Things had

to be discovered and re-discovered before anybody took much notice.

One thinks, in my field, of the interval when doctors on ships reported that they could prevent scurvy in the crew by making sure there were fresh vegetables or oranges or lemons around. It took at least another 200 years before Lind established this quite definitely with his experiments and, as you might imagine, another 50 years or so before the Royal Navy did anything about it.

MRS. BATEMAN:

May I ask you, Professor, if you will give us an example of what you consider a balanced day's diet.

PROFESSOR YUDKIN:

I am not sure that you want to practice this in the High Street, but a good test is to say to yourself, "Could I, with my ancestors, have obtained this food by picking it off a tree, digging it out of the ground or shooting it down with a bow and arrow or" – if you were very energetic – "digging a large hole and waiting for a mammoth to fall into it." You should eat meat, fish, fruit, vegetables, eggs and milk, those sorts of foods that are what you can see and what you can get if you are a hunter and food-gatherer. If you cannot get them precisely like that, then get them messed about in the minimum possible way. I think you can leave it then to your own taste buds to decide how much and in what mixture you would have these.

LADY LLOYD:

How about Perrier, which is a natural spring water and which has become so phenomenally popular? I have recently been working with the Health Education Council and they now say that carbonated waters are also fattening. Do you still advise it is better to drink ordinary water?

PROFESSOR YUDKIN:

I pay my water rates and I do not see why I should not drink water out of the tap. It is certainly not proved that just by putting some bubbles of carbon dioxide into the water it

becomes fattening in any way; carbon dioxide does not have any calories so it makes absolutely no difference. If they are sweetened that is something different again. The only people who, I think, would benefit from people drinking Perrier water are the people who bottle Perrier water.

MR. I. CHAPMAN:

I have no professional interest to declare. Professor Yudkin, having made very clear your views in relation to sugar consumption, I wonder if you could tell us what your views are in relation to salt consumption.

PROFESSOR YUDKIN:

There has been, for a long time, a reasonable amount of evidence that the amount of salt that many people eat is excessive. I hesitate there because I want to say that it seems as if some people are more susceptible to high salt intakes than others – it may be some people are virtually immune. But there is no doubt that there is a large body of opinion now which says that the amount of salt which many people eat is unnecessary and can be harmful, causing high blood pressure.

Something that is very interesting about salt is that it is unique because it is needed by the body, but on average, in most countries, we take something like ten times as much as we need. It is all very well saying we cannot possibly do any harm since we excrete the salt we do not need, because it does seem that in some people the fact we keep on taking salt and constantly having to rid of it end up by producing a high blood pressure.

MR. HEWITT:

You seem to suggest, Professor, that raw food is quite acceptable. Do we need to worry about our intake of cooked food or, more particularly, hot food and should we have to worry about local authorities providing a hot meal for our children at school at midday?

PROFESSOR YUDKIN:

I am sorry if I gave you the impression that there is

something especially advantageous or disadvantageous about raw food because I was not distinguishing on that point. In the sorts of communities in which we live, there are some foods it would be ridiculous to eat raw because of the risk of spreading infection. That is one important element.

As to whether it makes any difference if you have a hot meal or a cold meal, I think there is absolutely no advantage one way or the other. One can think of appallingly bad hot meals and one can think of extremely good cold meals, so I do not think that matters.

LORD LLOYD:

I am only an eater, not a nutrionist. I wonder whether you would just clarify for us, in relation to the model diet you suggested, what your views are in relation to fats and eggs, because at the moment there seems to be a great deal of concentrated criticism on those two articles of diet.

PROFESSOR YUDKIN:

I did not mention eggs although I did mention fats. I said there is a great deal of controversy. I think if one took a poll, one would find that the majority view is that animal fat specifically, by which I mean fats on meat and butter fats, are harmful if taken in the sorts of amounts that we tend to in this country. That is a majority view and it is by no means a universal view. I am in the minority about that.

There are also, and it is probably the same people, those who would say that one should not take more than perhaps two or three eggs a week. Possibly, if one is doing a Gallup Poll, one would find that there were some people who would not worry so much about eggs or about fat, but on the whole there are those who think that so-called saturated fats, hard animal fats, are bad for you, and also too many eggs, and there are others, like me, who eat at least one egg a day. I do not think we have had margarine in our house since I can remember.

QUESTION:

What about your substitute for sugar? It has been alleged that cyclamates are carcinogenic, is that true?

PROFESSOR YUDKIN:

There was a story, some ten years ago, that cyclamates, which were then available as an alternative to saccharine, were harmful because they caused cancer. The Americans banned them and within a week we followed suit. We banned them here and they are still banned, both in the United States and this country. They are still allowed in some countries, such as Germany and Switzerland – countries you would have thought were just as fussy as we are – so there are a lot of people who did not accept the evidence that cyclamates were harmful. The fact is that, at present, the only artificial sweetener that is used in this country, whatever its name – Sweetex, Hermesetas, or whatever – are all saccharine. From time to time you hear that they perhaps also are dangerous but I think that there is really no evidence for that any more than there was any real evidence that cyclamates are harmful.

MR. HARRIS:

There was an enforced lack of proper meat and various other things during the last war. Would you like to comment on the difference in health during that period of time?

PROFESSOR YUDKIN:

I am one of those who are extremely wary of making deductions from what the pundits call "epidemiological studies" of that sort, whether it is to do with changes at the time or whether it is to do with comparing one population with another, for the reason that you never get a situation in which there is only one thing that has changed.

Let us suppose – and it is not in fact true – by the end of the war there was less heart disease in this country than at the beginning of the war. You would say it is because we had less butter and I would say it is because we ate less sugar, somebody else would say it was because most of the healthy

people were away fighting the war and only the old dodderers like you and me were left behind, so naturally the death rate went up. With these sorts of figures one can be readily led into traps, so I would hate to try and draw any conclusions from what happened during the war, except to say that, apart from the rise in coronary disease, in general the health of the population of this country was far better at the end of the war than it was at the beginning. That was because one keeps thinking of rationing in terms of reduced consumption of important foods whereas rationing meant a more even distribution of important foods.

A SPEAKER:

How far do you think that food allergies are responsible for migraine or even more serious illnesses than that?

PROFESSOR YUDKIN:

To a small extent. I think it has always been known there are some people who are sensitive to particular foods but I think it is now, like so many things at different times, fashionable to talk about allergies. There is a new disease been invented – which will probably not last longer than a few years – which is total allergy. I have a cutting on my desk about a woman who has, over the last five years, eaten nothing but potatoes because she is allergic to everything else. You may believe that. I think that the current situation is that there is as much allergy to food as there always was; it may be something like 5% of the population or it may be a bit more or less but it is not nearly as important as is currently believed.

MR. COOK:

Professor Yudkin, the professional nutritionists, over the last two or three decades in this field have increased their influence and control not only within medical circles but also in the lay circles to an extraordinary degree. But what of the future? Do you think they will continue to exert and increase that influence or do you think they have shot their bolt?

Professor Yudkin:

I am hoping that they might increase their influence. I think that is very likely. There is now a new breed of person about, people who are professionally trained as nutritionists, beginning in 1954 when the first degree was established. You will now find the infiltration of nutritionists in many professions as, as it were, ancillaries, as well as people practising nutrition in posts as nutritionists. I am thinking, for example, there are enlightened food manufacturing firms that employ nutritionists now. So I would expect to see more and more influence by the nutritionists.

On the other hand, it is still true, as Lord Goodman said, that there is a large number of people who imagine that nutrition is something one knows instinctively and you can advise without necessarily having any formal training in it. I frequently meet people at dinner parties who come up to me and shake me by the hand, and say, "You are a nutritionist, I understand. Last week – " and then they tell me what they have just discovered. It happens to be something very different from what I know about nutrition, but they suppose that they are extremely knowledgeable and are prepared to give me advice on that and anything else you ask them.

Lord Goodman:

I am sure that, except for the unduly sensitive, this must have induced an appetite. I will ask Mr. Ballantine to propose the vote of thanks.